D. W.

X mas 1987

101 Great Scots

For Alexander, Louis
and Claudia

101 Great Scots

Allan Massie

Chambers

© Allan Massie 1987
Published by W & R Chambers Ltd Edinburgh, 1987

Illustrated by Janet MacKay

British Library Cataloguing in Publication Data

Massie, Allan
    101 great scots.
    1. Scotland — Biography
    I. Title
    920'.0411   DA758

    ISBN 0-550-20485-7

Typeset by Buccleuch Printers, Hawick

Printed in Great Britain at the University Press, Cambridge

Contents

Introduction

'As I take it, Universal History, the history of what man has accomplished in this
world, is at bottom the History of the Great Men who have worked here.'

Few modern historians would subscribe to Carlyle's view; indeed the most
influential and respected school of contemporary historians, the French
Annalistes, have banished the Great Man almost entirely; they prefer
demography and economic models. Fair enough; no one would deny that they
have added immeasurably to our understanding of the Past. Yet the reading
public is obstinate in its liking for biographies, and sometimes even
professional historians still oblige.

This book cannot claim to offer 101 biographies. These little essays are no
more than sketches. The portraits, like the judgements, are partial. I hope they
may instruct some, and entertain, though they cannot satisfy, all. The word
'entertainment' has been debased in our time, but the desire to offer the thing is
not ignoble; Macaulay hoped that his History might replace the latest novel on
a young lady's reading-table.

I hope that the book offers something in the nature of a biographical
history of Scotland and Scottish culture. Such an ambition can only be
incompletely achieved in this compass; to do it properly would require
perhaps five times as many Lives. There are sad gaps here. Medieval Scotland is
insufficiently represented; Gaelic Scotland even more reprehensibly so.
Ignorance of the language, and a consequent inability to appreciate its
literature, must be my only excuse. Yet it is also true that the materials which
would enable a non-Gaelic speaking Scot to come to a fuller understanding of
Gaelic Scotland are lacking. There are regrettably few women here. There
ought to be more ministers of the Church of Scotland, and more
agriculturalists. There are perhaps too many politicians and too many writers;
yet the first make an immediate impact and the second group offer the most
readily accessible indication of the state of culture of any given period.

If the book has a consistent theme, it is the diversity of Scotland. There are
two traditions of Scottish historical writing which have come close to annexing
our history and imposing their partisan interpretation of it. This is not
surprising for both represent parties long dominant in the history of our
country.

The first is the Whig–Presbyterian tradition, which saw the true expression
of Scottish nationality in Calvinism, the Covenant and the Kirk. It was a
tradition of stern, and often self-satisfied, virtue, narrow-minded, yet with its
own nobility. It tended to expunge all the achievements of medieval Scotland,
except the heroic legend of the Wars of Independence. It has survived in our
own century, in a new manifestation: though the Labour party in Scotland has
been supported by the voters of that section of the working-class which is

descended from the immigrant Catholic Irish, nevertheless Labour Scotland is the inheritor of the same morally self-righteous tradition. This Scotland was self-consciously democratic. The sense of the equality of all men which is a feature that has distinguished Scottish from English society has its roots in the Presbyterian culture with its emphasis on Bible study and its denial of priesthood; its insistence that there should be no intermediary between the individual man and his Maker.

With this tradition went another, which is the Unionist one. It was the Whigs who made the union with England, the Whigs who benefited by it, and the Whigs who most powerfully maintained it. The union appealed to common sense.

Naturally, in a country as diverse as Scotland, there have always been contradictory impulses. There was first Jacobitism, which meant different things to different groups. Effective Jacobitism was confined to the Highlands, where it was primarily an expression of hostility to the encroachments of the modern, commercial English-speaking world on Gaelic society. But there was another Jacobitism, most fairly described as 'literary Jacobitism', and this represented opposition to the Kirk and, by extension, to the incorporation of Scotland in the British polity. It was powerful among the Episcopalians and Catholics of the North-East, and it long survived the practical extinction of the Stuart cause.

The dominance of the Whig–Presbyterian tradition provoked a reaction. Burns was an early representative of this; so was Scott. In the twentieth century this has taken the form of an attack on the tradition as 'life-denying', and of a consequent reaffirmation of the values and achievements of pre-Reformation Scotland. Consequently much stress has been laid on language, and Knox and his fellow-Reformers have been seen as agents of the anglicisation of Scotland. In one sense this is undeniably true; yet the fact remains that for some four hundred years, their construction, the Church of Scotland, has been the institution which embodied the sense of national identity.

I hope that I have been able to do some justice to all these strands in our heritage. We have good reason in Scotland to be proud of the achievements of our forefathers. Few nations have contributed more to mankind than ours; a companion volume could be assembled of those of Scots descent who have flourished in other lands. Here, however, are one hundred and one of those who have made some noise in the world.

The greatest of Scotsmen, Sir Walter himself, introduced his first substantial work, *The Minstrelsy of the Scottish Border*, with these words: 'By such efforts, feeble as they are, I may contribute something to the history of my native country, the peculiar features of whose manners and character are daily melting and dissolving into those of her sister and ally. And trivial as may appear such an offering to the Manes of a Kingdom, once proud and independent, I hang it upon her altar with a mixture of feeling which I shall not attempt to describe.'

I am sensible that my own efforts are much feebler, this offering more trivial, but the spirit which animates the work and the mixture of feeling with which I offer it are, if the claim is not too vainglorious, similar.

ALLAN MASSIE
Selkirk, 1987

x

St Ninian

(fl. 5th century)

No reliable dates can be given for St Ninian, but he is reputed to have been the first to preach Christianity in Scotland. He is mentioned by Bede in his History of the English Church as 'a most reverend bishop and holy man of the British nation, who had been regularly instructed at Rome in the faith and mysteries of the truth'. Ninian, who is also known as Rinian, Trinian and Ringan (it is a ridiculous yet pleasing thought that in the second of these other identities he should have given his name to Ronald Searle's appalling schoolgirls) is, like most early saints, said to have been of royal birth. It was certainly in the beginning of the fifth century, when Rome had abandoned the northern part of Britain, that he worked in Galloway and tried to convert the Southern Picts.

Ninian's biography was written some eight hundred years later by Ailred, Abbot of Rievaulx. It is, not surprisingly, hardly reliable. According to Ailred, however, Ninian studied in Rome, where the Pope took note of him and thence despatched him to convert the people of western Britain who had not yet heard of Christ. On his way north Ninian visited St Martin of Tours and was later to name his first Church after him. He settled in Galloway and built there the first stone structure erected in Scotland. (This is incredible.) He was assisted in this by masons who had accompanied him from France. The white church, shining across the Bay of Wigtown, was known as Candida Casa or, in Anglo-Saxon, Hwitherne, which version survives as Whithorn.

Having converted the men of Galloway, Ninian travelled north to Perthshire where he met with equal success, the Picts rushing, according to Abbot Ailred, 'to renounce Satan with all his pomps and works and to be joined to the body of the believers by faith, by confession and by the sacraments'. It is, of course, unlikely that the Picts had so much as heard of Satan, but it is quite possible that many were baptised by the saint; modern missionaries have found it as easy to persuade the people to accept baptism as they have discovered it difficult to convince them to lead Christian lives. The Abbot of Rievaulx also assures us that Ninian 'ordained priests, consecrated bishops, distributed ecclesiastical dignities and divided the whole land into parishes'. The last of these was not accomplished in Scotland till the eleventh century at the earliest.

We might as well admit that we know very little of Ninian and are never likely to learn more. Yet in one sense we know enough. We know that he is the first man credited with introducing Christianity to Scotland; we know that something of the seed he planted grew, and that the south-west of Scotland remained Christian, or at least contained remnants of the Faith, in the dark century that succeeded the Roman withdrawal from Britain, and we believe that from this source sprang the impulse which took St Patrick to Ireland. At any rate it is reasonable to believe that from Ninian comes the oldest tradition of unbroken Christianity in these islands. The number of places, stretching from the Shetland Isles to the Solway, which are called by his name testify to the fame he enjoyed. St Ninian is the first saint of Scotland.

St Columba
(c. 521–598)

The Church of Scotland's kirk in London is called St Columba's and this reminds us that there is good reason for thinking that Columba, rather than Andrew, should be the patron saint of our nation. The legend concerning the arrival of St Andrew's bones, carried by St Regulus or Rule to that point of Fife that now bears his name, is some two hundred years older than the historically-established mission of Columba. Nevertheless it was Columba who brought Christianity to the Picts and Columba who established the holy place of Iona.

He was born in Donegal, at Gartan, reputedly of princely descent. According to his early biographers, Cumin and Adamnan, both monks of Iona who wrote within a hundred years of his death, he was given to the study of Scripture from youth. One of his teachers was St Ciaran who had himself preached to the Scots in Argyll and whose name is commemorated in the parish of Kilkerran. Around the year 550, Columba is said to have founded the abbey of Durrow but, a dozen years later, his involvement in a blood feud caused him to be excommunicated by an Irish Council. At the age of 42, in the year 563, he left Ireland, possibly devoting himself to missionary work as an act of penance, and sailed in a *currach* which was washed up on the island of Iona on Whit Monday. An artificial mound, in the form of an inverted boat, marks the spot where he landed.

The King of the Dalriada Scots, Conal MacComgail, granted Iona to Columba and his followers. He built a monastery there. Then he set out to convert the Picts. He journeyed to King Brude at his strong-place near Inverness. A contest with the pagan priests ensued, which owes something to Elijah's struggle against the prophets of Baal. Columba performed some miracles, which persuaded the king of the superior efficacy of the new religion. He and his followers submitted to baptism. No doubt their Christianity was superficial

3

but the process set in motion by Columba was never reversed. He made the north of Scotland nominally Christian.

Most of his life was passed at Iona, supervising his monks and training them for missionary work. This first monastery on Iona was built of logs but it included a church, a guest-house, the abbot's quarters and a granary. Columba frequently visited the mainland, either on pastoral work or to found a church. These churches were so numerous that he came to be called Colum kille or Colum of the Churches. He was also a man of letters, a writer of hymns and a transcriber of ancient manuscripts. The reputation of his library was celebrated throughout the Middle Ages. The Papal legate, Aeneas Sylvius (later Pope Pius II), who visited Scotland in the fifteenth century, hoped to find the lost books of Livy at Iona but was prevented from visiting the island. (Had the books been there in Columba's time, which is unlikely, they would probably have been destroyed in one of the many sackings of the monastery by the Norsemen in the intervening centuries.)

Columba's biographers assure us that he was 'of angelic appearance' and had a lovable disposition. There is a story of an old mare, used to bring milk to the monastery, that laid her head on his breast and wept a few days before he died. His death took place at the altar of his own church. His disciples buried him in Iona 'until in luminous and eternal brightness he should be raised again'. In fact, a hundred years later, his bones were carried off to Ireland. They were returned to Scotland and then lost.

His work, unlike his resting-place, endured. Dr Johnson, visiting Iona some twelve hundred years later, was pleased to feel himself 'treading that illustrious island which was once the luminary of the Caledonian regions whence savage clans and roving barbarians derived the benefits of knowledge and the blessings of religion'.

The Church established by Columba never died but in form and organisation it was to be superseded. Columba had established a Church which had no link with Rome. His followers, known as Culdees, did not seek one. They maintained their independent and idiosyncratic Christianity at least until the late eleventh century. For this reason, anti-papal Church historians have been inclined to credit them with possessing in equal measure the virtues of the primitive Church, as recorded in the Acts of the Apostles, and the sturdy independence of the Presbyterian Kirk. There is a good deal of fancy in this view because we know little in detail of the Culdees. However, Columba's monument is Iona and, in Johnson's words, 'that man is little to be envied whose patriotism would not gain force upon the plain of Marathon, or whose piety would not grow warmer among the ruins of Iona'.

Macbeth
(King, 1040–1057)

Everyone knows the story of Macbeth; of how he was a general of the venerable and admired King Duncan, of how he suppressed a rebellion and defeated the invading Norwegians; of how returning from the battle with his fellow-general Banquo, he encountered three witches on a barren heath near Forres. They, foretelling, addressed him as Thane of Glamis, Thane of Cawdor, and king that shall be, and they promised Banquo that his descendants would be kings. Macbeth was already Thane of Glamis by reason of his father's death, and was at once greeted by messengers from the king with the title Thane of Cawdor, the previous thane having been executed for his part in the late rebellion. Macbeth wrote to his wife, telling her of these matters and warning her that King Duncan was coming to be their guest. She incited him to murder. Macbeth, though at first reluctant, was at last persuaded and slew the king while he lay asleep in his chamber in Macbeth's castle. Responsibility for the crime was fixed on Duncan's sons, Malcolm and Donaldbain, who fled the country. Macbeth was made king but felt uneasy in his new office while Banquo lived. He therefore arranged his murder but was distressed to learn that Banquo's son had escaped. Now Macbeth's character deteriorated. Scotland suffered a reign of terror. Macbeth again consulted the witches who promised that he should be safe till Birnam Wood came to his castle of Dunsinane; they offered the further security that he should fear no man born of a woman. Though trusting them, his rule of terror did not abate. At last, Scottish refugees in England assembled an army with English help. They invaded Scotland. Approaching the tyrant's lair they disguised their advance by arming themselves with branches from Birnam Wood. A servant informed the king that the wood seemed to be approaching the castle. Macbeth realised that he had been cheated by the witches but nevertheless trusted in their last promise, only to be disillusioned when his adversary Macduff, the Thane of Fife, revealed that he had been 'from his mother's womb untimely ripped'. Fighting with desperate courage, Macbeth was slain by Macduff, who then carried the tyrant's head to the young Malcolm.

This is Shakespeare's Macbeth. The story is drawn from the chronicler Holinshed and perhaps from another source, William

Stewart's *Buik of the Chroniclis of Scotland*, which existed only in a single manuscript, but the historian Arthur Melville Clark has suggested that Shakespeare may have been able to consult it.

There is another version of the Macbeth story, however. In this Duncan was not an old man but a rough king in the prime of life. Macbeth was not a loyal general but, as Mormaer of Moray, the representative of another royal line with a good claim to the throne. Duncan was not murdered but killed in battle. Far from being a bloodthirsty tyrant, Macbeth was a wise and well-meaning king. He passed exemplary laws. He made a pilgrimage to Rome in 1050 and was the first Scottish king to do so. In 1054, however, Scotland was invaded by an English army led by Siward, Earl of Northumbria. They defeated Macbeth on the day of the Seven Sleepers (27 July). As a result of this defeat Macbeth lost control of the Lothians. Three years later, Macbeth was driven north by Siward, who had now been joined by Duncan's son Malcolm. Macbeth was slain at Lumphanan in Aberdeenshire. His stepson, Lulach, was made king but was himself killed a few months later at the Battle of Essie.

These are the two stories and there is no doubt which has the greater resonance. Is it possible to reconcile them?

First, the idea of unjustified rebellion and murder may be dismissed. Shakespeare, following Holinshed, appears to assume that primogeniture was established in eleventh-century Scotland. This was not so. The king was chosen, as also in Anglo-Saxon England, from the most suitable candidates among the royal house. Moreover, it appears that a system was already established whereby the succession alternated between two branches of the royal house; in this case one being represented by Duncan, the other by Macbeth. Therefore, when Duncan named his son Malcolm Prince of Cumberland (as he also does in the play), it must have seemed to Macbeth to be an attempt to pervert the succession, even to be a form of usurpation. That would justify his taking arms against Duncan.

Second, much of the record of Macbeth's crimes may be dismissed out of hand as the propaganda of the victorious party. It seems unlikely that Macbeth would have dared to leave the kingdom for the time necessary to journey to Rome, had he not been a securely established and popular king.

Third, the confusion of locations and the appearance of the witches are readily understood if we remember that Shakespeare's play was written for James VI and I, and so reflects some of the events of his reign in Scotland. Sir James Fergusson, in an essay, *The Man Behind Macbeth*, suggested that Shakespeare drew on the strange events connected with the king's cousin, Patrick Stewart, Earl of Bothwell, who consorted with witches at North Berwick and was accused of trying to engineer the king's death by means of magic. Arthur Melville Clark, in *Murder Under Trust: The Topical Macbeth*, drew attention to the similarities between the action of the play and the *cause célèbre* known as The Gowrie Conspiracy. This would account for Shakespeare's decision to locate the climax in Perthshire rather than Aberdeenshire. Both writers, even if their interpretations did not agree, made the case that the play of Macbeth drew more on the Scotland of the 1590s than on the Scotland of the eleventh century.

Yet, though Macbeth may have been innocent of murder and a good king, there is almost nothing in the dry chronicle of his reign which can compete in imaginative power with Shakespeare's play. Shakespeare's Macbeth is as persuasive as his Richard III; an example of Art imposing its version of the truth in History. Only one fact on the historical side may touch the imagination: both Macbeth and Lulach were buried in Iona, the ancient and revered burial-place of the Kings of Scots. Is it likely that the blood-stained hellhound of Dunsinane would have been laid to rest there?

St Margaret
(d. 1093)

The oldest building within Edinburgh Castle is a small and simple chapel to which is attached the name of St Margaret. She is also commemorated in the names of two villages that lie on either side of the River Forth, North and South Queensferry (the saint was also Queen of Scots), and in the little bay called St Margaret's Hope, where she first landed in Fife. For Margaret was not herself a Scot, but arrived as a refugee.

She belonged to the old royal house of Wessex and was thus a descendant of King Alfred. (Indeed it is through Margaret that our reigning Queen can trace her descent back to Alfred, beyond him to the legendary or near legendary Cerdic, the founder of Wessex, and thence to the god Woden.) But Margaret's more immediate descent had its own interest too. She was the grand-daughter of Edmund Ironside, who had been killed or murdered in 1016 while opposing the Danish king Cnut's conquest of England. Edmund's children, two boys called Edmund and Edward, were either expelled by Cnut or fled from him. Somehow they made their way to Hungary, where Edward, later known as 'the Exile' or 'Outlaw', married a Hungarian princess. About 1055 the king of England, the childless and pious Edward the Confessor, summoned his nephew the Exile back to England, perhaps with a view to making him his heir. The Holy Roman Emperor, whom the Exile had served, loaded him with jewels and other treasure and sent him on his way. The Exile died 'in mysterious circumstances' before meeting the Confessor. His son, known as Edgar the Atheling, was too young (apparently) to make a claim for the throne when the Confessor died; he and his sister Margaret were still living in England at the time of the Norman Conquest. As representatives of the old Saxon royal line, they could hardly be considered safe. Once it was clear that the Conquest was not going to be reversed, they decided to return to Hungary. Their

8

ship, however, was caught in a storm. It was blown north and into the Firth of Forth.

King Malcolm III (Canmore), the conqueror of Macbeth, who must have been approaching forty, welcomed them. He proposed marriage to the princess. No doubt politics came into it; the chance of allying himself to a family of such distinction (whatever its present misfortune) was too good to miss – but he may also have fallen in love with her. At any rate, if he was not yet in love, he seems to have been so soon after his marriage because Margaret quickly won an influence over him that is rare in what we know of royal marriages in the Middle Ages.

We have a biography of Margaret written either by Turgot, later Prior of Durham, or by Theodoric, a monk of that community. It is of course suspect, an example of special pleading; few medieval biographers were on oath to tell the truth. John of Fordun's *Scotichronicon*, drawing on other (now lost) material besides this biography, also tells how the messenger sent by Malcolm to interview the refugees was impressed by a lady whom he had not yet identified: '"whom, by reason of her incomparable beauty and pleasantness of speech, I took to be the chief of the party". . . . Nor was it wonderful that they should believe her to be the chief who was destined to be Queen of Scotland and heir of England.' This remark is likely to be a retrospective judgement. Malcolm and Margaret were married in Dunfermline, then his principal residence, by the end of the year.

She was clearly a remarkable woman. Her piety made a great impression. She could read too. Malcolm, who was himself illiterate, once found a manuscript which she admired and had it encased in gold, ornamented with jewels, to please her. She herself had brought to Scotland much of the treasure which the Emperor had given to her father and she kept a court of such magnificence as Scotland had never seen before. Nevertheless, she prayed long hours; she fed the poor and washed their feet. She took trouble over Saxon prisoners of war who were kept as slaves in Lothian households. She took charge of nine orphans and saw to their education. She attended to the building of Dunfermline Abbey. In short she behaved exactly as a medieval saint of noble or royal blood should. There is no reason, however, to disbelieve the account of her simply because it fits an approved pattern; saints too have their models and those who practise good works do so in the manner characteristic of their times.

Although Margaret herself became an exemplary figure, her importance in the history of Scotland goes far beyond her sainthood and is independent of it. First, by birth and inclination, she looked towards England and Europe and her influence contributed to the anglicisation of southern Scotland. For several centuries previously, the real question in Scotland had been whether the country would remain a Gaelic or Celtic kingdom or collection of princedoms like Ireland and Wales, or whether it would develop towards a monarchy on the English and Continental model. The reign of Malcolm saw a decisive tilt in the latter direction, decisive enough to withstand easily after Malcolm's death a renewed Celtic challenge in the 1090s from his brother Donaldbain. Margaret's legacy was considerable. Her daughter Maud (otherwise Matilda) would marry Henry I of England, son of the Conqueror, and her youngest son David would himself hold great estates in England. It is unthinkable that an Irish or Welsh princess or prince could have done so. Simply by being who and what she was, Margaret helped to ease Scotland into the mainstream of European civilisation.

Second, her influence was even more decisive in the matter of religion and church government. Here the struggle was between the Celtic or Culdee Church, the heir of Columba, and the Roman Church. As a daughter both of Hungary, a Roman outpost on the frontier of pagan Europe, and of England, there could be no question where Margaret's loyalty lay. Her particular arguments with the Culdees may seem remote and unimportant – the date of Easter, the desirability of taking communion then – but her insistence that Scotland should belong to the body of the Catholic Church was of incalculable value to Scotland – whatever admiration one may feel for the Culdees or nostalgia for their simple independence. It is unfashionable now to talk of higher and lower civilisations, but the modern fashion is a silly one.

Margaret was on her deathbed when news was brought to her that Malcolm had been killed in battle at Alnwick. She had foretold that his campaign would be unhappy and had asked for 'the black rood' to be brought to her. This was the most holy of all the relics that had been carried from Hungary to England and then to Scotland. It was a cross of gold bearing an ivory image of Christ and enclosing a portion of the True Cross. While Margaret was pressing it to her face, her son Ethelred entered with news of the death of his father and elder brother. At first, seeing his mother's condition, he told her all was well. She begged him by the Holy Cross to tell the truth and, when he did so, cried, 'I thank thee, Lord, that givest me this agony to bear in my death hour.' What other words could be used in the biography of one who would be a saint?

David I
(b. c. 1080, King 1124–1153)

David I was often called a saint. James VI, gazing on David's tomb in Dunfermline Abbey and remembering the quantity of royal lands that he had given to the Church, remarked that he had been 'a sair saint for the Crown'. The observation was not original. Sir David Lyndsay of the Mount had already written: 'King James I, roy of this regioun,/Said that he was ane sair sanct to the crown.' The charge was not unjustified; nevertheless David's reign inaugurated the great period of medieval Scotland, and the degree of civilisation that the country was to attain in the twelfth and thirteenth centuries owed much to him.

David was the youngest son of Malcolm Canmore and St Margaret and was the third to come to the throne. His sister Maud had been married to Henry I of England, the youngest son of the Conqueror. Before he was king, David was invested with the Honour or Earldom of Huntingdon, a complex of estates that stretched across some ten or eleven shires of the English Midlands. He married Maud de Senlis who was the daughter of the Saxon Earl Waltheof and of Judith, William the Conqueror's niece. These connections are worth pondering, for one can see in David a synthesis of the various strains which were to help to form medieval Scotland. He was the heir through Malcolm of the old Celtic royal house, through Margaret of the royal house of Wessex and through Judith of the new Norman kings of England. His connection with Waltheof fortified the 'English' or 'Inglis' connection, while his sister's marriage to the Conqueror's son and his own Earldom of Huntingdon brought him into the heart of Norman and feudal England. Many of the Norman families, of whom the Bruces and Balliols were only the most prominent, were introduced by David to form the aristocracy of feudal Scotland, some having been his vassals in England.

The boundary between the two kingdoms was not yet fixed. In the civil war that divided England on the death of Henry I, David intervened in support of his niece Matilda, known as the Empress because of her first marriage. Like other English barons, David, as Earl of Huntingdon, had sworn to accept her as queen. His oath, family feeling, and a natural desire to extend his own power and influence all prompted him to intervene on her behalf against her cousin Stephen of Blois, whom the majority of English barons had accepted as king. In two invasions he ravaged the north; in 1138 he penetrated deep into Yorkshire but was defeated at the Battle of the Standard near Northallerton. Despite this, Stephen was happy to make peace on terms favourable to David. By the Peace of Durham, David's son Henry was made Earl of Northumberland in succession to his grandfather Waltheof. Until David's death this fief was administered from Scotland. Of course it was no more part of Scotland than Normandy was part of England, but the Middle Ages saw nothing incongruous in the same prince being simultaneously king and vassal. Also, regardless of the terms on which Northumberland might be held, its possession by the heir to the King of Scots opened the possibility of the border between Scotland and England being eventually fixed on the line of the Tees rather than the Tweed.

Moreover David was able to take advantage of the weakness of England in Stephen's reign to establish the complete independence of Scotland. This had been in doubt in the reigns of his brothers. He struck his own coinage. He attempted to establish the independence of the Church in Scotland by seeking metropolitan status for his chief church at St Andrews and rejecting the authority of the Archbishop of York.

His many benefactions to the Church may have been intended to influence the Pope to decide in his favour; they were also evidence of his genuine piety which is attested by his biographer Ailred of Rievaulx. Even before David was king, he had invited monks, who belonged to a reformed Bendictine Order at the Abbey of Tiron in Picardy, to found an abbey at Selkirk. Later, apparently because the monks were discontented there, he re-established them at Kelso in 1128. The importance he attached to this foundation is shown by his choice of its first abbot, Herbert, who was also Chancellor of Scotland. Herbert later became Bishop of Glasgow. His successor at Kelso, Ernald, was first made the king's chaplain and then Bishop of St Andrews. As well as Kelso, David founded Melrose and Jedburgh Abbeys in the Borders and granted both establishments extensive estates. In the case of Melrose this eventually included all the lands of Ettrick Forest. Newbattle on the Esk and St Mary of Cambus-kenneth on the Forth also owe their foundation to him. It was David who converted the wooden church of Drumselch Forest outside Edinburgh into the Abbey of Holyrood. Monks from his foundation at Kelso established the great abbey of Arbroath. When one considers how these abbeys advanced civilisation by encouraging art and craftsmanship and how, even in their ruined state today, they delight the imagination and quicken one's sense of history, it may be said that, sore saint for the Crown though he may well have been, David I deserves our thanks more than any king of Scotland except Robert the Bruce.

Nor was David's contribution, which also included the introduction of the order of the Knights Templar to Scotland, limited to church affairs. In the internal peace which he maintained, commerce flourished. Many burghs date their origin or their first charters from David's reign. More than any of his predecessors he may be regarded as the true founder of the Kingdom of Scotland, which he found a cluster of more or less independent provinces and left as a recognisable feudal state. The 'Golden Age' associated with the two Alexanders in the thirteenth century would have been impossible without his civilising work and the structures which he established.

Personally David seems to have been an attractive figure. He was assiduous in the administration of justice. Like St Louis of France, he would make himself available to his most humble subject who had cause to plead or an injustice of which to complain. He encouraged all the arts of peace, including building in which he took an especial interest. According to his biographer, his chief recreation was gardening; he enjoyed working with his hands and occupied himself happily with planting trees and engrafting them. There are few more innocent and useful ways in which any man, let alone a man of power, can engage himself.

Michael Scott
(c. 1175–c. 1230)

His familiar spirit bridled the Tweed and split the Eildons in three; the latter was a strange legend to grow for the nearby Roman camp was known as Trimontium a thousand years before. Yet in the popular mind Michael Scott was the 'Wizard of the North', a prophet and magician perhaps confused with the old stories of Merlin. In reality, though much of his biography is sketchy, he stands forth as one of the most remarkable minds of his age.

His place of birth is uncertain. Some put it over the Border in Durham, but, although he studied at the cathedral school there, he is more likely to have been born in Upper Tweeddale where the Scotts originated. He proceeded to Oxford and then, in succession, to the Universities of Paris and Bologna. He studied mathematics, theology and law and, by his middle thirties, was master of all the knowledge of Christian Europe. Next he went to Palermo, where he became tutor to the future Emperor Frederick II, himself later to be known as 'Stupor Mundi', the Wonder of the World.

The court of Palermo was at that time the most remarkable in Europe. There could be read the rich tapestry of Mediterranean civilisation. Greek, Roman, Arab and Norman had all gone to make it. Scott learned both Greek and Arabic, to add to the Latin in which, like all educated men, he habitually wrote and, one presumes, thought. Frederick himself has been called the first modern man, but to say this is to disparage medieval civilisation unjustly. Rather, he and Michael Scott may be seen more fairly as representative of that civilisation with its zeal for knowledge, its breadth of culture and its ignorance of nationalism. Certainly Michael Scott, in forming the Emperor's mind, contributed to Frederick's fascination with the East. He wrote for the Emperor a handbook on astronomy and another on physiognomy, because he believed that 'the inward disposition of the soul may be read in visible characters on the bodily frame'. He also dedicated to the Emperor a translation of Aristotle's work on animals. It is pleasing to think that he shared a taste for natural history with the Emperor. Frederick built up a great collection of elephants, giraffes, dromedaries, panthers and rare birds; he also introduced the pheasant into Calabria and perhaps indeed into Europe.

The translation of Aristotle's text – from Arabic – was made at Toledo. Knowledge of Aristotle had disappeared from Western Europe. Michael Scott was among the first to reintroduce it by way of translations from the Arabic versions of Avicenna and Averroës. Such knowledge seemed dangerous to the Church and Scott's translations were censured; yet he was a potent influence, contributing to that reconciliation of Aristotelianism with Christianity which was to find its fullest expression in the work of the *Doctor angelicus*, St Thomas Aquinas, who was in fact related through his mother to Frederick II. St Thomas is known to have been taught by a devotee of Aristotelian thought at the University of Naples, which Frederick founded; his master might well have been himself a pupil of Michael Scott.

After some years at Toledo, Scott returned to Palermo where he continued as the Emperor's physician and astrologer. Pope Honorius II, presumably to please the Emperor, wrote to Stephen Langton, Primate of England, requesting him to confer a bishopric on Scott. He was duly elected Archbishop of Cashel but declined the preferment, reputedly because of his ignorance of Irish. If this was so, it showed a scrupulousness not often found among medieval clerics.

Towards the end of his life, he is said to have fallen into depression. It is to this period that various prophecies associated with his name are assigned. They may be apocryphal, however. Around 1230 he went to England to teach at Oxford. He is said to have returned to the Border lands and to have died there. Some place his death at Melrose, others in Cumberland. He was certainly dead by 1235, when the Latin poet Henry of Avranches wrote that 'he who had impugned Fate has himself submitted to his decrees'.

Scholar, scientist, astrologer and alchemist, Scott was in the forefront of human knowledge and cast a glamour over his time. Dante placed him in the fourth chasm of the eighth circle of Hell among the sorcerers and enchanters:
'Quell' altro, che ne' fianchi e cosi poco,
Michele Scotto fu, che veramente
delle magiche frode seppe il gioco.'
('That other, who is so thin about the flanks,
was Michael Scott who knew the trick of magic frauds.')

Others, however, revered him as a sage. Readers of John Buchan's *The Three Hostages* will recall that the villain Dominick Medina quotes a line: 'Sit vini abstemius qui hermeneuma tentat aut hominum petit dominatum (Let whoever seeks secret knowledge and dominion over men abstain from wine)'. Sandy Arbuthnot identifies this as coming from one of Michael Scott's unpublished papers in the

Bibliothèque Nationale in Paris. Sandy describes the paper as 'a manual of the arts of spiritual control – oh amazingly up-to-date, I assure you, and a long way ahead of our foolish psycho-analysts'.

'Se non è vero, è ben trovato', as the Italians say ('if it's not true, it's well imagined'), and a fine tribute from one Borderer to another.

Thomas the Rhymer

(c. 1220–c. 1297)

'True Thomas lay on Huntlie Bank,
  A ferlie he spied wi' his e'e,
And there he saw a lady bright
  Come riding down by the Eildon Tree . . .'

The 'lady' was the Queen of Elfland, who carried Thomas into the heart of the Eildon Hills where he remained for either three or seven years. Then, to avoid seizure by the infernal powers, he was permitted to return to upper Earth, where he delivered himself of many prophecies. He was still bound, however, to return to his royal mistress whenever she should summon him. Accordingly one day, as he was sitting in his tower of Ercildoune (Earlston), a messenger brought him news that a hart and a hind had left the neighbouring forest and might be seen walking up and down the village street. Interpreting this as a supernatural message, Thomas rose, followed the animals into the forest and was never more seen by men.

This legend has two curious features. In the first place, it is set in no remote past. Thomas Learmont of Ercildoune is an ascertainable historical figure, whose name is mentioned in contemporary documents such as the cartulary of the Trinity House of Soltra. His signature appears as witness to a deed whereby Peter de Haga of Bemersyde binds himself to pay rent of half a stone of wax annually to the Abbey of Melrose. Moreover, Thomas is the reputed author of the romance of *Sir Tristrem*, which Sir Walter Scott believed to be not only genuine but the oldest specimen of Scots poetry.

Secondly, whereas legends of figures such as Merlin are to be found widely distributed, those concerning Thomas, who lived in historical times, are concentrated within a narrow locality. All of the places mentioned in the 'Ballad of True Thomas' can be identified. Huntlyburn is still there, just outside Melrose, though the bank where Thomas lay is now desecrated by the new and repellently ugly District General Hospital. The Eildon Tree has gone but its position is marked by the Eildon Stone on the eastermost of the three hills. A nearby stream is called the Bogle burn. Thomas's tower has been identified with a ruin by the Leader at Earlston.

The poem of Sir Tristrem tells of the adventures of the Arthurian

Tristram and so belongs to the saga of the Morte d'Arthur, which has so many associations with the Borders. An English chronicle of about 1330 ascribes it to Thomas and the evidence for his authorship is examined in *The Romance and Prophecies of Thomas of Ercildoune*, edited by James A. H. Murray, the Editor of the *Oxford English Dictionary* (see p.199).

But it was for his prophecies that Thomas became most famous. These are more doubtfully authentic. Among them are the foretelling of the death of Alexander III, of the Battles of Bannockburn and Flodden, and of the accession of James VI to the throne of Great Britain. Thomas seems to have been accepted as a prophet very soon after his death. Scott writes that 'if we may believe Mackenzie, Learmont only versified the prophecies delivered by Eliza, an inspired nun of a convent at Haddington. But of this there seems not to be the most distant proof. On the contrary, all ancient authors who quote the Rhymer's prophecies uniformly suppose them to have been emitted by himself'. There is nothing improbable in this. The utterance of gnomic and vatic sayings, often the more obscure the better, was a natural consequence of the persistent belief in astrology and abstruse science. It was to reach its peak in the sixteenth and early seventeenth centuries with Nostradamus in France and the Rosicrucians, with whom the Emperor Rudolf surrounded himself, in Prague and Vienna.

In the nature of the genre, most of the Rhymer's alleged prophecies were gloomy. He is supposed, for instance, to have foretold the fall of Kelso Kirk when 'at the fullest'. An early fourteenth-century manuscript records a prophecy: 'when Rokesbourh nys no burgh'. Whatever the truth, Thomas of Ercildoune makes a great figure in Border legend.

There is one other curious possibility attached to him. In the seventeenth century, one of the Learmonth family went to Russia as a soldier of fortune. He established a branch of the family there and the name Learmonth was given the Russian form of Lermontov. The poet Mikhail Lermontov (whose novel, *A Hero of Our Time*, has been fairly described as 'that archetypal progenitor of the modern novel') belonged to the family. It is a nice fancy that links the inspired poet of medieval Scotland with one of the first two masters of Russian literature (the other, of course, being Pushkin).

John Duns, Duns Scotus
(1266–1308)

'Of realty the rarest-veined unraveller; a not
Rivalled insight, be rival Italy or Greece.'

So Gerard Manley Hopkins wrote of John Duns the Scot, known in his lifetime or immediately after his death as the *doctor subtilis* (the sharp-witted doctor). Yet this man was to be condemned and derided by Erasmus and the intellectuals of the sixteenth century, who stigmatised his followers as 'dunces'; the *Oxford English Dictionary* defines a dunce as 'an adherent of Duns Scotus, a hair-splitting reasoner, a cavilling sophist; one who shows no capacity for learning, a dullard, a blockhead'. Even when medieval philosophy became respectable again in the nineteenth century, pride of place was given to St Thomas Aquinas, whose teaching had been challenged by Duns Scotus; the *doctor subtilis* remained, as Dom David Knowles put it, 'the *fons et origo mali*, the chief exhibit in the chamber of horrors'. It took therefore a long time for Duns Scotus to be fairly appreciated.

Only the broad outline of his life is known and, except for the reminder it offers of the internationalism of the medieval intellectual community, it is of little interest. He was born in the village of Maxton in Roxburghshire, but he has been claimed by Duns in Berwickshire where there is a statue of him. He may have gone to school first in Haddington but was sent, at the age of eleven or twelve, to the Franciscan school in Dumfries, of which his uncle was guardian. In 1281 he was admitted to the Franciscan order in the church where, a quarter of a century later, Robert the Bruce was to murder the Red Comyn. He was ordained priest at Northampton in 1291 but clearly his intellectual abilities had already been noted by his superiors, as we find him studying at Oxford (1290–3), Paris (1293–6) and Oxford again (1297–1301). He was, it would seem, a medieval example of the 'lad o' pairts' and was giving lectures during this second visit to Oxford. He returned to Paris. There was at that time a quarrel between Philippe le Bel, King of France, and Pope Boniface VIII. The Pope's claims have generally been thought extravagant but Duns wrote in support of them, for which reason he was expelled from France. His banishment did not last long, however, because he returned in 1304 and became Doctor the following year. In 1307 he was sent to Cologne, where he died in 1308. This is doubtless a life which would be of great and detailed interest if we knew more about it; unfortunately we do not. It does, however, help to conjure up a picture of a Europe where national frontiers hardly existed and where there was therefore almost no restriction on the free movement of scholars, ecclesiastics, merchants or even certain sorts of labourer, from one country to another. The boy from the little village in Roxburgh could find himself teaching in Paris and Cologne; his great dead rival, Aquinas, had also taught in Paris and he had been the son of a German baron holding land in the Kingdom of Naples and Sicily.

'Duns Scotus', Knowles wrote in *The Evolution of Medieval Thought*, 'is by common consent a difficult thinker.' Indeed he may seem impossibly remote to anyone who has never concerned himself with medieval philosophy and theology, but the questions he pondered were to become staples of Scottish philosophy. He devised a metaphysical approach that was new and was to be of lasting influence, even in centuries when his own work was forgotten or disparaged. Dr George Davie wrote in the prologue to his book, *The Crisis of the Democratic Intellect*: 'It used to be noted that visitors to Scotland without a taste for metaphysics were liable to be nonplussed by the questions publicly debated, because of the tendency for arguments about mundane matters to develop into arguments about first principles and for ordinary problems about material things to turn into rarefied problems about the relation of matter to mind.' Duns Scotus may be seen as the father of 'metaphysical Scotland'.

The word 'metaphysics' frightens many, who are moreover uncertain whether the noun is singular or plural. (It is singular.) Chamber's *Dictionary* defines it as 'the science which investigates the first principles of nature and thought; ontology or the science of being; loosely and vaguely applied to anything abstruse, abstract, philosophical, subtle, transcendental, occult, supernatural, magical.' This is an admirable and capacious definition. Where Duns Scotus is concerned, his metaphysics might be described as 'the most subtle investigation of the first principles of nature and thought, and the relation of matter to mind'.

Duns occupied himself first with the question of God. Aquinas had perceived different orders of Being and found that Created Being was a reflection of God's Being; accordingly the mind could rise from Created Being to find its source in God. Duns found this unsatisfactory. To him, Being was univocal. It was a mistake to make any distinction between essence and existence. (*Falsum est quod esse sit aliud ab existentia.*) It is therefore impossible to go beyond the physical order of things; the First Mover is within the universe moved by him. All beings of which we have knowledge are in our experience dependent on something else; they are multiple and yet finite. Such beings require a cause which is necessary, single and infinite. Infinity must include all perfections (including existence) and this cause – necessary, infinite and yet single – must be God. To compress Duns's argument into a few sentences is to risk simplifying it out of meaning, but Duns did offer a satisfactory proof of God's existence within his own universe.

Duns agreed with Aquinas that reason could attain truth without any divine assistance. He held that the mind has a clear intuition of the individual. He elaborated what he called 'thisness' (*haecceitas*), an essential quality of each being or object below the generic and specific. Following this intuition Duns found a structure in things that corresponded to the structure of thought and, to use Hopkins' term 'inscape', he found an inscape of metaphysics covering the whole of being. He was therefore a realist, objects having a fixed actuality and their nature being identified by a metaphysical insight.

Duns laid great stress on the operation of will, in opposition to the Thomists who had held that it was a blind faculty. This brought him close to an ethical indetermination because he held that in the last resort only the commandment to love God was good in itself. All other acts were only good because they were commanded by God. There was no moral law beyond that commandment. It can be seen that, if God were removed from the argument, Duns's logic would have tended towards an existentialist freedom.

This was not the only respect in which Duns pointed the way ahead. He began the separation of theology and philosophy. His refusal to claim that we can go beyond our knowledge of this world, however metaphysically that world is perceived, hardened philosophy by bringing it back to its Greek roots. It has been said that he 'narrowed the capacity of unaided human intelligence' but this is, I believe, a mistake. Rather, he showed that a metaphysical interpretation of meaning was possible for the human intelligence without reliance on any knowledge of God. He found that there was indeed a gulf between the universe of sense, which we could understand, and the infinity of God. Human reason, he maintained in opposition to Aquinas, could only bridge that gulf by blind faith or by constructing arguments based on probability rather than knowledge. Although Duns himself did not question the truth of the Christian revelation, his writing may yet be seen as re-opening the way to a secular philosophy.

As the first metaphysician of 'metaphysical Scotland', Duns deserves to be better known. Like all the great philosophers, his arguments remain fruitful and stimulating even when his premises are rejected.

William Wallace

(d. 1305)

William Wallace was called by a contemporary 'for many years captain of the Scottish people against King Edward I of England'. Almost two hundred years after his death he became the subject of an epic poem in twelve books by Blind Harry. Because Wallace never compromised with the English he was the chief representative of Scottish popular nationalism; indeed Scottish self-consciousness of nationhood properly dates from Wallace and his successor Robert the Bruce.

Wallace was a Renfrewshire knight and was made a great man only by an accident of history. His name indicates a Welsh origin and his ancestors probably came from the Welsh marches as followers of Walter Stewart, the first of that family to acquire land in Scotland, sometime in the twelfth century. When Edward I deposed John Balliol, the king whom he had previously created, and himself occupied Scotland, he demanded that all freeholders do homage to him. Wallace's name is not to be found in the list of Stewart adherents who took the oath, and so he was probably outlawed. According to legend, however, it was the murder of his wife by the English which drove Wallace into what Edward would term a rebellion.

Certainly in May 1297 he killed the English sheriff of Lanark. Then, having joined with Andrew Murray who had been resisting the English in the north, he attacked the English commander in Perth. These successes gave the signal for a general uprising of all those who opposed the English. Wallace was made 'general of the army of Scotland', testimony surely to his ability and to the attraction of his character because, by birth, both Murray and William, lord of Douglas, would have been more obvious candidates for the position. Wallace justified his election by his subsequent choice of battlefield. He took up a strong position on the north side of the Forth, commanding the bridge at Stirling which for many centuries continued to be the strategic nodal point of Scotland as it offered the only passage for an army from south to north. The English, under the Earl of Surrey and Cressingham who was Edward's Governor of Scotland, were completely defeated on 11 September, 1297. For ten months Wallace was to be master of Scotland.

He still owed allegiance, however, to the imprisoned King Balliol and so, possibly also to allay the jealousy of the barons, contented himself with accepting the title of 'Guardian', which he was granted probably in the Kirk of the Forest in Selkirk. He raided Northumberland and established relations with the North German cities of the Hanseatic League, but he had little time to muster foreign support because in the followng spring Edward himself led the whole army of England against him.

Wallace by now had some cavalry – the main striking weapon of medieval warfare – under the command of Sir John Comyn, to bolster his force of spearmen. He determined to give battle, possibly rashly. Before the fight, which took place at Falkirk in 22 July, he told his men, 'I have brought you to the ring; now dance if you can.' His cavalry failed him, quickly abandoning the fight, but the spearmen held good, beating off several charges of the English knights. Then Edward withdrew his cavalry and unleashed for the first time that new and terrible force, the English longbow, which was to destroy the chivalry of France at Crecy, Poitiers and Agincourt. The Scots, deprived of mobility by the flight of their own horsemen, had nothing to offer in return but courage.

Wallace resigned the office of Guardian but did not abandon the national cause. He approached Philip IV of France in an attempt to renew the Alliance, first made in 1295, which had destroyed the wretched Balliol. Philip commended his 'beloved' William Wallace to the Pope but hardly matched his words with deeds. In 1303–4 the struggle seemed hopeless. Most of the nobles who had held out against Edward submitted to him. Wallace refused to do so but was now reduced to guerrilla warfare. In 1305 he was betrayed and handed over to Sir John Monteith, to whom Edward had entrusted the governorship of Dumbarton. Monteith despatched him to London. Wallace was arraigned in Westminster Hall and convicted of treason. He maintained that it was impossible that he should be guilty of this crime since he had never acknowledged Edward as his lord or as lord of Scotland. His claim was just, but disregarded. He was dragged through the streets of London to Smithfield for execution according to the grisly rites of hanging, disembowelling and beheading, which were the penalty of treason. This judicial murder was committed on 23 August, 1305. His limbs were sent to Perth, Dundee, Aberdeen and Stirling, as a reminder of the fate of traitors and a warning to others; they honoured the towns which received them.

Wallace's character is lost in the mists of legend but his achievements and his defiance stand forth, making him justifiably the authentic hero of Scotland, the one man with unsullied reputation who never compromised with the occupying power and never bowed the knee to the Hammer of the Scots.

Robert the Bruce
(b. 1274, King 1306–1329)

Robert the Bruce is often described as a Norman and his English connections are also stressed. Certainly the family originated or are first heard of in Normandy, in the vicinity of Cherbourg, but they were among the first Norman families to settle in Scotland. They arrived early in the twelfth century and Bruce himself was the seventh generation of the family to be born here. The Bruces were made Lords of Annandale. The future king's father also became Earl of Carrick by marriage.

Bruce's grandfather, also Robert, had claimed the throne on the death of Alexander III in 1286. His mother Isabel was the daughter of David, Earl of Huntingdon, who was the brother of Malcolm IV and William the Lion, the grandson of David I and great-grandson of Malcolm Canmore and St Margaret. Thus, through Isabel, the blood of the ancient Scottish kings and the royal Saxon line ran in Bruce's veins. His grandfather's claim was disregarded in 1286 but was advanced again after the death of Alexander's grand-daughter, the Maid of Norway. Bruce was then one of the two principal claimants, or competitors, as they were called, for the vacant throne. Edward I of England, who had been asked to adjudicate, preferred John Balliol, lord of Galloway. When, four years later, the much-oppressed Balliol turned against Edward, the Bruces took the English side but Carrick's suggestion that he be made king in place of Balliol was disregarded by Edward.

Wallace's rising transformed the situation. Young Robert the Bruce now adhered to the Scottish side, despite what Scott calls 'the vulgar tradition' that he was in Edward's army at Falkirk. In 1299, a year after that battle, Bruce was associated with Sir John Comyn of Badenoch in the Guardianship of Scotland. He remained in arms until 1302 when, the struggle apparently hopeless, he submitted to

Edward. It is necessary to make this history clear because Bruce has often been portrayed, in contrast to Wallace, as a mere opportunist. Certainly his opposition was neither as consistent nor as steadfast as Wallace's but it was firm enough. Even when he made his peace with Edward, he was not sufficiently trusted to be given any administrative authority in Scotland.

We do not know what effect Wallace's execution had on Bruce, but it can hardly have failed to make clear the penalty of unsuccessful opposition to Edward. Nevertheless, a few months afterwards, Bruce rode from Edward's court to claim the leadership of the national resistance movement. At Dumfries Abbey church he met Comyn of Badenoch (known as the Red Comyn), on whom had devolved the Balliol claim. They quarrelled and Bruce stabbed Comyn. Bruce ran out of the church, telling his friends that he feared he had killed Comyn. 'I'll mak siccar,' said Sir Neil Kilpatrick, dashing into the church to finish the deed. When the news of this sacrilege reached Rome, Bruce and his followers were excommunicated. However, as Sir Walter Scott put it, in a note appended to a passage in *The Lord of the Isles*, 'the thunder of Rome descended with little effect upon the Scotch mountains.'

Nevertheless, by this murder, Bruce had not only destroyed any hope of leading a united opposition to Edward but had also ensured that the extensive Comyn connection would fight against him. He hurried to Scone to achieve the authority of coronation. A crown was placed on his head by Isobel, Countess of Buchan, who, poor lady was to suffer sorely for her patriotic temerity; when she fell into Edward's hands a few months later, she was confined to an iron cage which was then suspended from the battlements of Berwick Castle. It was a makeshift coronation for Edward had removed the Stone of Destiny, on which kings of Scots were traditionally crowned, and also the crown, sceptre and robes.

Almost immediately afterwards the little army he had gathered was surprised and scattered in Methven Wood. Bruce fled into the wild hills of Atholl and then, with winter approaching, withdrew still further to the little island of Rachrin off the Mull of Kintyre. He sent his queen and the ladies of his court to Kildrummy Castle on Donside, in the charge of his brother Nigel. That winter the castle was taken by the English and all became Edward's prisoners.

Bruce's recovery from this low point was slow but steady. He had to contend with Scottish enemies, such as the Macdougals of Lorn and other Comyn connections, as well as the English. Undoubtedly the death of Edward I in 1307, and the succession of the brave but incompetent Edward II, eased his position. Gradually Bruce and his lieutenants, his brother Edward, his nephew Thomas Randolph of

Moray, and Lord James Douglas, regained the castles held by the English. By 1313 they had taken all but Stirling. That year, Edward Bruce, who was besieging Stirling, negotiated a treaty with its governor, who promised to surrender the castle if he was not relieved by Edward within a year.

The Battle of Bannockburn (23–24 June, 1314), which was provoked by this agreement, was the decisive battle of the war. It determined that Scotland would survive as an independent kingdom. It was won against the odds, for not only were the Scots outnumbered three to one but it was to prove the only battle of the age in which the English longbow was mastered. The keys to the victory were the superior morale and training of the Scots army and the mastery that Bruce showed in his choice of ground and disposition of his forces.

After Bannockburn, Bruce pursued three objectives. First, he had to reassert royal authority in the kingdom. His personal prestige and sense of justice made this possible. He even reconciled the Balliol and Comyn factions but this reconciliation did not long survive his death. Second, he set himself to acquire foreign recognition, partly perhaps to put pressure on England to acknowledge Scotland's independence. The Declaration of Arbroath (1322), the noblest statement of that claim, was addressed to the Pope and secured his recognition and the lifting of the sentence of excommunication passed on Bruce after the murder of Comyn. Bruce swore that he would go on a Crusade when the affairs of Scotland were settled. Peace with England, his third objective, was longer in coming.

Bruce recaptured Berwick in 1318. (His wife Elizabeth de Burgh and the Countess of Buchan had been released earlier in an exchange of prisoners after Bannockburn.) He invaded the north of England and won other battles at Bydand (1322) and Stanhope (1327). However, it was not until the deposition and murder of Edward II threw the affairs of England into confusion that the English were ready to recognise the independence of Scotland. Peace was made at Edinburgh in March 1328 and later confirmed in the Treaty of Northampton. Bruce's young son, later David II, was married to Edward III's sister Joan in an attempt to ensure good relations between the two countries. This was to prove to be as futile as most such royal alliances.

Bruce died in 1329, reputedly of leprosy. He had been unable to fulfil his crusading vow but his heart was removed from his body (which was buried in Dunfermline Abbey) and, placed in a casket, was carried on a Holy War by his general and friend, Lord James Douglas. On his way to Jerusalem, Douglas paused in Spain to assist Alfonso of Castile in his struggle against the Moors. When attacked by enemy cavalry, Douglas threw the casket containing the heart of Bruce into the press of battle and charged after it. 'Now pass thou onward as thou wert wont', he is said to have cried, 'and Douglas will follow or die.' The casket was later found near the body of Douglas and was at last brought back to Scotland to be buried in Melrose Abbey.

To Wallace and Bruce Scotland owed its survival as an independent nation. It is proper that their statues should guard the gateway of Edinburgh Castle. Bruce's achievement was celebrated in the epic poem, *The Brus*, written about 1375, by John Barbour, Archdeacon of Aberdeen. Robert II awarded Barbour a gift of £10 for this expression of Scots patriotism. Its praise of Freedom is memorable:

> 'A! Fredome is a noble thing!
> Fredome mayss man to haiff liking,
> Fredome all solace to man giffis;
> He levys at ess that frely levys.'

These lines are Bruce's true memorial.

James I
(b. 1394, King 1406–1437)

'If God grant me but the life of a dog, I will make the key keep the castle and the bracken-bush the cow.' This statement of intent was reputedly made by James I on his return to Scotland from English captivity in 1424. He strove hard to make it good and came so close to success that he was murdered by those who feared and resented his authority.

James inherited a long-turbulent Scotland. There had been no capable ruler since the Bruce died almost a hundred years before. The land was feebly governed and riven by factions. It was an early example of what the historians call 'bastard feudalism', a state wherein great men (and in Scotland lesser men too) maintained private armies and levied private war.

James's elder brother, David, Duke of Rothesay, had been murdered by his uncle, the Duke of Albany. His father, the aged and incompetent Robert III, fearing for his younger son's safety, had resolved to send him to France. The plan characteristically miscarried. The prince's ship was intercepted by English pirates who, knowing a good thing, passed him on to their own king. Henry IV received him with smiles, in the knowledge that possessing this hostage would help to secure his northern frontier. 'Assuredly,' he said, 'if the Scots had been polite they would have sent him to me for his education since I also know French.' James's father died of shock or weakness on receiving the news of his capture.

James was kept in England, part prisoner and part guest, sometimes more the one, sometimes apparently the other, for eighteen years. Henry V carried him with him on his French Wars, which no doubt contributed to the education of the Scots king. Henry's reason for requiring his company was political, however. There were Scots, under the Earl of Buchan, fighting in the French army. If the royal standard of Scotland could be flown over the English tents, these Scots could be branded traitors. Indeed, at the siege of Melun in 1420, James issued a command to the Scots in the army of the Dauphin of France to lay down their arms. When the city fell, a number were hanged for having borne arms against their sovereign.

James's stay in England was not without benefit. In particular he received a good education. It helped to make him a poet. *The King's Quhair* was a long poem of 197 seven-lined stanzas, written in the metre which Chaucer had used in 'The Clerk's Tale' and which on James's account came to be called *rhyme royal*. It celebrated his love for Joan Beaufort, the grand-daughter of old John of Gaunt. The poem follows literary convention – the poet looks from a window and sees his lady walking in a garden – but it has a delightful freshness and real virtuosity. It shows that James had read Chaucer well but it is no mere imitation of the master. It has a native exuberance such as derivative work never possesses.

James married Joan Beaufort. It was a political as well as a love match. It may indeed have been the main condition of his return to Scotland. Joan's Beaufort uncles, particularly Henry, Bishop of Winchester, who was one of the chief men in the English Council of Regency for the infant Henry VI, must have seen in the marriage a means of weakening, even breaking, the Scottish alliance with France. Other conditions were set. A sum of £4000 was demanded to cover the costs of the king's eighteen years' residence in England – to where he had been brought, and kept, against his will, as a prisoner. The money was to be paid in five instalments. With rare generosity the first instalment was remitted, to serve as Joan's dowry. Thus did the Beauforts provide for their niece at the expense of two kingdoms.

Back in Scotland James soon made up for lost time. He arrested and punished some turbulent lords, no doubt partly as evidence of intent. He had himself crowned at Scone. He summoned a Parliament to Perth, which passed a flurry of legislation. It imposed new taxes. It took measures to preserve the country's natural wealth: a closed season for salmon was decreed; rooks must be destroyed to save the corn; archery was encouraged and football forbidden; duties were imposed on the export of horses, sheep and herring, and customs duties and town rents were reserved for the crown. Most significant, it was decreed that any rebel should suffer the forfeiture of his lands.

This promise of firm government dismayed many of the nobility who were little accustomed to royal interference. A rebellion broke out in the West and was suppressed. Then James arrested his uncle, old Albany, his cousin Murdoch, who had for some years been his companion in English captivity, and Murdoch's father-in-law, the Earl of Lennox. We do not know the precise charges nor the defence, but sentence of death was passed on the accused and carried out. The courtly poet was showing himself a ruthless king.

In this respect James fitted perfectly into the pattern of late medieval and Renaissance princes, who were quite capable of combining high culture with judicial severity. Machiavelli, as we know, drew from life not from imagination. Characteristically, in the midst of this onslaught on his nobility, James found time to take an interest in St Andrews University which had been founded in 1412. He suggested that it should be moved to Perth, which he seems to have preferred to Edinburgh as the capital of Scotland. It is unfortunate that Perth did not supplant Edinburgh; it had the advantage of being further from the English border and closer to Gaelic-speaking Scotland. James indeed seems to have had some sympathy with the Highlanders. Although he broke the power of the Lord of the Isles, he treated him and other recalcitrant rebel chiefs more tenderly than he did the Lowland lords who defied him.

James's assertion of the royal authority caused resentment to fester. There were too many families who had suffered at his hands and feared worse. A conspiracy was formed, the leaders being Sir Robert Graham of Strathearn and the aged Earl of Atholl. In February 1437, James was a guest at the Abbey of Blackfriars in Perth. He amused himself by playing tennis, perhaps to lose weight. (The future Pope Pius II, who had come to Scotland on a diplomatic mission the previous year, thought him too fat.) Irritated by the loss of tennis balls down a drain which ran from the Abbey cellars, he ordered the drain to be stopped up. The decision cost him his life. The conspirators broke into the king's apartments, having first removed the bolts from the door. The attempt by young Catherine Douglas to delay them by using her arm as a bar allowed the king time only to descend to the cellars through a trap-door. He found himself caught there. As he had been preparing for bed, he wore only his night-gown but he resisted his murderers bravely. Twenty-eight wounds were later counted on his body. His heir was a boy of six, and so the pattern of Stewart rule was set – a turbulent minority followed by a few years of energetic royal government ended by untimely death.

William Dunbar
(c. 1460–1520)

In the flowering of Scottish poetry which belongs to the century and
a half before the Reformation, the three chief figures are Henryson,
Dunbar and Gavin Douglas. Of these the greatest is Dunbar. He has
the widest range and the most remarkable virtuosity, and is equally
capable of soaring flight and colloquial directness. Perhaps he lacked
Henryson's acute sense of character, which makes the generally
inappropriate term 'The Scottish Chaucerians' applicable to him, and
perhaps he left no single work as substantial as Douglas's translation
of *The Aeneid*, but he has qualities which the others lack and in which
even Chaucer himself is deficient. In Dunbar we can see not only the
rich culture of the Middle Ages, but also, as when we read Dante and
Petrarch, that everything that is meant by the Renaissance was in fact
a development of medievalism, not a contradiction of it. John Buchan
considered that Dunbar 'ranks with the Ballads, Burns and the
Waverley novels as one of Scotland's four main contributions to
letters'. When Hugh MacDiarmid set himself to revive the Scotch
tongue and poetry, his slogan was 'back to Dunbar'. Such
recognition of Dunbar's achievement and importance represents a
fairer assessment than the absurd observation of the American critic,
Russell Lowell, that 'he who is national enough to like thistles may
browse there to his heart's content'. The lazy parochialism of this
judgement may be exposed by any quotation from Dunbar:

> 'Hail, more decore than of before,
> And awetar be sic sevyne,
> Our glore forlore for to restore,
> Sen thou art quene of hevyne!
> Memore of sore, stern in Aurore,
> Lovit with angellis stevyne,
> Implore, adore, thou indeflore,
> To mak our oddis evyne.
> Ave Maria, gratia plena!
> With lovingis loud ellevyn,
> While store and hore my youth devore,
> Thy name I sall aye nevyne . . .
> Imperiall wall, place palestrall,
> Of peerless pulcritud;

Triumphale hall, hie tour royal
Of Goddis celsitud;
Hospitall riall, the lord of all
Thy closet did include;
Bricht ball cristall rose virginall
Fulfillit of angell fude!
Ave Maria, gratia plena!
Thy birth has with his blude
Fra fall mortall originall
Us raunsound in the rude . . .'

The clashing syllables of this passage from 'Ane Ballat of Our Lady'
combine the magnificence of medieval Latin with the energy of the
vernacular. It is marvellous stuff that deserves to be sung out.

Dunbar could speak in other voices too:
'When that the nycht dois lenthin houris,
With wind, with haill, and havy schouris,
My dule spreit dois lurk for schoir;
My hairt for langour dois forloir,
For aik of symmer with his flouris . . .'

A poetic commonplace perhaps, but how elegantly and easily it is
turned. He had the true poet's regard for his masters:
'O reuerend Chaucere, rose of rethoris all,
As in oure tong ane flour imperiall,
That raise in Britain evir, who redis rycht,
Thou bearis of makaris the triumph riall;
Thy fresh anamalit termes celicall
This mater coud illumynit have full brycht;
Was thou nocht of our Inglisch all the lycht,
Surmounting eviry tong terrestriall,
All fer as Mayes morow dois mydnycht?'

Yet he was capable too of the direct and Rabelasian speech of the
'Daunce of the Sevin Deidly Sinnes':
'Syne Sweirness at the secound biddynge
Cam like a sowe out off a middynge . . .'
and of the sombre philosophy of 'All Erdly Joye Returnis in Pane'
and of the grim 'Lament of the Makaris'. His mastery of the verse
paragraph, a sure sign of a high and accomplished culture, is nowhere
clearer than in 'Hermes the Philosopher':
'Thou seis thir wrechis set with sorrow and cair,
To gaddir gudis in all thair lyvis spece,
And when thair baggis are full, thair selfis are bair,
And of thair richness bot the keping hess;
Whill otheris come to spend it that hes grace,

Whilk of the wynning no labour had nor cure;
      Tak thow example, and spend with meriness:
      Without glaidnes availis no tresour.'

We know little of Dunbar's life but, although it would be fascinating
to learn more, the lack of knowledge does not affect the appreciation
of his genius any more than it does in the case of Shakespeare. Dunbar
was probably born in East Lothian and he certainly studied at St
Andrews. He may have been a Franciscan novice but later took
priest's orders. He served on various embassies to France and
England, the latter to arrange the marriage of James IV to Margaret
Tudor. This he celebrated in 'The Thrissell and the Rose'. He
received a pension from the Court but his name disappeared from the
Treasurer's Accounts after Flodden.

No Scottish poet equals his technical mastery and yet it is almost
by chance that the bulk of his work survives. A small collection was
published by Chapman and Myllar in 1508 but other poems were
found only in a number of manuscript collections. The first collected
edition did not appear until 1834.

Master of a wide variety of moods and forms, Dunbar is a poet
who delights. He also offers the clearest evidence that Scotland in the
late fifteenth century was a country of copious and exuberant culture.
Edwin Muir wrote of 'Dunbar's beautifully patterned and figured
verse' and pointed to 'the immense loss in technical skill which
Scottish poetry suffered between Dunbar and Burns, the loss of the
whole art of poetry'. It is hard to dispute this judgement. Even those
who question it must confess that mastery of the whole art of poetry
is to be found in Dunbar and nowhere else in Scottish literature.

James IV
(b. 1473, King 1488–1513)

There was a fifteenth-century French saying, 'fier comme un Ecossais (proud as a Scotsman)'. It might have been coined with James IV in mind. His reign saw the brief flowering of Renaissance Scotland and James seemed worthy of its splendour. He encouraged and patronised art and science; he built nobly; he created a navy; he travelled all over his kingdom; he was handsome, intelligent, generous and glittering. The great scholar, Erasmus, who was for a time tutor to one of James's illegitimate sons, said of James: 'He had a wonderful intellectual power, an astonishing knowledge of every-thing, and unconquerable magnanimity, and the most abundant generosity.' The Spanish ambassador, Pedro de Ayala, reported to King Ferdinand and Queen Isabella that the King was a remarkable linguist, of keen intellect, always busy yet keeping time to read, handsome, temperate, devout, and an effective ruler. Kings are, of course, there to be flattered and, when a king condescends to a commoner, it is natural that he should be praised in return. However, Ayala, writing in cipher to his employers, had little need to dissemble. It is fair to conclude, therefore, that this was indeed the impression that James made on those who knew him. Likewise the long list of mistresses suggests that James was just as attractive to women as his descendant Charles II was to be.

Yet this was the king who was also known at 'James of the Iron Belt'. As a mere boy of fifteen, he had been seduced into giving his countenance to a rebellion against his father, the unfortunate James III. That had resulted in the king's murder by a priest or a man posing as a priest, and James IV suffered lasting guilt on this account, wearing an iron chain round his waist to the end of his life as a reminder of the sin he had committed. That was more surely than superstition and suggests that James's character was more compli-cated than it appears.

As king he strove, like all the Stewarts, to impose order on his turbulent kingdom and to extend the authority of the Crown. He subdued the Highlands, but only temporarily. He then found himself obliged to fall back on the resource of assigning lieutenancies to the Earls of Argyll and Huntly, which achieved order at the expense of increasing the power of these two chieftains. He performed his judicial duties punctiliously. One of the complaints directed at his father had been that he neglected these.

One cannot easily judge the king's responsibility for all the achievements of his reign. It was, of course, James's good fortune that he was the contemporary of a poet like Dunbar who shed lustre on his age. James's Chancellor, William Elphinstone, Bishop of Aberdeen, may deserve the credit for the foundation of a university in that northern city and for the passing of the Education Act of 1496 which commanded that the eldest sons of landowners should acquire 'perfyte Latyne' and then study law. The establishment in 1506 of the first printing press in Edinburgh by Chapman and Myllar would doubtless have happened without the king's encouragement. On the other hand, he can surely claim credit for the new palace at Holyrood. The Great Hall of Stirling Castle was constructed in his reign. A fine hunting lodge was built in the deer park of Falkland Palace. The building of Scotland's first navy, which so greatly impressed contemporaries, though it proved of little value, was certainly the king's own work. It was said that the forests of Fife were stripped to build his flagship, the *Great Michael*.

There was a streak of knight-errantry in James. He loved tournaments, although these occasions which were once the training-ground for warfare had, with the development of artillery and the longbow, become mere sport. This fanciful attitude, this preference for appearance rather than reality, was evident also in his foreign policy. Although he was king of a poor country on the extremity of Christendom, he proposed himself as leader of a crusade against the Turks at a time when the crusading spirit had long ago been replaced by considerations of commerce and realpolitik in those parts of Europe somewhat closer to the Sultan's power. It was perhaps this same spirit which made James apparently ready to accept the claims of the imposter, Perkin Warbeck, who asserted that he was Richard of York, the younger of the Princes who had disappeared in the Tower. For some years James kept Warbeck at his court. He even invaded the north of England on his behalf.

James's policy towards England was indeed inconsistent, almost as if he were divided between reason and fancy. Reason was uppermost when he sent ambassadors, who included Dunbar, to treat for the king's marriage to Henry VII's daughter, Margaret

Tudor. Dunbar was not alone when he saw, in the union of the thistle and the rose, a new dawn; that marriage was eventually to lead to the union of the crowns. In the year before the marriage, James signed a Perpetual Peace with England but it lasted only ten years. Then, in 1512, while Henry VIII was campaigning in France as a member of the Holy League which Pope Julius II had cobbled into being against the French king, James imprudently renewed the Auld Alliance. Whatever the benefits of civilisation that the French connection had brought to Scotland, there had never been the least military or political advantage. James invaded England the following year and proved the truth of the one adverse criticism which the Spanish ambassador had directed against him: 'He is not a good captain because he begins to fight before he has given orders.' This was not all that was deficient in his generalship; he abandoned a strong position in response to the Earl of Surrey's appeal to his chivalric generosity. By his blunders and rashness he brought down on Scotland the greatest disaster for more than two hundred years. He himself was killed at Flodden, doubtless fighting bravely, but more died at Flodden than the king and so many members of the nobility. The great promise of Renaissance Scotland perished also on that muddy hillside.

Gavin Douglas
(c. 1474–1522)

The word 'poet' having lost all sense of its original Greek root in modern English, it is well we have the Scots word 'makar' to remind us of its meaning. This is particularly important when considering a poet like Gavin Douglas, whose principal work lay in translation. That is an art we too easily despise, but we do so because, seduced by the theory that art is a means of self-expression, we forget simply that a poet is one who makes things. Accordingly, since a translator is not an 'original' artist, we are inclined to set him aside as of little account. If Gavin Douglas is to some extent an exception, this is simply because he is seen as having considerable importance in the history of the Scots tongue. His version of the *Aeneid* is after all the longest piece of verse we have in Scots, and, clearly, interesting for that reason, especially perhaps as Douglas seems to have been the first makar to call the language he wrote 'Scottis' rather than Inglis. This interest is, of course, legitimate and proper enough, but, along with our disregard for translation, it obscures the fact that Douglas's principal importance is that he is a very fine poet, who, while losing something of the tenderness and mystery of Virgil, has nevertheless given us more of Virgil than we can find in any other version in any variant of our tongue, and moreover, given us what is a great poem in its own right.

The question of translation is important, because it is partly the evidence of Douglas's *Aeneid* which persuades us of the richness of the culture of sixteenth-century Scotland. Ezra Pound, a warm admirer of Douglas, observed that 'a great age of literature is perhaps always a great age of translation, or follows it'. This is not surprising; where there is a real interest in literature, and where talented poets are to be found, it is natural that there should be curiosity about the problem of rendering the literature of another country, and particularly that of the Ancient World, into the vernacular – both because this represents a challenge to the poet, and because he wishes to make the original which he admires available to readers. A great age of translation is evidence of a wide diffusion of culture.

Douglas was a great poet, a contemporary of Dunbar, and therefore flourishing at the period when Scots had attained a wholeness, a copiousness and flexibility which made it possible for an undertaking such as the translation of a work of the highest art to be attempted. Ezra Pound thought that Douglas was not only a great poet, whose works should be made available, but that his *Aeneid* was greater than Virgil's, 'as Douglas had heard the sea'. The reason given is a silly one, and the argument pointless, not only because Pound did not possess sufficient Latin to evaluate Virgil, but because such a comparison can mean nothing and must be irrelevant. What is important is that Douglas and the language he employed were both up to the task. The means at the poet's disposal were both strong and natural. At no subsequent point of the history of the Scots tongue could this have been said, and so Douglas's *Aeneid* shows very clearly what we lost, when English in its southern form became the language of discourse after the Reformation. For a generation perhaps Scots remained capable of being used for great poetry – Mark Alexander Boyd's sonnet 'fra bank to bank, fra wood to wood I rin', and Alexander Hume's 'On the Day Estivall' are two examples – but thereafter it dwindled into provincialism till MacDiarmid tried to revive it as an artificial language this century. It is the tragedy therefore of Douglas's *Aeneid*, that it stands at the tail of a tradition when it should rather have nurtured and enriched it. We are faced with the paradox of a great work with no real successor.

Of Douglas as a man we know little with certainty. He had a public career which is well documented. He belonged to the branch of the family known as the Red Douglases, and was a younger son of old Bell-the-Cat, the fifth Earl of Angus. He is said to have been born at Tantallon Castle near North Berwick, and he attended St Andrews University in the early 1490s. He may have studied in Paris. Like many younger sons he was destined to a career in the Church. In 1503 he was Provost of St Giles, and in 1515 became Bishop of Dunkeld. After Flodden (1513) his nephew the Earl of Angus married the Queen-Mother Margaret Tudor, and Douglas was caught up in the struggle for control of Scotland that raged between Angus and the Duke of Albany. In 1517 he headed an embassy to France to try to arrange the marriage of the boy James V with a French princess, but on his return he found Albany established as Regent, and was exiled to England, where he died, apparently of the plague, in 1522.

All this is interesting but not important. His version of the *Aeneid* is important. Even those who denigrate translation admire the Prologues which he wrote for each book. They are fine, but their originality is no great matter and the body of the poem is finer still. There might be a hope for Scottish culture when Douglas's *Aeneid* becomes standard reading in our schools; pigs will fly sooner.

George Buchanan
(1506–1582)

Matthew Arnold believed that culture could spread sweetness and light: George Buchanan was one of those who prove that this is not necessarily the case. He was a man of profound and wide learning and considerable creative gifts but he was also narrow, self-righteous and intimidating.

Buchanan may be seen as the bridge between the Renaissance and the Reformation. His education was that of a humanist but his temperament that of a bigot. Yet, full-grown before the Reformation broke Europe in two, he is a reminder of its earlier unity. As such, he serves also as an illustration of the truth that the Protestant Reformation was at the same time an act of revolt against certain aspects of humanism, and more importantly, the development of its spirit of individual inquiry.

He came from Stirlingshire. His father's death impoverished the family, as his mother was left with eight children to rear, but an uncle sent him to the University of Paris to study Latin in 1518. He remained there for four years and achieved such a knowledge of the language that it became his natural medium of writing. In 1525 he enrolled at St Andrews as a poor student. The following year he accompanied his master, the historian and philosopher John Major (otherwise known as Mair), back to Paris, where he graduated as Master of Arts in 1528. For the next few years he taught at the College of Sainte Barbe in Paris.

Back in Scotland in the middle 1530s, he became tutor to James V's bastard son, Lord James Stewart, the future Earl of Moray. This was a significant appointment. Moray was later to become the leader of the Protestant Lords of the Congregation and Buchanan's patron. However, Buchanan's stay in Scotland was short-lived. He wrote a satire, called *Franciscanus*, directed at the future Cardinal Beaton. Although, according to one account, he was encouraged in this by the King, the ecclesiastical authorities accused him of heresy. He fled to England and was convicted in his absence.

He seems to have found no opportunity in England and so proceeded to France, where he taught at the new College de Guyenne in Bordeaux. There he wrote two tragedies in Latin, *Jeptha* and

Baptistes. They established him among the foremost writers of his day. (*Jeptha* was translated into Scots by Robert Garioch in our time.) In 1547 he moved to Portugal, to lecture at the University of Coimbra, but was accused of heresy by the Inquisition and imprisoned. It may have been in prison that he wrote a version of the Psalms in Latin verse. His imprisonment did not last long; he was lecturing again in Paris in 1553. Being a polymath, like most humanists, he displayed his versatility by publishing an elaboration and defence of the Ptolemaic Theory of the Universe, *De Sphaera*, as well as by writing a marriage ode for Mary, Queen of Scots and Francis II of France.

By now Buchanan was a thoroughly convinced reformer. It was natural, therefore, that news of the establishment of Protestantism in Scotland should bring him home. Queen Mary herself returned the next year and Buchanan was appointed her tutor. Mary was nineteen, a widow and a reigning queen, and it might be thought that she had little need of a tutor. However, Buchanan read with her in the evenings. He was perhaps the most distinguished Scottish scholar; being also a convinced Protestant, it may be that it was hoped that he would convert the queen. Their relations seem to have been friendly. She granted him a pension of £500 Scots from the revenues of the Abbey of Crossraguel in Ayrshire and in 1566 he became Principal of St Leonard's College in the University of St Andrews. He was now sixty and, it seemed, secure for life. The following year he was Moderator of the General Assembly of the Kirk. However, the murder of Darnley and then Mary's marriage to Bothwell turned him against the queen. He seems to have believed that she was implicated in the murder. At any rate, his long alliance with Moray held. When, after Mary's flight to England, Moray decided to charge his half-sister with the murder of her husband, Buchanan obligingly composed his *Detection* of her iniquities. Charitable judges find in it 'a feeling of personal moral outrage' but moral outrage is better not expressed by one who can treat fact with the cavalier disregard that Buchanan displays. His *Detection* dishonours him as a scholar but suggests that he had a considerable talent for gutter journalism.

Buchanan had his reward, being appointed Keeper of the Privy Seal of Scotland in 1570. He was also made tutor to the young James VI, a post that he held from the time the boy was four till his thirteenth year. Buchanan was a harsh master. James later said that he 'trembled at the approach' of another man who reminded him of Buchanan. One of Buchanan's pleasures was to blacken the character of the boy's mother. However, although he was strict and probably sadistic, he was also efficient. Six hundred volumes were assembled for James's education and he became a first-class scholar. From the age of five, he was studying Latin and Greek.

As Buchanan grew older, he seemed to become more vigorous. He composed a tract, *De Jure Regni apud Scotos*, which was a justification of the imposition of limits on Monarchy, written especially, of course, with reference to the deposition of Queen Mary. He also composed a *History of Scotland* in twenty volumes, which is at its most interesting and least reliable when it deals with events in his own lifetime.

Buchanan wrote principally in Latin, still the language of international scholarship. There are also, however, two pieces in Scots, one an attack on the Hamilton family, the other a satire on Maitland of Lethington who, like the Hamiltons, had adhered to Mary. Both of these were intended to appeal to a wider and more immediate public and both, in their vigorous use of Scots, show how the language might have established a prose literature if the Reformation had not come to Scotland from England.

Buchanan is one of those whom it is impossible to like, even when one admires his range of scholarship and his energy.

John Knox
(c. 1513–1572)

John Knox is perhaps the most misunderstood figure in Scottish
history. Everything that people have disapproved of in post-
Reformation, Calvinist Scotland has been fathered on Knox. He has
been taken as representative of the most narrow bigotry. At the same
time, he is often seen, because of the part that he undoubtedly played
in the Reformation of Scotland and in the formation of the Scotch
character and Scotch society, as a nationalist and patriot. He has been
regarded as a misogynist because of his publication of *The First Blast
of the Trumpet against the Monstrous Regiment of Women*. All of
these views are equally false.

The word 'Regiment' has often been misunderstood as meaning
'clan' or 'the whole body of the sex', whereas Knox meant
'Government'. His blast was directed at Mary Tudor whose
accession to the English throne had deprived him of the comfortable
prospect of a bishopric. In his private life, Knox's relations with
women were affectionate. He enjoyed their company and their
admiration. He married twice, the second time at the age of fifty-
nine. His bride, Margaret Stewart, daughter of Lord Ochiltree, was
only sixteen. Stevenson thought that we might 'remember Knox as
one who was very long-suffering with women, kind to them in his
own way, loving them in his own way – and that not the worst way, if
it was not the best – and once at least, perhaps twice, moved in his
heart of hearts by a woman, and giving expression to the yearning he
had for her society in words that none of us need be ashamed to
borrow'. Queen Mary, one may note, was disgusted by his second
marriage, not because of the difference in age but because the girl was
noble and Knox was not, and perhaps because Knox had been
ordained a Catholic priest.

Although Knox undoubtedly played the leading role in the
Reformation, it is hard to see him as a patriot, let alone a nationalist.

Professor Gordon Donaldson is surely correct when he writes that Knox 'was perhaps the chief agent in all time in the anglicisation of Scotland, in both its politics and its culture'. The Reformers were the party which preferred an English to a French alliance; indeed they could not have come to power nor maintained themselves in power without English support. Their propaganda was conducted in English and by English means, rather than in Scots and by Scots means. Their Bible, psalter, service-books, and all the official documents of their Church, were written in English. Knox himself had been prominent in the English Reformation of Edward VI's reign. He had been offered an English bishopric and declined it only because of his 'forewight of trouble to come', the 'trouble' being the probable succession of the Catholic Mary Tudor. Moreover, he had tried to return to England on Mary's death in 1558, only to find himself unwelcome because Queen Elizabeth had been offended by the trumpet-blast. (Knox had not had the 'forewight' to see that there might be a Protestant queen. Otherwise, being a cautious and politic man, he might have moderated his tone.) His first wife was English and he sent his children to be educated in England.

However, the greatest absurdity is the charge that it was Knox who made Scotland a narrow, gloomy, Calvinist country opposed to art, secular culture and any joy. This is not only a caricature of Knox and his achievement but also ridiculously unhistorical. The fact is that the sixteenth century saw a strong, reforming Puritanism everywhere: in Rome as well as in Scotland. Most of the Scottish laws which tried to reform private life and to impose on it a stricter morality were passed before the Reformation. Even Sabbath observance – that feature of Scottish Calvinism – can be traced back to the Catechism approved by the last Roman Catholic Archbishop of St Andrews, John Hamilton. Knox himself thought that Sunday was quite a good day for a dinner-party and after the Reformation he permitted the taverns to be open on Sunday except during the hours of church services.

It is popularly believed too that Knox and his followers were responsible for the destruction of many of the churches of Catholic Scotland. Most of those lost were actually burned by invading English armies: the transepts and choir of the abbey church of Holyrood in 1544, the Border abbeys during the 'Rough Wooing' that culminated in the battle of Pinkie in 1547. Few churches were built in the century after Knox but this was partly because Scotland was well supplied with places of worship. Knox can no more be blamed for that than he can be praised for the great flourishing of domestic architecture in that same century. It is worth observing in passing that this flowering contradicts the impression that the

Reformers were 'against art'. Knox himself attended the theatre, had a hand in writing the text of a pageant, and enjoyed music. It is far too simple to blame Knox for the complex causes of Scotland's changing culture.

What is left of Knox when the myths are stripped away?

John Knox was born in Haddington, probably educated at St Andrews and ordained a priest. At St Andrews he seems to have been taught and probably influenced by the humanist historian, John Major, who wrote, among other works, a *History of Greater Britain* which advocated the union of England and Scotland. Like many humanists, Knox became a Reformer. It is important to realise that the Reformation grew out of the Renaissance, however much it was to react against certain elements in that movement. Knox was associated with the Reformer George Wishart, who was burned at St Andrews in 1546. The following year he attached himself to the group of Reformers who had revenged Wishart by murdering Cardinal Beaton and seizing the castle of St Andrews. When the French recaptured the castle, Knox was taken prisoner and sentenced to the galleys. He was released early in 1549 and went to England. His prominence there has been noted already. He quickly removed himself when Mary Tudor came to the throne and retired first to France, then to Geneva, where he came under the influence of Calvin. There, in what he called the 'most perfect schole of Christ', he imbibed and accepted the doctrines of predestination and the Elect which were to be features of Scottish Presbyterianism. But these doctrines, deriving from St Augustine, are a recurrent strain in the history of Christianity. The fervour with which they were adopted in Scotland owes more to something native in the national character than to Knox.

His political importance dates from his return to Scotland in May 1559 and specifically from the sermon he preached in Perth a week later. This made him the intellectual leader of the Protestant Party but its success was due to several factors: to the formation of the group of nobility who called themselves 'the lords of the Congregation'; to the hostility to French influence, amounting to control, which had been spawned by the Regency of the Queen Mother Marie de Guise; most of all, to the military and political support of England. Knox became Minister of St Giles in Edinburgh, which brought him into frequent contact with Mary Stuart in her return as queen. The opposition of Knox and Mary, of stern Morality against warm-hearted Romance, has been taken by many writers as a constant theme in Scottish history and as a representation of a division in the Scottish character. It must be said that this notion owes more to a fanciful projection than to the facts of history. Mary herself was more of a Puritan, more

44

of a politician, and less of a Romantic than this antithesis suggests. Nevertheless, inasmuch as both Mary and Knox are taken as symbolic rather than historical figures, it has proved fruitful.

Knox himself was a prudent rather than a fearless politician. He approved of the murder of Rizzio, although there is no reason to think he was party to it, but when it failed to lead to the overthrow of Mary, he retreated first to Ayrshire and then to England till any danger was past. In like manner he deemed it advisable to withdraw from Edinburgh in 1571 when the castle was held by supporters of the deposed queen.

Knox wrote a *History of the Reformation of Religion in the Realm of Scotland* which was completed after his death and published in 1586. It does not underplay his own part in affairs. Even so, it hardly removes the impression that Knox's importance was more symbolic than actual. It is perhaps fair, therefore, that history should have employed irony at his expense and accorded him a popular reputation for narrow bigotry. The popular conception of Knox is false; the picture of his influence is unhistorical; much of the opprobrium directed at his memory should rather be addressed to the Covenanters of the seventeenth century.

Mary, Queen of Scots
(1542–1587)

The drama of her life, the cruelty of her death and the courage and dignity with which she faced it, have made Mary Stuart a figure of romance. No amount of critical investigation nor psychological enquiry can alter that. She is, for all time, the unhappy and maltreated queen.

There is always some truth in legends and this is the case with Mary. Had it not been so, she could neither have won the devotion of so many in her life nor have retained her interest for succeeding centuries. Nevertheless, as frequently happens, the reality is at least as strange and compelling as the legend.

The first fact to grasp about Mary is that she was a politician. She was born a queen and very soon circumstances ensured that her ambitions would extend beyond Scotland. She was taken to France for her own safety when she was only six. She represented, through her mother Marie de Guise, the French interest in Scottish politics. Consequently those who favoured an English alliance were ranged against her. This opposition was rendered acute by the ideological division of Europe. England, thanks to Henry VIII's marital difficulties, had embraced the Reformation; France was divided and would suffer miserable civil wars as a result. In France the Catholic champions were Mary's own family, the great House of Guise. Scotland in the 1540s was still Catholic but Protestantism was winning adherents, both among religious enthusiasts and among the nobility who saw how their English counterparts were enriching themselves on the spoils and properties of the Church. Henry VIII proposed that the infant Mary should marry his young son Edward and then sent an army north to burn the south of Scotland and so encourage the Scots to agree to his proposal. Mary was taken to France to escape this 'Rough Wooing'. She was thus committed to the French alliance and the Catholic Church, and was betrothed to the Dauphin of France.

In 1558 her cousin Elizabeth became Queen of England but, in Catholic eyes, Elizabeth was illegitimate. (At one point her father had also bastardised her by Act of Parliament.) Accordingly, in Paris Mary was proclaimed Queen of England and Ireland. Although she was compelled to relinquish this claim according to the terms of the Treaty of Leith in 1560, and thereafter concentrated her attentions on trying to make Elizabeth acknowledge her as her heir, Mary never abandoned the claim in her own mind. In her last letter, written to Henry III of France the night before her execution, she wrote of her 'God-given right to the English crown'.

Before the Treaty of Leith was signed, Mary had also been Queen of France and was now widowed. She returned to Scotland in 1561. She was not yet twenty.

She came back to a land convulsed by the Protestant Reformation. She had been brought up in the most elegant court north of the Alps and found Scottish manners rude. Yet she was well enough prepared. Like Elizabeth, she was highly educated and she had been schooled by her uncle, the Cardinal of Lorraine, in the arts of politics. She made no attempt to re-impose Catholicism, though she maintained her right to practise her own religion. She debated with John Knox and, reading his complacent account of these conversations, it is hard not to believe that the Queen had the better of the argument. She worked in friendly manner with her half-brother James Stewart, whom she made Earl of Moray, despite his leadership of the Protestant Lords of the Congregation and her knowledge that he maintained close relations with Elizabeth and received money from her. When the Earl of Huntly tried to mount a Catholic counter-revolution, she rode against him and suppressed the rebellion.

The cold-hearted Elizabeth, who remarkably combined extreme egoism with an absence of dynastic ambition, eschewed marriage. Mary could not do so. From the first, the question was: 'Whom shall the Queen marry?' Elizabeth insulted her by proposing her own favourite and lover, Robert Dudley, who was believed to have murdered his wife to make himself available for the throne of either England or Scotland. Mary declined this singular honour and instead married in 1565 her cousin, Henry, Lord Darnley. Everyone agrees that it was a disastrous choice. Darnley was a pretty boy but weak and, as it proved, vicious. Mary undoubtedly fell in love with him, the emotion precipitated perhaps by the experience of nursing him through an attack of measles. There may also have been something motherly in her feelings – he was a year younger and much younger in experience and judgement. He does not seem to have been in love with her; if he was, it did not last long.

The marriage alarmed Elizabeth. Darnley was, nominally at least, a Catholic. Moreover, as a descendant of Henry VII, he had a claim to the English throne. Elizabeth was now ready to encourage the disaffected Protestant lords, especially Moray who saw his influence over his half-sister wane. Meanwhile, Mary had made a friend of an Italian called David Rizzio, who had arrived in Scotland on a diplomatic mission from Savoy. She appointed him her secretary and seemed to rely on his company and judgement. A conspiracy was formed, which included Darnley; Rizzio was brutally murdered, in sight of the Queen, in Holyroodhouse. Mary was pregnant and, after the murder, was threatened by the noble gang with 'being cut into collops and thrown over the wall'.

The murder of Rizzio revealed to Mary the danger of her position and the vile cruelty of those who surrounded her. She did not repine for long, however, but set herself to redeem her position. Her son was born and she patched up relations with Darnley: 'My lord,' she said, 'God has given you a son, begotten by none but you. . . . This is a son who (I hope) shall unite the two kingdoms of Scotland and England.' Nevertheless, any trust between her and the Protestant Lords of the Congregation was broken. Almost inevitably, she turned to the Catholic Earls of Huntly and Atholl and, more and more, to the Earl of Bothwell, a rough Borderer who, though a nominal Protestant, seemed at least to have the virtue of loyalty.

The association with Bothwell was to ruin Mary but it is hard to see how she could have chosen otherwise. Darnley was no support at all; many of the nobility, including Moray, were her open enemies. The year between Rizzio's murder on 9 March 1566 and Darnley's on 10 February 1567 was crowded and confused. We shall almost certainly never establish the truth concerning the murder of Darnley. The most plausible explanation is that a plot was laid to murder both Mary and her husband and that this was discovered by Bothwell who, seeing the means of using it to his own advantage, then stepped in to organise only Darnley's murder. Contemporary opinion declared him guilty, though he was able to overawe the court that tried him, and so secure his acquittal. Opinion also branded Mary as his accomplice but there is no evidence to support this; the fact that her enemies later resorted to forgery to prove their case seems rather to disprove it. Moreover, Mary's position was weakened by the murder of Darnley, whereas there would have been little opposition to her divorcing him. Indeed both Moray and Maitland of Lethington, the most intelligent of her advisers, had recommended divorce: 'We shall find the means that your Majesty may be quit of him,' Lethington said.

In April 1567, Mary was abducted by Bothwell on her way from Linlithgow to Edinburgh. He had eight hundred horsemen with him. Mary consented to accompany him to Dunbar to avoid bloodshed. At Dunbar Bothwell raped her. We have her own word as evidence in a letter written to the Bishop of Dunblane: 'As by a bravado in the beginning he had won his first point, so ceased he never till by persuasion and importunate suit, accompanied not the less with force, he had finally driven us to end the work begun at such time and in such form as he thought might best serve his turn.'

They were married in mid-May, Bothwell having abruptly divorced his wife. Mary's unhappiness was evident. She was in effect Bothwell's prisoner. Forces gathered against them and two armies met at Carberry Hill outside Musselburgh. There was hardly a battle. Bothwell's troops abandoned him. With Mary's permission, he fled, leaving her to her enemies. They brought her into Edinburgh, where the city mob shrieked out, 'Burn the hoor!'

Her humiliation was complete. She was taken to Loch Leven Castle, where the rebel lords compelled her abdication by threatening her with death if she refused. There too she miscarried of twins. Her spirit revived. She persuaded her gaoler's son, young Will Douglas, to aid her escape. She gathered a little force, mostly of Hamiltons, but was defeated again at Langside, outside Glasgow, and fled in fear for her life to England.

Her arrival embarrassed Elizabeth but also offered her an opportunity to extend her influence over Scotland and so safeguard her northern border. Mary's enemies brought accusations against her and provided evidence in the form of the Casket Letters. No-one has seen these ingenious documents since the sixteenth century and it seems probable that the so-called 'originals' were never offered for impartial examination. However, Elizabeth established a Court of Inquiry. This exculpated Moray and the Protestant Lords of the charge of rebellion (as it had to do, since Elizabeth had aided that rebellion) but it also found nothing proven against Mary, though the proceedings were used to blacken her reputation. It is significant, however, that the senior English commissioner, the Duke of Norfolk, proposed that he should marry Mary himself; that suggests that he had found nothing to make him think her guilty of murder and adultery.

Mary's imprisonment lasted nineteen years. There were conspiracies on her behalf, some of which she encouraged. (Norfolk lost his head on account of one of them.) Meanwhile, in France the religious wars broke out and the division between Catholic and Protestant Europe sharpened. Mary, as a symbol of the Catholic cause and as the Catholic claimant to the English throne, could not escape involvement. Elizabeth, who was cold-hearted but not cruel, resisted several demands that the Queen of Scots should be put to death. (She was far more ready to consent to assassination than to a quasi-judicial execution.) Finally, her minister and spymaster, Walsingham, employed agents who entrapped Mary into giving her approval to a plot against Elizabeth's life. She was subjected to a State Trial, which offered a parody of justice, and sentenced to death. Elizabeth signed her death warrant, endeavouring to do so in such a manner as would acquit herself of all responsibility, and the sentence was carried out on 8 February 1587. Mary met death with absolute courage and composure. Everything in accounts of this judicial murder, except for the queen's bearing, is utterly disgusting.

Andrew Melville

(1545–c. 1622)

Andrew Melville was John Knox's successor as the leading figure in the Scots Kirk. He is best remembered for his defiance of James VI. He told the King that the Kirk possessed an authority which derived directly from God; it was therefore superior to the authority of the civil power. There were two kings and two kingdoms in Scotland. One was Christ Jesus, whose kingdom was the Kirk, and of that kingdom James was 'not a king, nor a lord, nor a head, but a member'. He also told the King that he was nought but 'God's silly vassal'. Such reproofs made James all the more determined to impose episcopacy on the Church. He triumphed in his lifetime and Melville in fact spent a number of years imprisoned in the Tower of London. Melville's teaching was maintained by the Covenanters throughout the seventeenth century and remained influential in the General Assembly afterwards. (Subsequent generations, however, refrained from addressing monarchs in Melville's imperious and insolent tone.) Melville also made other lasting contributions to Scottish life.

Belonging to the first generation to be brought up in Protestant opinions, Melville entered St Mary's College, St Andrews, after schooling at his native Montrose, in the Reformation year 1559. He studied afterwards at Paris and Poitiers before moving to Geneva, where his master was Calvin's successor, the great theologian Theodore Beza. This course of education should remind us that Calvinism did not represent a clean break with the humanist tradition. On the contrary, it was understood as a development of that tradition and Melville, like Buchanan, was an accomplished Latin poet. He spent perhaps a dozen years in study on the Continent. On his return to Scotland in 1574, he was appointed Principal of Glasgow University.

Although the Reformers had regarded as vital the reform of the three universities, Glasgow, St Andrews and King's College, Aberdeen, nothing had been achieved in the quarter-century since Catholicism was overthrown. At Glasgow Melville quickly introduced a new curriculum and reformed the old system of teaching. Previously each 'regent' had taken his class through the entire course; now Melville introduced specialist instructors. In 1577 the university received a new charter which embodied Melville's reforms. It remained the basis of education there for three centuries.

In 1579 he moved to St Andrews to carry out the reforms of the colleges there. St Mary's College, of which he became Principal, was now devoted exclusively to theology. Melville insisted on the importance of the study of Biblical languages, without which a true understanding of the Bible was impossible. In this, too, he showed himself an heir of the humanist tradition: Erasmus, for instance, had attacked the authority of the Vulgate by turning back to the Greek Testament from which St Jerome had made his translation.

After his release from the Tower, Melville was not allowed to return north. Instead he went to the Protestant Academy at Sedan, where he taught for the last ten years of his life.

Melville's contribution to the development of Scottish academic life was considerable. He assimilated Scots university education to the practices of the Continental universities where he had studied (and perhaps taught) himself. Nevertheless, the chief interest of his career may now lie in the reminder it offers that the early leaders of Scots Presbyterianism were by no means the uncouth and barbarian fanatics of some popular legend. The true heritage of Presbyterianism is to be seen in men like Melville – cultured, cosmopolitan scholars and intellectuals – rather than in the narrow-minded and yet extravagant ranters of the later Covenanting period.

John Napier of Merchiston
(1550–1617)

The tower of the old castle of Merchiston is now incongruously encased in a modern building that somehow manages to be bland and crude at the same time. The result is ridiculous, and yet for another reason which has nothing to do with architecture, it is not ridiculous at all; it is in fact appropriate. For the modern building is the Napier College of Commerce and Technology, and the old castle was once the home of one of Scotland's earliest and most distinguished mathematicians, whose fame in his own day was so great that he was commonly reputed to be a master of the black arts, whose familiar was a cockerel the colour of jet.

John Napier was born at Merchiston, a family estate lying to the south-west of the Borough Muir of Edinburgh. He was educated at St Andrews University, and then travelled and studied on the Continent. He adhered to the Reformed Religion, and in 1593 published a poem, 'A Plaine Discovery of the Wholwe Revelation of St John', which has few merits. He took no part in public life, but occupied himself with his studies, though when he succeeded to the family estates comparatively late in life he interested himself in agricultural improvements, being one of the pioneers of the use of fertilisers.

Like most scientists of his time, he was versatile. The art of war (in which so many members of later generations of Napiers were to be prominent) aroused his curiosity. He devised burning mirrors, bullet-proof jackets and advanced engines of artillery. None of these proved of practical use. It was as a mathematician that he made his principal contribution to science. He invented a simple calculator, known as 'Napier's Bones' and, most important of all, worked out the system of logarithms which he set out in his 'Mirifici Logarithmorum Canonis Constructio', published two years after his death.

Napier is a strange and interesting figure. On the one hand with his reputation as a necromancer and the oddity of some of his speculations, he seems to look back to the late Middle Ages, not of course far behind him. On the other hand the genuinely scientific nature of the main line of his work anticipates the Enlightenment.

53

The width of his interests, as well as the acuity of his mind, suggests that he would have been quite at home in the Edinburgh of the 1750s. He had very considerable creative ability, and a profoundly inquiring mind. He lived, however, in an age when the public mind of Scotland was corrupted by its obsession with theology. The first half of the seventeenth century is a curious period of our history. In some respects it is a noble one; yet it is also an aberration. The theocracy which the Kirk struggled to establish was ready to suspend natural laws to point up moral lessons. It was a time of 'neurotic superstition', as John Buchan put it, and in such an atmosphere the spirit of rational scientific inquiry could not find a fertile soil. A man like Napier was therefore doomed to work in isolation (which contributed to his eccentricity): he was denied the support and encouragement of his intellectual equals who preferred the minute and scrupulous investigation of Old Testament texts to the examination of the physical world. His powerful mind therefore had no immediate influence, for his contemporaries had other matters with which to occupy themselves; he founded no school and left no disciples. It was to be more than a hundred years after his death before Scotland would produce the engineers who could benefit by his work, and whose own work would transform the economy and appearance of the country.

James VI and I
(b. 1566, King 1567/1603–1625)

In the banqueting hall at Whitehall the great baroque ceiling, designed by Inigo Jones and painted by Rubens, showed James VI and I dispensing justice amidst the clouds. James liked to be known as the British Solomon but he is better remembered, unfairly, as 'the wisest fool in Christendom'. The most intelligent and successful of the Stuarts, he is also the only one to have attracted ridicule. For this, the memoirs of Sir Anthony Weldon are responsible. It was Weldon who told how King James's clothes were ludicrously padded against dagger-thrusts; who retailed stories of James's slobbering fondness for his favourites Robert Carr, whom he made Earl of Somerset, and George Villiers, who was created Duke of Buckingham. Yet James was a much more remarkable man than the popular image would suggest.

James suffered a miserable upbringing. He was starved of affection, was ever in danger and was bullied by his tutor, George Buchanan, whose magisterial methods were a disgrace to the humanism he affected. The excessive fondness, for which Weldon, a scurrilous and untrustworthy gossip, reproached James, was perhaps the result of this wretched childhood. It is a common observation that those who are denied love in youth will grow up either harsh and incapable of giving love themselves or else conspicuously tender. James, to his credit, was the latter.

As King of Scots, poor, without military resources, bedevilled both by a turbulent nobility and by the arrogant Calvinist ministers, one of whom, Andrew Melville, insolently informed him that 'a king was no more than God's silly vassal', James managed to impose his will on the kingdom and bishops on the Church. His life was frequently in danger, whether from the Gowrie Conspiracy or the witchcraft practised by his demented cousin, the Earl of Bothwell, but he survived and, after his translation to the English throne, could truthfully boast that he ruled Scotland more easily with his pen than his ancestors had done by the sword.

The throne of England was James's ambition and it is a pleasing irony that the Union of the two kingdoms, which Edward I and Henry VIII had sought to achieve by war, should at last have been accomplished by the prudent and politic pacificism of King James. Had he had his way, that Union would have been made more complete. However, the English Parliament, though prepared to swallow a Scotch king, jibbed at an incorporating Union which, it was believed, would loose a still greater flood of needy Scots upon them.

It is certainly true that James relaxed on attaining his ambition. He might indeed have echoed the Borgia Pope, Alexander VI, who said, 'God has given us the Papacy. Let us enjoy it.' James, secure in his rich, new kingdom, was much happier to devote himself to revelry and to hunting (in which activity he daily disproved the allegations of physical cowardice) than to the business of state. He began to drink too much, and not only on occasions such as the state visit of his brother-in-law, the King of Denmark. It was observed that he was forever sipping sweet white wine. All the same, it rarely incapacitated him. He was extravagant too, where Queen Elizabeth had been notably mean, and his geniality lacked the dignity which had been one of the few redeeming qualities of the generally repellent Tudors. He found himself in financial difficulties, especially after the death of Robert Cecil, Earl of Salisbury.

He quarrelled certainly with Parliament, though the House of Commons had been growing obstreperous even in the last days of Queen Elizabeth. Parliamentarians disliked the king's pedagogical lecturing. This may be held against him but the more bitter quarrels of his last years were the result of his adherence to a policy which was perfectly justified.

One of his first acts had been to bring to an end the war with Spain. This was wise, for the only justification of that war had been the threat to England's interests, and this had in fact been removed by the defeat of the Armada in 1588. Thereafter the war was expensive, unrewarding and indeed damaging, as Spain encouraged disaffection in Ireland. James, however, was a man of peace. He believed that there were no fundamental problems in Europe that could not be allayed by diplomacy. The outbreak of the Thirty Years War in Germany seemed to prove him wrong and many of his subjects wished him to intervene in support of the Protestant cause, which was represented by his son-in-law Frederick, Elector Palatine of the Rhine, who had accepted the throne of Bohemia against James's advice. James refused to do so, and he was quite right. Perhaps he over-estimated his ability to win the friendship of Spain and to mediate in the war, but we who in our century have learned that the glamour of war is a mockery and its horrors real can only approve his intention.

James made two permanent contributions to our national life. The first of these was wholly admirable. It was at his instigation and at his command that the Authorised Version of the Bible was rendered into English. The noble sonority of the Epistle Dedicatory records our permanent debt to King James for this work:

'For when Your Majesty had once out of deep judgement apprehended how convenient it was, that out of the Original Sacred tongues, together with comparing of the labours, both in our own, and other foreign languages, of many worthy men who went before us, there should be one more exact Translation of the Holy Scriptures into the English tongue; Your Majesty did never desist to urge and to excite those to whom it was commended, that the work might be hastened, and that the business might be expedited in so decent a manner, as a matter of such importance might justly require.'

Inasmuch as the King was, in the original sense of the word, the author of what is commonly known as the King James Bible, he contributed more to the culture of his people than any other monarch can claim to have done. It has been rightly said that the Authorised Version and Shakespeare's plays are the greatest works in the English language; King James commissioned the first and encouraged the second by according his royal patronage to Shakespeare's Company.

The other venture with which James is associated has turned out less happily. This was the plantation with Protestant settlers of recalcitrant Ulster, where the O'Neill earls had long waged a war which the English called a rebellion. These colonists, mostly Scots Presbyterians, established themselves firmly and so the division of Ireland and the troubles with which the United Kingdom has since been afflicted may be held to be ultimately the responsibility of King James.

This maligned king was a good scholar, an indifferent poet, a loving father, a man whose sense was greater than his dignity, a wit and a humorist. The portrait of him drawn by Scott in *The Fortunes of Nigel* is admirable. His grandson, Charles II, inherited much of his wit and good sense but unfortunately James's son Charles was denied both, and so lost his throne and his head.

Archibald Campbell,
8th Earl and 1st Marquess of Argyll
(1604–1661)

John Buchan, in his biography of Montrose, observed that in every national crisis there is some personal antagonism 'where the warring creeds seem to be summed up in the persons of two protagonists'. Argyll and Montrose were such. Argyll won the battle in their lifetime but Montrose conquered posterity. Montrose has glamour, Argyll none. Argyll's cause seems to us distant and repugnant, a narrow and intolerant fanaticism. Nevertheless there is a case to be made for him.

Argyll was head of the most powerful of the Highland clans but his was a difficult inheritance. His father, the seventh Earl, fell into debt, married a Catholic as his second wife, was himself converted to the Roman Church and spent many years in exile. He disliked and distrusted his heir, the son of his first marriage to a daughter of the Earl of Morton, and went so far as to warn the King against him.

The young Argyll was unprepossessing. He had lean Campbell features, thin red hair and a decided squint. But his intellect was sharp and he was capable of exercising considerable charm. For a period in 1650 the young Charles II fell under his spell.

The most important moment of his life came during the Glasgow Assembly of the Kirk in 1638, when he was converted to the extreme Presbyterian doctrines. Duplicitous, even hypocritical, though he was in his political dealings, his religious sincerity cannot be questioned. Nowadays zealotry such as Argyll's is easy to reprove or mock. This is strange, for our own times and our own country offer many examples of fanatical intolerance at least equal to his. It may be said in Argyll's favour that at least he believed his faith to have the authority of Almighty God behind it, while our modern zealots can claim no authority beyond their own opinions which they bolster by reference to 'democratic rights'.

At any rate, from 1638 Argyll's course was set. He believed in theocracy, in the authority of the Kirk guided by righteous nobles among whom he was chief. He was consistent in this faith, though it led him on a tortuous course. It persuaded him to resist Charles I and crown Charles II, to collaborate with Cromwell and then defy him, to assert the right of Scotland to determine its own form of Church government and then try to impose that same form on an unwilling England.

The outline of his life can be briefly told. Until 1638 he was concerned principally with his own estates and made no political mark. Thereafter, by reason of his position and his talent, he emerged as the political chief of the Covenanters. His power, however, was always qualified. The Kirk's ministers, conscious of being in hourly contact with the will of the Almighty, did not easily tolerate any secular leader. Likewise, in the confused politics of the time, there were always other noblemen ready to dispute Argyll's position.

Nevertheless he was one of the formers of policy and the Solemn League and Covenant signed with the English Parliament in 1643 was his master stroke. As events turned out, it was a piece of brilliant folly which was to ruin Scotland and eventually Argyll but the reasons for making the agreement seemed cogent. Charles I's plan of reforming the Scots Kirk to the model of the Church of England had provoked national opposition. This found expression in the National Covenant of 1638 and the subsequent Bishops' Wars which seemed to have secured Presbyterianism in Scotland. Few, however, believed that Charles had accepted this willingly. He was now engaged in war with his English opponents. It seemed likely that if he won that war he would renege on his promises to the Scots. In 1643 his victory was probable. Argyll and the leading ministers of the Church were convinced that their cause depended on the fortunes of the English Parliamentary armies. They further believed that there could be no security for Presbyterianism in Scotland unless the Church in England was reformed on similar lines. Therefore they entered into a military alliance with the English Parliament and extracted as their price the promise of the establishment of Presbyterianism in England.

The alliance was expedient but it was short-sighted and ignorant, for Presbyterianism was a weak cause south of the Border. The Church of Scotland was essentially a national church, a theocracy determined to guide the whole people and legislate them into godliness. South of the Border many of the firmest opponents of Charles had ceased to believe in a national church at all. They were as fanatical as the Scots Kirk, but their fanaticism took a different and more independent form.

The rise of Cromwell and the nature of the New Model Army broke Argyll's policy. From the moment that the King surrendered himself to the Scots army in May 1646, Argyll was fighting against the tide of events. Montrose's campaign in 1644/5 had shaken his power in Scotland and involved him in personal humiliation, but the effect of that could not be compared with that of the now evident refusal of the new masters of England to accept Presbyterianism. The Scots, it seemed, had kept their part of the Solemn League and Covenant; they had served the interest of their English allies, who now refused to serve theirs. Soon there was dissension and division in Scotland. Some were now ready to trust the king and to come to an agreement with him. The result was the Engagement and the Second Civil War of 1648, from which Argyll stood aloof.

The execution of Charles I offended the Scots, Argyll among them. He now embarked on a desperate and uncharacteristic gamble: the restoration of Charles II. Charles, however, played a double game. He was unwilling (and who can blame him?) to surrender himself to the Covenanters. Montrose came to Scotland with the king's commission as Lieutenant-General, even while the Covenanters' ambassadors negotiated terms with Charles. Montrose's capture and hasty execution destroyed the hopes of pure Royalists. Argyll watched his great rival carried up the Canongate of Edinburgh. As he drew back behind the shutters, an English voice cried out, 'It was no wonder that they started aside at his look, for they durst not look him in the face these seven years.'

Charles arrived in Scotland and for a few months it seemed that Argyll might yet succeed. He had the King in his hands and even came close to arranging that Charles should marry his daughter, Lady Anne Campbell. But Argyll was now at the mercy of the forces he had encouraged. Charles was assailed and insulted by fanatical ministers, who disgusted him with the cause he had reluctantly embraced. Even Argyll, although he wrote the sermons that his own chaplain would deliver, found the more extreme of his allies to be 'madmen'. Cromwell then broke the Covenanting party at Dunbar (September 1650); Argyll still arranged Charles's coronation as a Covenanted king at Scone but he had lost control. When Charles marched south the following summer, it was at the head of an army which included Engagers but from which Argyll was missing.

Argyll had no choice but to acquiesce in the English occupation of Scotland which followed Charles's defeat at Worcester. Everything for which he had played had been lost. The Scottish Parliament was abolished. Even the General Assemblies of the Kirk were forbidden. He had become once again a mere clan chief, of little consequence as a national politician.

He was in friendly correspondence with Charles shortly before the Restoration of 1660 but he had many enemies. Whereas an Act of Indemnity and Oblivion was quickly passed in England, there was no such Act in Scotland. When Argyll travelled to London, hoping to be received by the king, Charles declined to see him and he was arrested.

One charge of acceding to Charles I's execution could not be sustained; at last the only charge that could be brought convincingly against him was that he had concurred with Cromwell and the usurpers in opposition to those who had appeared for the king. Even this was doubtful until General Monk, who had been Cromwell's own commander in Scotland before he had determined to restore the king, produced letters from Argyll. These, according to Bishop Burnet in his *History of his Own Time*, were written 'in a strain too zealous to make it believed that his compliance was feigned or extorted from him'. Thus Argyll was condemned to death on evidence supplied by Monk, who had served Cromwell far more zealously than Argyll had ever done but whose change of heart in 1660 had been rewarded with a dukedom.

It was thought that Argyll might die 'timorously', as he had never been famed for physical courage. He disappointed his detractors. The night before his execution he wrote to the king, 'justifying his intentions in what he had done in the matter of the Covenant, protesting his innocence as to the death of his father, wishing him a long and happy reign, casting his wife and children upon the royal mercy, and praying they might not suffer for his fault'. On the scaffold, he told his advocate that 'he would not die as a Roman braving death, but he would die as a Christian without being affrighted'. His head replaced that of Montrose's on a spike on the west face of the Tolbooth.

Monuments to both Marquesses now confront each other on either side of the aisle in the High Kirk of St Giles. It is fitting that both should be commemorated there. Each was in his way a patriot. Even if Montrose remains by far the more attractive character and stirs the imagination as Argyll can never do, his great antagonist is also worthy of our respect and admiration.

Sir Thomas Urquhart of Cromarty
(1611–1660)

A vein of swaggering extravagance runs through Scottish history; 'fier comme un Ecossais' ('proud as a Scotsman') was not a French proverb for nothing. The extravagance can rise to the sublime and topple over into absurdity. Many of our eccentrics have walked, or rather danced, a tightrope between magnificence and buffoonery, few with a more nimble spring than Sir Thomas Urquhart of Cromarty.

His father was a laird, able to send his son to King's College, Aberdeen and to finance several years' residence in France and Italy, from which the younger Urquhart returned in 1636. He had put these years to good use, learning sufficient French eventually to translate Rabelais, most difficult and magniloquent of authors, though admittedly with the assistance of a native French speaker called Motteux.

Urquhart might have settled to a life of rich, easy and abstruse scholarship but for the outbreak of the Bishops' War three years after he had inherited his estate; that and the subsequent Civil War brought him prison, exile and impoverishment. He was an Episcopalian and a Royalist, and fought against the Covenanters at Turriff in 1639. The triumph of the Covenant forced him to flee to London, where Charles I knighted him in 1641. His father died the following year, in which there was peace in Scotland; he left his estates embarrassed, but Urquhart returned to live in the tower of Cromarty. There he passed some years in study and writing. All his books are curiously titled, as might be expected: in 1645 he published *Trissotetras* a work on mathematics, especially trigonometry, which made use of Napier's logarithms. He took no part in Montrose's wars, probably because Montrose had been a Covenanter in 1639. It was characteristic of Urquhart that the one Royalist campaign in which he declined to participate should have come closest to success.

He fought later, however, either in the Engagement of 1648 or in the Worcester campaign of 1651 (accounts differ). At any rate he forfeited his estates and suffered a spell of imprisonment in the Tower of London.

He had, however, been able to salvage his books, or some of them, and during his imprisonment he completed two works :

Pantochronochanon and *Ekskubulauron* or *The Discoverie of a most Exquisite Jewel*. The first is a work of genealogy concentrating on Urquhart's own family. This was immensely distinguished, for he was able, with some ingenuity, to trace his descent through a Greek prince of the third century before Christ, named Esormon of Achaea back to Adam; the Queen of Sheba making a happy appearance on the distaff side. It would be nice to know how much of this nonsense Urquhart believed; very little, I should say.

The Jewel is principally a learned and witty attack on Scotch Presbyterianism, and the pretentions of the theocracy which then guided and controlled Scotland. By way of contrast, however, Urquhart also recounts the life-story of his hero James Crichton of Cluny (1560–1585), a Renaissance polymath known as 'The Admirable Crichton', soldier, duellist, poet and scholar, the subject, incidentally, of a novel by Harrison Ainsworth. While it is probable that Urquhart exaggerated the virtues and graces of his hero, he also started an argument which has never ceased between those who saw the Reformation in Scotland as a great and godly event which opened up the possibility of establishing Israel north of the Tweed, and those who deplored it for its narrowing and stultifying effect. This struggle between Renaissance grace and Humanism and the Presbyterian virtues can perhaps never be brought to a conclusion, if only because there is evident right on both sides, but it has been differently interpreted, and with different emphasis, in different periods. If the nineteenth century backed Knox and the Kirk, many in the twentieth century, especially writers, have lamented what was destroyed in the Kirk's triumph. It is partly a matter of temperament, and the one comforting reflection is that Scotland may have been richer for the division of opinion.

After his release from prison Urquhart retired to the Continent, and engaged again on his translation of Rabelais. Like all the greatest translations this is a work of art in its own right. It is hardly faithful except to the spirit of the original. It has been observed that Urquhart found even more adjectives than Rabelais. What appealed to him in Rabelais was not only the Frenchman's exuberance and fecundity of language, but his resolute opposition to the follies of his age, and, in particular, the attempt of the Counter-Reformation (so similar to the Reformation itself in its restrictiveness) to put a clamp of humanity. There was between Rabelais and Urquhart the fellow-feeling and community of spirit which successful translation demands.

Urquhart died still in exile in 1660. A fit of wild laughter on hearing the news of the king's Restoration is said to have been the cause, and the story is too good to be disbelieved.

James Graham, Marquess of Montrose
(1612–1650)

On the 21st May 1650 Sir Archibald Johnston of Warriston who, twelve years previously, had hailed the signing of the National Covenant as 'the glorious marriage day of the Kingdom with God', sneered at one of the first signatories of that Covenant, now condemned to death, for the care he took of his hair on the morning of his execution. 'My head is still my own,' replied the Marquess of Montrose. 'To-night, when it will be yours, treat it as you please.' The night before, 'amid the smoke and wrangling of the guards', he had written these lines:

> Let them bestow on every airth a limb,
> Then open all my veins, that I may swim,
> To Thee, my Maker, in that crimson lake;
> Then place my parboiled head upon a stake,
> Scatter my ashes, strew them in the air. –
> Lord, since thou knowest where all these atoms are,
> I'm hopeful Thou'lt recover once my dust,
> And confident Thou'lt raise me with the just.

Nine years before he had sworn to 'carry fidelity and honour with me to the grave'. Now, as he marched to the scaffold, the notary public, John Nichol, thought him more like a bridegroom than a criminal, and another observer, James Fraser, wrote that 'he stept along the streets with so great state, and there appeared in his countenance so much beauty, majesty, and gravity as amazed the beholder, and many of his enemies did acknowledge him to be the bravest subject in the world, and in him a gallantry that braced all the crowd'.

In politics Montrose might fairly be described as a Moderate, but it has proved almost impossible for men to write of him with moderation. For Whig historians, he was variously 'a vainglorious butcher', 'an infamous ruffian, but eminent loyalist', one who at best 'played his heroic role to perfection'. His admirers have exalted him as the Paladin of Scotland, the noblest soul and wisest mind in the heroic and distracted seventeenth century. No doubt the truth lies as it usually does in between, but Montrose is a figure capable of conquering all reservations, and, for me, there is no Scotsman to compare with him, among those tested in the extremities of action. This therefore is a biased account and, for a corrective, the reader must look elsewhere.

The Graham lands lay in Perthshire, Angus and Stirling, fringing the Highland Line, but they were a family which had always looked south rather than north. One Graham had fallen by Wallace at Falkirk, another at Flodden and a third at Pinkie. The young Montrose seemed to have been born in more peaceful times, for the Union of the Crowns had been effected, and James VI could now boast that he ruled Scotland more easily with his pen, than his ancestors had by the sword; both Montrose's grandfather and father served him as Chancellor.

The boy attended St Andrews University. He was a good scholar, whose favourite reading was Walter Raleigh's *History of the World*, Caesar's Gallic Wars, and Lucan's *Pharsalia*. He married Margaret Carnegie, daughter of the future Earl of Southesk in 1629, and four years later made a tour of France and Italy. On his return in 1636 he presented himself at Court but, through the jealousy of the Duke of Hamilton, his interview with the king was cold. Hamilton was a futile fellow, the man of whose execution an old woman said, 'Folks say that his head wasna a very gude ane, but, puir gentleman, it was a sair loss tae him,' and his jealousy of Montrose, though understandable, was to impair the Royalist cause in Scotland.

Montrose came home to find the country in turmoil. Charles I's attempt to compel Scotland into religious uniformity with England was properly resented as an infringement of national liberties. This seemed clear to Montrose, and he was, as recorded, one of the first to sign the National Covenant, that great statement of defiance and affirmation of the fundamental laws of the Kingdom. He never departed from his view that the Covenant was justified. In the ensuing war he commanded a Covenanting force against the Royalists of the north-east, who were mostly Episcopalians and Roman Catholics. It was a minor campaign, but it showed that Montrose was a born soldier.

The next four years are confused ones. In this period a gulf widened between Montrose and other Covenanters which was both political and personal. On the personal level, he aroused the enmity of Argyll; on the political, he began to move towards the king. Though he had been so fervent a Covenanter that the king's English Minister Strafford had recommended he be imprisoned, he now found that the Covenant which in his view had been established to rectify the balance in the State, threatened itself to disturb it. Montrose had clear ideas about the nature of Sovereign Power which he set out in a letter written either to Lord Napier or to Drummond of Hawthornden, and about the immutable nature of fundamental law. His position was that the recognition of a Sovereign Power was essential to the stability of the State, and that while Charles had previously exceeded his Prerogative, it was now being infringed by the Parliament in England and by Covenanters in Scotland. Montrose has been called a turncoat, but he found himself in a position common in revolutionary times: the man who stands his ground and holds his opinion steady may find his former confederates move beyond him, and those to whom he was first opposed arrive at his position. The Solemn League and Covenant, by which the Scottish Estates and Kirk moved into a formal alliance with the English rebels, decided him. When he stood before his accusers in Parliament in May 1650, he re-affirmed his loyalty to the National Covenant, and said of the Solemn League: 'How far religion has been advanced by it this poor distressed kingdom can witness'.

Nevertheless, in the Spring of 1643 the Covenanters, probably on the advice of Argyll, who had the wit to recognise ability even among those he disliked, tried to draw him back to their side, with an offer of military command and the payment of his debts. The Moderator of the Kirk, Alexander Henderson, a man whom Montrose respected, pressed the offer, but he could not accept. That summer he travelled south to warn the King that the agreement between the Scots and Parliamant was about to be ratified, and that this would mean the despatch of a Scots army to England. He urged the King to commission him to raise troops in Scotland.

Eventually he was given the position of the king's lieutenant-general in Scotland, but there were no troops available. He crossed the Border in August 1644, in disguise, with only two companions, to try to slip through the Covenanting Lowlands and 'raise Scotland for the King'. It was a desperate venture; it led to his Year of Victories.

Somewhere in the western or central Highlands there was, he knew, a force of Ulster Macdonalds, under the command of one Alasdair, son of a hero called Colkitto (which name was also to be applied to Alasdair). They were all that had been sent of a force promised by the Earl of Antrim, and they were fighting men of rare quality. Alasdair is the true hero of Montrose's Wars in Gaelic legend, and it is possible that Montrose's English-speaking biographers, following the account of his chaplain Wishart, have not given him his due. Yet that the Gaelic claims made for Alasdair are exaggerated is probable: in a long career of warfare, he showed boundless courage, but no force he commanded gave evidence of a strategic or even tactical grasp, except for his year under Montrose's command.

Between August 1644 and August 1645 Montrose's little army, ever-shifting in its composition and never amounting to more than

5000 men, won victories at Tippermuir, Aberdeen, Fyvie, Inverlochy, Auldearn, Alford and Kilsyth. They performed prodigies of valour, and the winter march from Blair Atholl into the Campbell country of Argyll (which they laid waste) and back through Glencoe and up through the Great Glen before doubling back through Lochaber to Inverlochy was one of the great feats of warfare performed in these islands. At Auldearn Montrose anticipated Napoleon's battle-plan for Austerlitz, and Kilsyth made him Master of Scotland, placing him, as he hoped, in a position to restore the King's Cause which, after Naseby, seemed lost in England.

But at this point the bubble burst. His army, after the manner of Highland armies, scattered; Alasdair left, promising to return, to pursue private war in the West. Montrose hoped to raise more troops in the Borders, and so march to help Charles, but he had hardly begun the task, when he was confronted by General David Leslie with at least 6000 men. Montrose had less than a quarter of that number when he was surprised and his forces scattered at Philiphaugh outside Selkirk. The Covenanters honoured their grim God by slaughtering three hundred Irishwomen who had been among Montrose's camp-followers. The ministers' lust for revenge on the man and army which had so terrified them was such that Leslie himself was provoked to ask one of the men of God: 'Mr John, have you not once gotten your fill of blood?'

Montrose's great adventure was at an end. He retired to the Continent where his fame had preceded him. The Cardinal de Retz welcomed him as a Roman hero reborn. Cardinal Mazarin offered him the captaincy of the King's Guard and the rank of Marshal of France. The Holy Roman Emperor gave him the crimson baton of a Marshal of the Empire. He disregarded such honours and put aside temptation; he had given his sword to his own king and to one cause alone.

Charles's execution on January 30, 1649 affected him deeply: he fainted when he heard the news. A few days later Wishart found these lines on a table in his room:

> Great, good, and just, could I but rate
> My grief, and thy too rigid fate,
> I'd weep the world in such a strain
> As it should deluge once again.
> But since thy loud-tongued blood demands supplies
> More from Briareus' hands than Argus' eyes,
> I'll sing thy obsequies with trumpet sounds,
> And write thine epitaph in blood and wounds.

He had himself painted in black armour, and those about him found that he had the air of a 'fey' man.

Charles II was already in communication with Montrose's enemies when his Captain-General set off on his last mission. The young king was cynically backing both horses, but Montrose's enterprise was misconceived, ill-prepared and misdirected. Montrose's intention was to hold the extreme north of Scotland, where he hoped that Mackays and Mackenzies would join the little force he would bring from the Continent, and so compel Leslie to undertake a dangerous march against him. But the campaign had hardly begun before his little army, made up principally of raw recruits, was surprised, their intelligence being poor, and scattered at Carbisdale in Ross. A few days later Montrose was betrayed by one Neil Macleod of Assynt, in whose house he had taken refuge. Macleod's price was £25 000 Scots, four-fifths to be paid in coin, and the balance in oatmeal. Highland tradition has it that two-thirds of the meal was sour.

Montrose had to be despatched quickly, before the king with whom the Covenanters were negotiating could reach Scotland. Fortunately the Estates had attainted him and outlawed him in 1644, and it was that sentence which was carried out.

The Gaelic poet Ian Lom Macdonald wrote:

> I'll not go to Dunedin
> Since the Graham's blood was shed,
> The manly mighty lion
> Tortured on the gallows
>
> That was the true gentleman,
> Who came of line not humble,
> Good was the flushing of his cheek
> When drawing up to combat.
>
> His chalk-white teeth well closing,
> His slender brown not gloomy! –
> Though oft my love awakes me,
> This night I will not bear it.

John Maitland, Duke of Lauderdale
(1616–1682)

He was the 'L' of Charles II's Cabal, in effect the Viceroy of Scotland for almost twenty years. Bishop Burnet in his *History of His Own Times* offered an unattractive portrait: 'He was very big; his hair red, hanging oddly about him; his tongue was too big for his mouth, which made him bedew all he talked to; his whole manner was boisterous, and very unfit for a Court.' Burnet was his enemy, but even he admitted that Lauderdale was very learned, 'not only in Latin, in which he was a master, but in Greek and Hebrew. He had read a good deal of divinity and almost all the historians, both ancient and modern, so that he had great materials. He had with these an extraordinary memory and a copious but unpolished expression'. Charles II's first minister, the historian Clarendon, disliked Lauderdale even more than Burnet did, and said that 'he had courage enough not to fail where it was absolutely necessary, and no impediment of honour to restrain him from doing anything that might gratify any of his passions', but Charles himself said that he would 'venture Lauderdale with any man in Europe for prudence and courage'. As was usual in the seventeenth century he was deeply versed in theology, but in the Chapel Royal a preacher once cried to him, 'My lord, my lord, you snore so loud you will wake the King.'

Clearly an interesting man, and one hard to evaluate. The difficulty is made all the greater when his political career is considered.

He was an early Covenanter, and one of those who negotiated the Solemn League and Covenant with the English Parliamentary rebels in 1643. This was one of those ill-starred ventures which seemed a masterstroke at the time. It appeared necessary to the Scots Covenanters that they associate themselves with the rebels in England, for they were sure that, if Charles I was once successful there, their own liberties, in protection of which they had signed the Covenant and fought the Bishops' Wars, would be again in danger. The weakness of the agreement with the English Parliament amounted, however, to folly, for by the terms of the Treaty the English were bound to establish Presbyterianism in their own country, which few had a mind to do, and those few lacked the means. It is to Lauderdale's credit that he came to realise this.

He was never more than a limited rebel. He took up arms to protect the liberties of Scotland and its Church. He changed sides when it seemed that, as a result of the Cavaliers' defeat, these liberties were in no danger from Charles, but were hardly secure from the English Army.

He fought at Worcester for Charles II and was captured after the battle, spending years in English prisons, being released only a couple of months before the Restoration, when Charles appointed him Secretary of State for Scotland. The years in prison undoubtedly influenced Lauderdale, and the man who emerged was much changed from the young Covenanter. He had read Thomas Hobbes's *Leviathan*, that cogent argument for absolute power in a state, and had indeed in the late 1640s conversed with Hobbes in Paris. He had seen the extravagant follies of the all-powerful Kirk. He had also seen Charles I replaced by a republic and that republic fall under the rule of a dictator. That seemed to confirm him in the belief that popular government could be as regardless of law and custom as an untrammelled king; his reading of classical history supported this opinion. Between 1642 and 1660 traditional forms of government had been destroyed, but all the attempts to replace them had been defective or undesirable. Lauderdale concluded therefore that a return to the system of monarchy, supported by a loyal aristocracy, offered the best hope of stability.

The position in Scotland was, however, complicated by the question of the Church. Lauderdale was himself still a Presbyterian, but he could not fail to see that the assertion of the liberties of the Church from state control, which he himself had made, had resulted in the disturbance of civil peace and the denial of all authority other than the Kirk's own. Logic, therefore, drove him to the acceptance of a form of modest episcopalian government of the Church (which had been James VI's position) because only in this way could sufficient control be exercised over the Kirk to prevent it from subverting the Crown. He had also, as a nobleman, been disgusted by aspects of Presbyterian egalitarianism; he had concluded, or he came to conclude, that it was not merely a matter of James VI's 'No Bishop, no King', but also of 'No Bishop, no Aristocracy'.

The refusal of the extreme Covenanters to accept his settlement drove Lauderdale's Government into more and more repressive measures. He found himself caught in the classic trap of the moderate. Personal resentments no doubt played a part in the increasing difficulties which he encountered in the late 1670s, but there was more to it than that. Lauderdale was attempting to impose a policy which lacked popular support, and found only a few ädherents beyond Court circles. Moderate Presbyterianism was the desire of the Scottish people, but it was a form of Church Government which sat ill with the Royal Prerogative that Lauderdale upheld.

He was a Scottish patriot who resented English interference in the affairs of Scotland, but he became ever more doubtful if Scottish prosperity was possible within the existing structure which debarred Scots from free trade with England and with English colonies. He came to believe that a Union between the two Parliaments was necessary to achieve this. In October 1670 he submitted the proposals of the Scottish Commissioners for Union which would have 'united the entire Parliament of Scotland with the Parliament of England'. These were set aside because the king was too busy with 'other weighty matter' (the French Alliance). So, according to the Memoirs of the future Lord Advocate, Sir George Mackenzie of Rosehaugh, 'it stopt rather to the wonder than the dissatisfaction of the two nations', and was not to be revived in Lauderdale's lifetime. However, his reluctant arrival at support for the Union is interesting if only because the arguments he advanced were to be those put forward when it was achieved forty-seven years later. Lauderdale, with all the advantages of exercising a very complete mastery in Scotland, while having the ear of the king, as no Scottish minister had between 1688 and 1707, yet found the existing structure unsatisfactory from the Scottish point of view.

Lauderdale fell from power in 1679 as a result of manoeuvres at Court and his own failure to suppress the extreme dissident Covenanters. He had been made a peer of England some time before, and retired to Tunbridge Wells to try to restore his health, broken by hard work and overindulgence. (He drank heavily and was said to be able to eat a whole sheep at a sitting; of course seventeenth-century sheep were fairly miserable specimens.) He died in 1682. No one had ruled Scotland for so long in that century, and no one is so hard to assess. He has been called traitor, tyrant, turncoat, timeserver; but a dispassionate analysis of his career suggests that he was a patriot and a man of sense.

Lord Stair

(1619–1695)

Scots Law is unique and of central importance in our cultural history. It is an amalgam of Common Law, Feudal Law and Roman Law, 'systematised', in the words of Lord Cooper, quondam Lord President of the Court of Session, 'by resort to the law of nature and the Bible, and illuminated by many flashes of ideal metaphysic'. The result was a Law which was 'self-reliant, severely practical, invincibly logical, with a metaphysical bent.' No body of Law can ever have a single author, and indeed Lord Cooper speaks of 'the forgotten architects of our system'; yet, if there is no author, Scots Law can claim a father in James Dalrymple, first Viscount Stair, whose *Institutes of the Law of Scotland* (1681) represents the most complete codification of Scots Law and sets out its fundamental principles. Stair's Institutes are the Old Testament of Scots Law.

Stair was born in Ayrshire, son of a laird, and after study at Glasgow University, arrived in Edinburgh to pursue a legal career, in time to be caught up in the fervour of the Covenant. He served as a captain in the Covenanting army before teaching philosophy at Glasgow from 1641. In 1648 he became a member of the Faculty of Advocates.

He acted as secretary to the Commissioners appointed by the Estates to negotiate with Charles II in 1649–50. This did not prevent him, seven years later, from being appointed a commissioner for the administration of justice by General Monk, who considered him 'a very honest man and a good lawyer'. He was certainly the latter. Nor did this adhesion to the Republic debar him from honour and office under the restored monarchy; why indeed should it, when his patron Monk had been the chief agent of the Restoration and was rewarded with a dukedom. Dalrymple's rewards were more modest: he merely became a knight and a judge. He was constitutionally a moderate, and he had certain scruples. In 1663 he resigned his office rather than take an oath renouncing the possibility of rebellion. Others did not hesitate to swear an oath which made nonsense of the past quarter-century of their political life, but Dalrymple would not. However, Charles II, appreciating his valuable qualities, allowed him to add a reservation to the oath, and he was thus able to return to office, accept a baronetcy and, seven years later, the office of Lord President of the

Court of Session. In 1674 he became a Privy Councillor, and throughout that decade was carefully active in the suppression of the extreme Covenanting rebels. According to Macaulay, whose brief portrait of Dalrymple has all his customary brilliance, 'he had a wonderful power of giving to any proposition which it suited him to maintain a plausible aspect of legality, and even of justice; and this power he frequently abused.' However, Macaulay adds, 'he was seldom in his place at the Council Board when anything outrageously unjust or cruel was to be done.' In 1681 he resigned office, ostensibly to avoid taking the oath prescribed by the Test Act, but it may be because he foresaw that the Government's policy of repression was likely to fail in the long run. He went into exile in Holland; his wife has been suspected of attending conventicles, by no means the worst charge levelled at her, and he himself was perhaps suspected of sympathy with the rebels, especially since the Government had become more extreme.

In Holland he made himself useful to William of Orange, who valued his advice, and though distrusted by many of the Covenanting exiles (with good reason), he encouraged Argyll's rebellion in 1685, and assisted him with his advice. On its failure a prosecution was launched against him in Edinburgh, but his eldest son, John, had remained loyal to James VII and thus safeguarded the family estates. In 1688 Dalrymple returned with William of Orange, was reappointed Lord President and created a Viscount. For the next few years he and his son, by this time the Master of Stair, were William's most trusted ministers in Scotland, and it was the Master who bore the chief responsibility for the Massacre of Glencoe.

The Dalrymples were unpopular with the nobility who resented their rise, and with the Whigs who distrusted their history. Lord Stair, however, was admired as a jurist and his son as a formidable debater and skilful politician. The father's wisdom aroused some distrust too; it was said that he was in league with the Devil, that familiar accusation of seventeenth-century Scotland. Even graver accusations were directed at Lady Stair who was compared to the Witch of Endor and had also been seen, in the guise of a cat, sitting on a cushion beside the Lord High Commissioner. This is improbable but the fate of several members of the family lent credibility to the suggestion of 'dark dealings with the fiendish race'. One of Stair's sons had died of poison; a daughter had stabbed her bridegroom on their wedding night; one grandson had killed another.

There is much to be savoured in the home life of the Father of Scots Law.

Sir George Mackenzie of Rosehaugh
(1636–1691)

A nickname can distort biography and history. Sir George Mackenzie of Rosehaugh was called by Covenanters 'the bluidy Mackenzie', and it is as the bearer of this name that he appears among the persecutors of the Righteous, assembled at the Devil's table-board in 'Wandering Willie's Tale' in *Redgauntlet*. Anyone who only knows him as such may be surprised on mounting the broad staircase of the National Library of Scotland to find him commemorated in a stained-glass window. But the commemoration is justified, for Mackenzie was the founder of the Advocates' Library which in 1925 became the National one, and he was a remarkable man whom Dryden described as 'that noble wit of Scotland'. Partisan feeling, Mackenzie's reputation reminds us, can make short work of justice.

He was a son of the second Earl of Seaforth and born in Dundee. His education was extensive, at Aberdeen, St Andrews and Bourges. He was called to the Bar in 1659, and, despite his youth, defended the Marquess of Argyll two years later. He made the case for Argyll skilfully and convincingly, but Argyll's enemies were determined he should die, whatever the evidence or the law. The case made Mackenzie's reputation and he advanced under the patronage of Lauderdale, until he became Lord Advocate in 1677. As such he was responsible for conducting the prosecution of Covenanting dissidents at the height of the Killing Time, and during the greatest or most acute crisis Charles II's government experienced. No doubt he was sharp in his prosecution, but there is no evidence that he exceeded the law of the land. He had earlier advocated religious toleration (*Religio stoici*, 1663), but toleration was not the point at issue. Those whom he prosecuted were political revolutionaries who had rejected the king's government and declared Charles deposed. Mackenzie's subsequent career suggests that he was a man of honour: he lost office under James VII because he resisted the king's claims to be able to set aside the law in favour of his fellow-Catholics. Yet in 1688 he remained loyal to James and opposed the Revolution.

Mackenzie was a distinguished jurist. In 1678 he published the *Laws and Customs of Scotland in Matters Criminal*, and in 1684 the *Institutes of the Laws of Scotland*. The latter work was to be superseded by Stair's *Institutes* but forms the basis of Stair's work.

Mackenzie presented Scots law as existing within a European framework of a generally accepted Common Law, which itself derived from Roman Law. His work helped to mark the difference between Scots and English Law, and with Stair he helped Scots Law to maintain its distinct identity after the Union.

He wrote history. His *Memoirs of the Affairs of Scotland during the Reign of Charles II*, though not published till 1821, is the most valuable source for the reign as seen from the Government side; it makes the case for regarding Lauderdale as a patriot, and indeed Mackenzie had defended him before the Privy Council on the occasion of his fall from power. He also defended the royal authority in *Jus Regium*, intended as an answer to Buchanan's *De Jure Regni*, written a hundred years earlier. Moreover, he was an enthusiast for the Scots language, proclaiming its superiority over both English and French. English he considered a weak courtly 'invented' language, whereas Scots was natural, bold, 'firy'; it was spoken by both the 'commons' and 'by learned men and men of Busynesse'. Not for the first or last time one sees in Mackenzie that the Jacobite Right (if such an anachronistic term be permitted) was capable of a more robust patriotism than the Whigs, whose natural tendency was to seek closer accord with England and efface the distinction between the two countries.

As a young man Mackenzie also wrote what appears to have been Scotland's first novel. *Aretina* is a pastoral romance, no more readable, I would suppose, than the generality of that tedious and outmoded genre; but the third book is said by Trevor Royle in his *Companion to Scottish Literature* to be a coded history of Scotland from the reign of James VI to that of Charles II. That might repay study.

All in all, Mackenzie was clearly a man of unusual intelligence with an unusual range of interests; but the nickname marks him.

John Graham of Claverhouse, 1st Viscount
(1649–1689)

John Graham or Grahame of Claverhouse, created Viscount Dundee in November 1688, only eight months before his death at Killiecrankie, played but a small and, as it turned out, insignificant part in history; yet his name is far better known, and was more greatly reviled, than that of many more influential politicians and soldiers. He entered into romance and legend, forever caught by Scott in the picture presented in *Wandering Willie's Tale* where, in the Devil's Antechamber, 'there was Claverhouse, as beautiful as when he lived, with his long, dark, curled locks streaming down over his laced buff-coat, and his left hand always on his right spule-blade, to hide the wound that the silver-bullet had made. He sat apart from them all, and looked at them with a melancholy, haughty countenance.' One can see in this picture the re-creation of Claverhouse as a Byronic hero.

He was a connection of the great Marquess of Montrose, but himself hardly more than a bonnet laird, who, after attending St Andrews University, sought his fortune as a professional soldier. He served, like many Scots, in both the French and the Dutch armies (though these were engaged against each other). Macaulay pours scorn on a story of an altercation he is said to have had with William of Orange. According to this, Claverhouse, then a Captain, saved William's life by remounting him at the Battle of Seneff. William promised him promotion as a reward but then gave the promised commission to another. Whereupon Claverhouse boxed his ear. The punishment for such an offence was the loss of the right hand but the Prince of Orange merely said, 'You saved my life; I spare your right hand; now we are quits.' Macaulay is doubtless right in discounting the tale; the fact that it was told, and believed, tells us something of Graham's temper, and the regard in which he was held.

He returned to Scotland in 1677 and was given a command against the rebel Covenanters, which he held throughout the period known as 'The Killing-Time'. He was defeated by a Covenanting force at Drumclog in 1679, which hurt his professional pride, though experienced soldiers were not lacking among the Covenanters. Later that year he was chiefly responsible for the Covenanters' defeat at Bothwell Brig, and he then became the chief agent in the

Government's campaign of suppression. No period in Scottish history has aroused stronger feelings than this. The Covenanters saw themselves as 'a suffering remnant of the House of Israel' and persuaded posterity that they were martyrs for their religion. In a sense this was true, and one of the enduring and potent images we carry with us is of the little psalm-singing conventicle worshipping their Lord in the western hills, while outposts scan the tops for the appearance of Claverhouse and his Godless dragoons. There is truth in this picture or it would not prevail. On the other hand there is deception also. These Covenanters were men who rejected the lawfully constituted authority, who approved of murder as a political act and had indeed committed it: the assassins of Archbishop Sharp were the heroes of the movement. Also, the Covenanters were committed to overthrowing the monarchy and established religion and to constructing their own state, which would have been even more intolerant than that which persecuted them. For Claverhouse they were simply rebels, who had put themselves beyond the protection of the law and deserved to be extirpated.

Claverhouse was by repute cruel or at the very least indifferent to cruelty. He was said to have murdered one John Brown of Priesthill at the door of his own house in the sight of his pregnant wife. He was also said to have made a pact with the devil; bullets rebounded from his body and even his horse had a charmed life. The extravagance of one charge does not necessarily disprove the other, but must cast some doubt on it. What seems to have made him a figure of such sinister import is that he combined personal beauty and grace of manner with an indifference to the suffering of others. But torture was permitted by the law of Scotland, and the lords of the Privy Council, such as the Lord Advocate Mackenzie, were more guilty of the cruelties of the Killing-Time than Claverhouse. As for his dragoons and dragonnades, the words have a sinister ring also, but the dragoon was simply the mounted infantry-man of the time.

Claverhouse was moved by personal ambition as much as by any political zeal. He made several requests to the Privy Council for forfeited estates (and got some of them) and he seems to have been careless in accounting for the fines he collected. In this again he was far from exceptional; all seventeenth-century politicians hoped to profit from the misfortunes of their opponents and most did so.

When the Revolution came in 1688, Claverhouse's position was difficult but not desperate. Many who had served King James made their accommodation with King William. Claverhouse was in Whitehall when King William arrived and, though he was among the few whom the Scottish Whigs requested William to omit from the general amnesty he proclaimed, the king, perhaps remembering that Dundee (as he now was) had served under him, refused to do so.

Dundee, therefore, took his place in the Convention which met in March 1689 in Parliament House to consider the settlement of the kingdom. The position of the Royalists (as the Jacobites were still called) was far from hopeless. Dundee and Lord Balcarres held King James's Commission; the Duke of Gordon still held Edinburgh Castle for the exiled king; and there may even have been a majority of moderate royalists among the lords of the Convention.

However, two things drove Dundee from the constitutional path. First, his own life was in danger. Many of his Covenanting enemies had gathered in Edinburgh and the Estates refused to guarantee his safety from those who sought to revenge themselves on him. Second, a letter from King James to the Estates was so ill-judged and so adamant in its refusal to admit grievances or offer compromise that the moderate Royalists were alienated and King James's support disappeared. Even so, had Dundee been as unscrupulous and as lost to a sense of honour as the lave of Scotch politicians, he could have made an accommodation with William and the Whigs. He declined to do so and turned to arms.

He left Edinburgh precipitately and rode to the Highlands. There he found support among those clans whose hostility to the Campbells now expressed itself as loyalty to King James. He delayed some months, hoping that James would send him some regular troops from Ireland, which he now occupied with an army of 40000 men. The king reglected to do so. Dundee, mindful of what his kinsman Montrose had achieved with a Highland army, waited at the Pass of Killiecrankie for the Government troops under General Mackay, a veteran of William's wars in the Netherlands. The victory of the Jacobites was complete, but Dundee, rising in the stirrups to rally his inexperienced cavalry (a small force of Lowland lairds and about forty of his old troopers), was shot under the left arm and died in the hour of victory. He was buried at Blair Atholl in an unmarked grave. His death confirmed the Revolution in Scotland. Macaulay judged that 'during the last three months of his life he had approved himself a great warrior and politician; and his name is, therefore, mentioned with respect by that large class of persons who think there is no excess of wickedness for which courage and ability do not atone.' A smug judgement; Dundee casts a glamour over the period. Scott thought the popular picture of him false. Writing to the Duke of Buccleuch about Hogg's novel, *The Brownie of Bodsbeck*, he said, 'Hogg has slandered Clavers to please the Cameronians [as the extreme Covenanters were called] who do not read novels, and therefore will not be pleased.'

Andrew Fletcher of Saltoun
(1653–1716)

Andrew Fletcher of Saltoun was one of the most remarkable political thinkers that Scotland has produced. Like many theorists he himself was an indifferent politician.

He belonged to a family of East Lothian lairds and was tutored by Gilbert Burnet. Burnet later had as his pupil the Princess Mary (daughter of James, Duke of York, and of the future wife of William of Orange) and wrote the *History of His Own Time*, in which he described Fletcher as 'a Scotch gentleman of great parts and many virtues, but extravagantly passionate'. The young Fletcher studied first at Edinburgh University and then abroad. In 1678 he was a member of the Convention of Estates, representing either Haddingtonshire or East Lothian. He was opposed to the Stuart government, being against the maintenance of a standing army or the granting of taxation powers without extracting reforms from the government. In 1683 he went abroad to join opposition politicians in the Netherlands.

In 1685 he took part in Monmouth's rebellion, an act which certainly calls into question his political judgement because the rising was ill-prepared and foolish. His participation was cut short when he killed the Mayor of Taunton in a quarrel, an act which similarly calls his temper into doubt. He fled again to Holland but returned three years later with William of Orange. However, his support for William soon withered when he saw how negligent the King was of Scottish interests.

Fletcher was an intellectual. In the 1690s he published pamphlets on politics and economics: *A Discourse of Government with relation to Militias* (1697) and *Two Discourses concerning the State of Scotland* (1698). However, it was his part in Scotland's last Parliament and in the debates on the proposed Treaty of Union that make him of enduring importance. His long opposition to a strong monarchy had made him aware of the dangers of a Stuart restoration. His keen mind foresaw difficulties which an incorporating union might present. He, therefore, cast round for other means of resolving the crisis which had been created by the English settlement of the throne on the House of Hanover and the Scots' reluctance to follow suit. He advanced two schemes, both ingenious.

The first was to impose a scheme of limitations to the power of the Scots king. This would, he thought, remove English fears if the Scots chose a king of their own, and Scots fears if they devolved the Crown on the Hanoverians. His explanation of Scotland's ills was clear. 'Since the Union of the Crowns all our affairs have been managed by the advice of English ministers, and the principal offices of the kingdom filled with such men as the court of England knew would be subservient to their designs; by which means they have had so visible an influence upon our whole administration that we have, from that time, appeared to the rest of the world more like a conquered province than a free independent people.' There is an enduring validity to this argument, and his conclusion was that there was no way 'to free this country from a ruinous dependence upon the English court, unless by placing the power of conferring offices and pensions in the [Scots] Parliament so long as we have the same king as England'.

This argument was acute but it approached too close to Republicanism to convince. He was, therefore, driven towards the idea of Union. Yet his roving and speculative mind jibbed at the proposed 'incorporating union'. Observing that the Scots had certain interests which were distinct from those of England, he said that they 'deserved no pity if they voluntarily surrender their united and separate interest to the mercy of a united Parliament, where the English have so vast a Majority'. He sensed that power in the State was passing from king to Parliament and so asked in effect how Scottish interests could be protected in a united Parliament, when it had proved impossible to defend them in the Dual Monarchy. There Scottish ministers were supposedly independent but in reality they depended for their continuance in office on their 'subservience to the designs' of English ministers. 'This', he argued, 'will be the issue of that darling Plea of being one and not two; it will be turned upon the Scots with a vengeance, and their forty-five Scots members may dance round to all eternity, in this trap of their own making. . . .'

Hence, Fletcher, finding his scheme of Limitations unacceptable, turned to Federal Union. As conceived by him, this amounted to little more than the expression of amity and removal of discord. He envisaged two independent kingdoms linked by a Treaty of Friendship which would remove Scotland's commercial grievances and would allay English fears of an independent Scottish foreign policy which might endanger England's security. The disparity between the two nations made Federalism chimerical.

Fletcher opposed the Act of Union to the end. When it was passed, he retired from politics and turned to farming and agricultural improvements. He remains a figure of enduring importance, however, because his arguments, though directed to the immediate political crisis, remain the best exposition of the case against the Union. Anyone arguing that case finds himself returning to Fletcher for refreshment.

William Paterson
(1658–1719)

Banking is of comparatively recent origin in both England and Scotland; the name Lombard Street in the City of London recalls the long dominance of Italian bankers there, though the greatest Italian banks were to be found in Florence and Genoa rather than Milan. Germany and the Netherlands had great banking houses by the beginning of the sixteenth century. It was not, of course, to be wondered at that a poor country like Scotland should be backward in developing a banking system; yet, when at last it did so, Scots quickly became so adept and made so many innovations of lasting value in banking, that our late arrival in the field is worth noting.

To William Paterson goes the credit of having been a founder of both the Bank of England (1694) and the Bank of Scotland (1695). Paterson was born, apparently in Dumfriesshire, in 1658. Nothing is known of his early life, but he settled in London and became a merchant trading with the West Indies. He could not have done this from Scotland, since the Navigation Laws barred all but English residents from engaging in trade with English colonies. The Revolution of 1688 and the subsequent war with France put a great strain on public finances, and in particular made a high level of government borrowing necessary. Various schemes to expand and stabilise credit were propounded, among them a highly chimerical Land Bank. Paterson submitted his own scheme in 1691, though it made no progress for three years, by which time the Government's need for credit was acute. It was then taken up by Charles Montague, the Chancellor of the Exchequer, and Michael Godfrey, a leading London merchant. Their patronage helped the scheme to find favour with the leading members of the Whig party.

Paterson's scheme was that £1,200,000 should be borrowed by the Government at 8%. To encourage subscription of the loan, the subscribers were to be incorporated as the Governor and Company of the Bank of England, with the power to trade in bills of exchange, bullion and forfeited pledges; the Bank was forbidden to lend money to the Crown without the authority of Parliament. It is not too much to say that Paterson's scheme stabilised the Revolution settlement; everyone knew that James II would, if restored, repudiate the debt.

Paterson was one of the first directors of his bank, but he was not re-elected. After trying his fortune briefly in Germany, he returned to Scotland. He had made friends with Fletcher of Saltoun, to whom he unfolded his new scheme: to plant a Scottish colony on the Isthmus of Darien in Panama. This scheme he had been maturing for more than ten years, and he believed that he had discovered the means of making any nation rich. He easily persuaded his fellow-countrymen, all the more because he had at first the support of those English merchants who hated the monopoly enjoyed by the East India Company. The Company of Scotland trading to Africa and the Indies was therefore established, and all Scotland was hit by investment fever; some £220,000 sterling were subscribed.

Paterson's project was of the utmost simplicity, and should perhaps have been distrusted for that very reason. He argued that enormous profits could be made if trade between Asia and Europe could avoid the long slow route round Africa. A colony established at the narrowest point of the Americas, where the strip of land was no more than a bridge between the Atlantic and the Pacfic, could capture the bulk of Indian trade. He had, he averred, himself been to Darien, and no substantial obstacle existed to the establishment of a colony. This was foolish, for Spain claimed the land, and retained the monopoly of trade.

The Darien scheme was a disaster; yet there is no reason to think Paterson dishonest. It depended on English support, but there was no reason either to think that this would be forthcoming. Paterson himself accompanied the first expedition to Darien and suffered terribly from its failure.

He was, however, nothing if not resilient. His prostration was only temporary. He was soon busy with new schemes: for the Consolidation of the National Debt, for the Establishment of a Sinking Fund. In the Union debates of 1707 he lent his advice to those in favour of the Treaty, and was invited to assist in framing its fiscal provisions. This led him to break with his old friend Fletcher, but to Paterson Union made good sense. He had had to move to London himself in the first instance in order to share in the expansion of England's empire; he had seen his greatest project broken on English hostility; he drew what must have seemed a logical conclusion.

Rob Roy Macgregor Campbell
(1671–1734)

In 1603 the Clan Macgregor was outlawed, and its members forbidden to bear the name Macgregor, which is why Rob Roy had, as Alan Breck informed one of his sons, 'the ill-taste to clap the name Campbell tae his ain'. Naturally, the outlawry of the Macgregors caused the clan neither to cease to exist nor to disperse, but it had otherwise quite the opposite effect of what was intended. Deprived of their legal rights, or now only able to hold them by the goodwill of others, the Macgregors were driven into criminal attitudes, if not acts. Moreover, since they inhabited the Southern Highlands, the Braes of Balquidder and the country around Loch Lomond, they were to be found at that dangerous point where the more or less civil society of Lowland Scotland marched with the Highland clans which had never really been brought effectively within the law of Scotland. Dr Johnson expressed surprise that the most lawless clans should be found nearest the Lowlands, but in fact it is precisely in such frontier areas that robbery and blackmail may flourish, as the example of the Borderland before the Union of the Crowns shows very well.

Nothing is known of Rob Roy's early life, though he is said to have taken the lead in an affair known as the Hership of Devastation of Kippen in 1691. (This was, as far as bloodshed goes, a mild affair, only one man being killed.) He lived for some years under the protection of the Duke of Montrose, and followed the trade of cattle-dealer. Inasmuch as there was a cash economy in the Highlands it depended on the export of black cattle to the Lowlands and England, and Rob won a considerable reputation as a man who could win his clients a good price. In these years of prosperity the Duke of Montrose confirmed his right to the properties of Glengyle and Inversnaid, and Rob Roy might be known neither to history nor legend but for an unfortunate event which took place in 1712. There was a depression in the cattle market, and he was cheated by a partner, and found himself insolvent. He was not, however, penniless for he had been entrusted by clients with a considerable sum amounting to some £1000 sterling in order to buy cattle in the Highlands; one of these clients was Montrose. Faced with his own difficulties, and this temptation, Rob Roy made off, exchanging the career of a more or less respectable dealer for that of a bandit.

The Duke was aggrieved. He took legal action against Rob, attaching his landed property and driving his wife out of the house she occupied. From this time Rob Roy made private war on the Duke of Montrose. He found an ally and protector in the Duke of Argyll, for the Campbells and the Grahams had many scores to settle. Moreover, Argyll, like other great men, found it useful to have a man like Rob, who was not too careful of the law, at his disposal. If Rob Roy was in his conduct something of a *mafioso*, Argyll as a great Highland chief was *un gran' mafioso*. Each found the connection valuable. Rob could retreat into Argyll's estates if pressed by the law; Argyll could use Rob to persuade recalcitrant tenants or political opponents to fall into line.

Rob professed himself a Jacobite, even though Argyll was a Whig, and so cast a veneer of political commitment over his crimes. All those who supported the Revolution Settlement or the Union with England were thus classed as legitimate targets; unless, of course, they were prepared to buy him off. The blackmail he practised is what we should call a protection racket. It had one bare justification: since Rob Roy had no monopoly of depredation, he might actually be called upon to give real protection. In general, however, the knowledge that a farm or estate was being 'protected' by Rob would deter competitors.

Though a Jacobite, his performance in the Fifteen was equivocal. He joined the Earl of Mar, who sent him to Aberdeenshire to recruit among the Macgregors settled there, and he later acted as the Jacobite army's guide on its march from Perth to Dunblane; but, since his patron Argyll was commanding the Hanoverian army, and since Rob was probably too sagacious a man to be impressed by Mar's leadership or the Jacobites' prospects under his command, it seems likely that he played a double role. Certainly, in a letter written to Field-Marshal Wade after the Rising, he claimed not only that he had been forced into rebellion 'to avoid being flung into prison' (on account of the action the Duke of Montrose had brought against him) 'had I followed my real inclinations in joining the king's troops at Stirling', but that he had 'sent his Grace the Duke of Argyll all the intelligence I could from time to time, of the strength and situation of the rebels'. This may be easily believed. As to his conduct at

Sheriffmuir, the old ballad no doubt gives an accurate enough picture:

> Rob Roy he stood watch
> On a hill for to catch
>   The booty, for aught that I saw, man;
> For he ne'er advanced
> From the place where he stanc'd
>   Till nae mair was to do there at a' man.

Duncan Forbes of Culloden
(1685–1747)

Scott's Waverley novels may be read as an act of reconciliation or synthesis. They show how Scottish history and culture were formed through the clash of opposites, and how such struggles do not result in the entire victory of one party but lead to the development of a new society which partakes of both. He revealed how history is deformed by the partisanship which would reserve all truth and virtue to one side. His own sympathies were Tory and Jacobite, but he makes the Whig and Hanoverian case too, and he shows how the richness of a culture depends on its ability to make use of those who were defeated.

There were men who exemplified this in their own lives. One of the chief of these was Duncan Forbes of Culloden; there is irony in the fact that his family estate should also have been the name and site of the battle which led to the destruction of the old Highland society, for it was part of Forbes's life's work to try to avert that by bringing all Scotland comfortably within the polity of the new Union. He affords one of those rare instances of a politician who was not deformed by partisanship, and who saw his task as something wider and more humane. Forbes is a stumbling-block to Scottish Nationalists because none could deny his patriotism and readiness to defend Scottish interests any more than they could deny his commitment to the Union with England and the Hanoverian succession.

He was born in or near Inverness in 1685, and, like many Scots aspirant lawyers, received part of his education in the Netherlands at the University of Leyden. He was admitted advocate in 1709, two years after the Union. He attached himself to the Duke of Argyll, and by Argyll's influence became Sheriff of Midlothian. During the 1716 Rising he garrisoned Culloden Castle and defended it against the Jacobites. He was made advocate-depute, and in that capacity challenged the Crown's decision to send accused Jacobites out of Scotland for trial. Though himself a Government officer, he flatly declared this to be illegal, for he was jealous in defence of the liberties of Scots Law which had been reserved by the Treaty of Union. He even collected money for the defence of accused Jacobites.

87

Despite this show of independence his rise was rapid. He was successively Solicitor-General in 1717, a Member of Parliament from 1722–1737, and Lord Advocate from 1725. Then, when the office of Secretary of State for Scottish Affairs was discontinued, the administration of Scotland devolved on Forbes as Lord Advocate; for twenty years he was the chief figure in Scottish Government, and made himself responsible for the defence of the rights and interests of Scotland. His independence was displayed again in 1737 after the Porteous Riots in Edinburgh which had alarmed the Government. Ministers brought in a bill which would deprive the city of Edinburgh of certain privileges; Forbes, though the principal law-officer of the Crown in Scotland, opposed his own Government's bill in the House of Commons. Again, his virtue was recognised, and he did not suffer for his honesty, becoming in the same year Lord President of the Court of Session.

When a new Jacobite rising broke out in 1745 Forbes was firm in his opposition. He dissuaded a number of Highland chiefs from joining the Prince (for which they had good reason to thank him subsequently), and, when a shortage of supply was felt, supplied Government troops from his own resources. In all, he is said to have expended £30000 in defence of the Hanoverian regime. This money was never repaid. The reason for the Government's negligence and ingratitude to its greatest servant is unclear, but Cockburn's explanation is probably he correct one.

Having observed that Forbes was distressed by this treatment, Cockburn said: 'The mere money he probably never thought of, but the sentiment conveyed in the refusal was hard to bear. On this subject he was silent. But he had induced others on his credit to advance funds for the exigency of the day, and he openly remonstrated against not being able to do justice to them. He was thanked by His Majesty, but this is sometimes the coldest form in which an old servant can be discarded. No cause was ever found sufficiently plausible to be openly stated in defence of this conduct, but when we recollect the characters of the Duke of Cumberland and of Forbes, we cannot doubt that one of the popular accounts is the true one, which ascribes it all to his having plainly, and even in the king's presence, expressed his decided disapprobation of the violence of the royal army after the battle of Culloden.'

Cockburn's explanation is almost certainly correct. Forbes had reproached Cumberland for the barbarity of his conduct, and was not likely to be forgiven. In this, as in everything else, Forbes showed himself to be a man of humanity and judgement. Some doubtless will think the ingratitude with which he was treated was no more than to be expected by one who had supported a Union in which Scotland must always be a junior partner, but those who adhered to the Stuarts, such as Lord George Murray, could have told similar tales of royal ingratitude.

Forbes never seems to have wavered in his view that the Union was on balance beneficial to Scotland. Neither is there any case in which he can be shown to have neglected Scotland's interests. He believed in the letter of the Treaty and was quick to resent any infringement of it. He was a man of great benevolence and culture, a friend of Ramsay, James Thomson (of 'The Seasons'), Pope, Swift and Arbuthnott; in these friendships too he showed himself able to transcend party divisions.

He died in 1747 and was buried in Greyfriars Churchyard. A bust by Roubillac adorns Parliament House. He was a great man who has been too much forgotten.

Alexander Macdonald
(Alasdair Mac Mhaighstir Alasdair)
(*c.* 1695–*c.* 1770)

Every Scot who has no Gaelic is in that sense deprived of part of his inheritance. This knowledge arouses and compounds the feeling of guilt, and may also make him aware of a certain inferiority. There is a whole and important area of our history and culture which we have to take on trust, and much of it is hidden from us. This can lead us into absurdity too. I have heard fellow Scots who could neither read nor speak Gaelic proclaim Sorley Maclean to be the greatest living European poet. No one can possibly make such a judgement, unless he is capable of reading all the languages of Europe, but it is particularly ridiculous when the speaker is ignorant of the language in which his admired poet writes. Translation can only give an indication of quality, and it is probably true to say that translators contribute as much to their own language as they do to an understanding of their poet. Those of us who read Sorley Maclean's work only in translation can only have a dim appreciation of his genius, and this is equally true of his great predecessors.

By common consent Alexander Macdonald (Alasdair Mac Mhaighstir Alasdair) is among the greatest of these. He also bestrides the old world of Gaelic Scotland which was finally broken at Culloden and the new one which came into being after the failure of the Rising. He was born in Moidart, the son of the Episcopalian minister of Ardnamurchan. He was a close kinsman to the Clanranald chiefs, and a cousin of Flora Macdonald. Little is known of his early life, though he may have been out in the Fifteen, for he was a lifelong Jacobite, and may have studied for a time at Glasgow University. He was employed by the SPCK (Society for Promoting Christian Knowledge) as a teacher and catechist; for the Society he compiled the first Gaelic–English Dictionary. Sometime in the 1740s he became a Roman Catholic, and for some years before the Forty-Five he worked as a Jacobite agent. He served in the Prince's army as a captain, though he must by now have been well over fifty. He is reputed to have taught the Prince some Gaelic. He contributed a journal, written in English or at least translated by himself into that language, to Bishop Forbes's collection of Jacobite lore *The Lyon in*

Mourning. He spent some years in retirement after Culloden, but in 1752 was able to return to Moidart and lived near Arisaig till his death.

The earliest of his poetry to survive dates from about 1740. It belongs to a characteristic Gaelic tradition, but also shows that he had read James Thomson's poem 'The Seasons', one of the Augustan classics. Alasdair's nature poems are acts of celebration, distinguished by close observation and, we are told, rare metrical and linguistic virtuosity. In this period he also wrote 'The Author's Entreaty to the Muses', which reveals him to have been a self-conscious craftsman.

The verse of his second period is what we should term 'committed'; that is to say, it is written to promote the Jacobite cause and to revile its enemies. (In one poem the Hanoverian King George is addressed as a German cannibal.) Some of the poetry is hortatory, some satirical. 'The standpoint,' according to Professor Derrick S. Thomson, 'can be a clan one or a Gaelic nationalist one, Scottish, British or European (exceptionally).' At the very least the range and content of this poetry should disabuse anyone of the notion that Gaelic poetry is either a naïve outpouring of emotion, or wedded to a melancholy mood.

In his last period he wrote what is accepted as his greatest work, a long poem called 'The Birlinn or Galley of Clanranald'. This describes a voyage from South Uist to Carrickfergus in Ireland, and is a celebration of courage displayed in adversity. The poem begins with the blessing of the vessel, proceeds with a description of the rowers and their task, and then gives a vivid account of the voyage and the hardships they endured. Professor Thomson calls it 'a hard, clear, many-faceted intellectual and poetic diamond'. Again we have to take this judgement largely on trust. Hugh MacDiarmid made a verse translation in 1935, which gives any reader the sense of the poem, and only the most well-disposed more than the sense. I do not think anyone who read his translation without realising that it was a translation and without a predisposition to extract great poetry from it would find anything remarkable. Yet those who have the Gaelic are united in their judgement that this is great poetry. We have, I think, to accept their judgement.

David Hume
(1711–1776)

An old woman found a middle-aged gentleman stuck in a marsh on the outskirts of Edinburgh. He called on her for assistance, but thinking she recognised him, she asked if he was not 'Dauvit Hume, the atheist'. It was not a moment suitable for philosophical discussion, so he admitted the charge. Whereupon she commanded him to recite the Lord's Prayer before he should receive her help. Being a perfect sceptic, Hume complied. It is an instructive story, an endearing and characteristic one.

Hume is the greatest of Scotch philosophers, and one of the two greatest figures of the Enlightenment. Adam Smith was the other. Hume was also a thoroughly engaging and sympathetic man, whom Mrs William Adam, the wife of the architect and mother of Robert, described as 'the most innocent, agreeable, facetious man I ever met with'. He was fond of cooking and company; the first he described in 1769 as 'the Science to which I intend to devote the remaining Years of my Life; . . . for Beef and Cabbage (a charming Dish), and old Mutton and old Claret, no body excels me.' His correspondence is full of affectionate raillery, much of it directed against the English; he has had the misfortune, common to humorists, of finding his jokes taken seriously.

He was born and died in Edinburgh, but came from a Berwickshire family, whose estate was at Ninewells. He read law briefly, with little pleasure, and spent two years in business at Bristol, with no more. His father then provided him with the means to live three years in France, mostly at Rheims. He studied philosophy and in 1739, at the age of twenty-eight, published his masterpiece, the *Treatise of Human Nature*. (It is usual enough for philosophers, like mathematicians and lyric poets, to flourish young.) The Treatise was to be revised and expanded, but remains the best expression of his thinking.

Hume considered that our beliefs about the world were the consequence of certain tendencies inherent in our nature, the most important of which was the imagination's ability to make associations between otherwise distinct ideas. It was the imagination which, by the way it worked, enabled us to bridge the gaps in our experience, and so build up complete pictures of what would else be fragmentary. His theory of causation depended likewise on the imagination. He pointed out that we may not observe necessary connections, but that we project on the world our assumption that a sequence which has occurred in the past will be repeated. (We believe that the sun will rise tomorrow because we have known no day on which it has not done so, and though we may be quite ignorant of the properties of clouds, we associate a cloudy sky with the possibility of rain.) In this way we are able to construct a rational model of the world without relying for our understanding of it on any theory of divine intervention.

Hume's philosophy, therefore, enabled men to make sense of the world and of human society in purely human terms. He banished metaphysics from philosophy, and theology from the discussion of moral and social conduct, and what he had to say about the sympathetic mechanisms which order our relations with other men and women made it possible for philosophers to consider men living in a society which was held together by cultural, and not simply political, bonds. In this he developed Hutcheson's theory of sympathy, just as his empirical starting-point was the work of Locke and Berkeley; he took that further by applying it to our knowledge of our own natures as well as of the material world.

No philosopher exists quite in a vacuum. In such discussions Hume and those who followed him were exploring ideas which were widely current: Montesquieu in *L'Esprit des Lois*, for instance, was also developing the idea of cultural association being as important as political structures. But these ideas had a special force in Scotland as a society which had recently acquiesced in the resignation of its political independence and the devaluation of its political structures, but which yet felt itself to be distinct.

Hume was a public man too: he was Librarian to the Faculty of Advocates, Secretary to the British Ambassador in Paris, and Under-Secretary of State for the Northern Department in London. His reputed atheism denied him university Chairs. This does not seem to have dismayed him; his philosophy was sufficiently robust to allow him to accept misfortune.

He wrote a five-volume *History of England*, which was a great success and made him better known as an historian than philosopher. He recognised that 'this was the historical century', and, with a mixture of surprise and pride, that Scotland 'was the historical nation'. His own history, and those of the other philosophical historians of the Enlightenment, marked a new development in the art. He believed that society developed, unconsciously, through distinct stages each characterised by a different economic structure.

(In this Hume, like Montesquieu, anticipated Marx.) His theory was progressive and determinist: it allowed for the natural involuntary development of societies. It was neither facile nor optimistic, for Hume and his fellows realised that a relapse to barbarism was as possible as an advance to a higher civilisation, but his insistence that man's history could not be satisfactorily studied without reference to social structures deepened the subject and rescued it alike from chance and mere adherence to chronology.

He did much to clear the mists from the study of history and economics. He showed for instance that theories of a real social contract were unnecessary. The utility of government justifies its existence. Consent is no necessary fiction; governments cannot continue without it, however it be obtained. In economics he expounded the theory that the value of money is determined by international trade. If an economy were closed and entirely self-sufficient, then the quantity of money in circulation would be immaterial, since prices would rise or fall accordingly. But in international trade, where the quantity of money cannot be determined by government, real value is established; this was a powerful argument for free trade, fully developed by Adam Smith.

Hume is a figure of unusual attractiveness. It was hard to find anyone who knew him who did not like and revere him. He is our only philosopher of a truly European reputation. More than that, however, he is a fine example of how intelligent men can flourish and develop their intellectual abilities in an apolitical society. Eighteenth-century Scotland presents this strange paradox: the surrender of political independence caused a thousand flowers to bloom. Such a stroke of fortune is, however, only possible when government is minimal. Energies which in the sixteenth and seventeenth centuries had been directed towards narrow and bitter controversy were free to roam speculatively, and the weight of government was not yet such as to oppress or restrict them.

James Burnett, Lord Monboddo
(1714–1799)

Monboddo believed that men had once had tails, but had lost them, and that the orang-utang was an undeveloped human being, lacking only speech. This was a remarkable belief to hold in the middle of the eighteenth century, and one which exposed Monboddo to a good deal of mockery. Yet it was also quite consonant with the general tenor of the Scottish Enlightenment. Monboddo might be described as a primitive evolutionist; yet he was more complicated than that, for he also agreed with Rousseau in thinking the savage happier than the civilised man, and the savage's way of life in many respects more admirable.

Like so many of the great figures of the Enlightenment, Monboddo was a lawyer and a laird. He came from the north-east and was brought up on the family estate in Kincardineshire. He attended school locally at Laurencekirk. There was a tradition of scholarship there, for an earlier schoolmaster had been Thomas Ruddimen, the author of *Ruddiments of the Latin Tongue*, published in the year of Monboddo's birth, and Laurencekirk was also the birthplace of the poet and philosopher James Beattie, a friend of Monboddo (even though they disagreed) and of the judge and agricultural improver Lord Gardenstone, who built a model manufacturing village there, and wrote, as Boswell put it, 'a pamphlet upon it, as if he had founded Thebes'. So Monboddo had good reason to feel a strong local pride.

He proceeded to King's College, Aberdeen, and thence to Edinburgh and Groeningen universities, and was called to the Bar in 1737. He became Sheriff of Kincardineshire in 1760, and a Lord of Session in 1767. He was a member of the debating club called 'The Select Society', which met every Wednesday in the Advocates' Library for 'the pursuit of philosophical inquiry and the improvement of the members in the art of speaking'. It was the principal focus of intellectual activity in Edinburgh, and it would be hard to exaggerate its influence and value.

Monboddo's principal interest was the history of society. In this inquiry his master was the Frenchman Montesquieu, whose importance as an influence on the Scottish Enlightenment was central. His two principal books were *Of the Origin and Progress of Language* and *Antient Metaphysics*. Each was published in six volumes, spread over the last quarter-century of his life, the publications overlapping. His sensational claims about tails and the orang-utang naturally aroused the greatest interest, and were equally naturally received with considerable scepticism. This tended to obscure his central thesis which was somewhat more valuable. He questioned the origin of language as recorded in the myth of the Tower of Babel recounted in Genesis. Language, Monboddo held, originated from necessity and proceeded to develop naturally; it was not an arbitrary gift of God. In his *Antient Metaphysics* he took up a position which was to be central to the Scottish Theory of Education, asserting that a full cultural development was only possible if science and philosophy were both studied; they were not mutually exclusive but complementary.

Monboddo was in many ways an eccentric and untypical figure; his ideas embarrassed some of his distinguished contemporaries like Lord Kames, and yet they were perhaps more fruitful. Certainly his foreshadowing of Darwinian ideas of the origin of the species was a remarkable achievement of intuition. He won for himself the status of a celebrity in London, which he used to visit annually, riding there till he was past eighty. He was finely inconsistent, for he was able to combine his evolutionary theories with a belief in the decadence of human society.

Something of his flavour may be got from the account of Dr Johnson's visit to Monboddo which Boswell gives in his *Journal of a Tour to the HEBRIDES*. Boswell 'knew that Lord Monboddo and Dr Johnson did not love each other . . . yet I was also curious to see them together' (Monboddo was a friend of Boswell's father). He, therefore, engineered the visit, and a comic occasion it proved to be. The occasion buried their hostility and they vied with each other in paying compliments. Even so, it began stickily. Lord Monboddo drew Johnson's attention to an old tower marked with the arms of the House of Douglas, to which his great-grandmother belonged, and said, 'In such houses our ancestors lived, who were better men than we'. Johnson could not let such an assertion pass: 'No, no, my lord. We are as strong as they and a great deal wiser.' But they were able to agree about Homer and the value of the history of manners, squashing poor Boswell when he put in a word for military history. Then they were able to find more common ground in deploring the decrease of learning in both Scotland and England, though both were, one would have thought, themselves proof to the contrary. Johnson: 'Learning is much decreased in England, in my remembrance.' Monboddo: 'You, sir, have lived to see its decrease in

England, I its extinction in Scotland.' So much for the Enlightenment! On this firm basis of nonsense even an argument in which Johnson defended the greater happiness of the London shopkeeper than of the noble savage could not disturb the good feeling, and they parted on friendly terms, Monboddo sending his black servant with them to guide them on their way. Johnson confided in Boswell that he was 'much pleased with Lord Monboddo today. He said, he would have pardoned him for a few paradoxes when he found so much that was good: but that from his appearance in London, he thought him all paradox'.

Charles Edward Stuart, Bonnie Prince Charlie
(1720–1788)

Lord Rosebery declared that 'every Scot is a Jacobite at heart'. An exception should be made for Campbells but the opinion is at least half true. The most vivid pictures presented to us by our historical imagination are Jacobite, as are our best-loved and most character-istic songs. Jacobitism represents pure spirit as opposed to dull mercantile efficiency. It has all the romance of a lost cause. It enshrines loyalty that acts without hope of reward. It breathes a tender and melancholy nostalgia and, at the same time, a defiance of the odds. There can be few 'modern' Scots who have not at some time found themselves susceptible to its charms despite the fact that, while it was a live political cause, the great majority declined to permit their hearts to rule their heads.

Prince Charles was Jacobitism incarnate. He had no other aim in life but the restoration of his family and when this failed he disintegrated. His collapse may be taken as criticism of his character but it was also the expression of his utter identification with his cause.

The '45 was an impossible romance. It was a schoolboy's adventure which came close to overthrowing an established dynasty. The Prince's escape after Culloden stretches credulity. It offers occasion for pride too. A price of £30000 was laid on his head at a time when the total cash income of the Highland counties can hardly have amounted to that sum. No-one was found to betray him, although one minister disgraced the name of Macaulay by showing himself eager to do so.

Charles Edward was not the pretty boy some portraits suggest but a tough, athletic and wilful young man. He stood 5 ft 10 inches and had dark red hair, and was twenty-five when he embarked on his great adventure. He was no more than half-educated for he had resented his tutors, but he had trained himself for war and was devoted to golf, tennis and shooting. His mother was Polish. His great-grandfather, John Sobieski, had saved Vienna and Christendom from the Turk in 1685, the same year that his paternal grandfather became James VII of Scotland and II of England. Charles had something of the impossible gallantry of the Poles about him. Allied to his Scots blood it made for an audacious nature that was capable of contemplating, and almost achieving, what more sober and sensible men would never have dreamed of undertaking.

The war between Britain and France which broke out in 1742 seemed to give him his chance. Nobody believed that the Jacobites could still be restored without French help. When that help was not forthcoming, Charles was still prepared to try. One Antoine Walsh, a Franco-Irish shipowner of Nantes, lent him a brig. The Prince landed at Loch nan Uamh, between Moidart and Arisaig, on the 25 July 1745. He had with him seven men, an improbable collection of mostly sexagenarian adventurers and failures.

The Highland chiefs told him to go home. He answered grandly, 'I have come home.' Some of them – Macdonalds of Clanranald, Glengarry and Keppoch, Lochiel and his Camerons, Stewarts of Ardshiel – were driven by shame to join him. He had perhaps six hundred men when he raised his standard at Glenfinnan on 19 August. Within the next few weeks, some fifteen hundred more joined him. Sir John Cope, the Hanoverian general, was out-manoeuvred and Edinburgh occupied.' Then, when Cope had managed to ship his troops south, the Highland charge scattered them at Prestonpans. Charles was master of Scotland.

James VIII was proclaimed and for a few weeks Holyroodhouse became again what it had only briefly been before: a royal palace, full of gaiety and dancing. Charles, displaying high spirits, charm and clemency, refused to allow public rejoicing for his victory over his father's subjects. The army grew with the enthusiasm of victory and left Edinburgh at the end of October. The Prince marched at the head of his troops, as he would continue to do throughout their advance. On 8 November they crossed into England.

They had chosen the western route by way of Carlisle because they believed that the English Jacobites of Cumberland and Lancashire were eager to rise in support. Unfortunately the English adherents of the Stuarts were mostly no more than dinner-table Jacobites and little support was forthcoming. The choice of the western route was in fact a blunder. The octogenarian Marshal Wade was at Newcastle with some inferior troops. A victory over Wade on

English soil might have encouraged Charles's English supporters and intensified the panic already developing in London, where King George was packing his bags ready to slip off to Hanover.

The opportunity was lost. Instead, they marched as far south as Derby. They were dismayed by the lack of support and aware of the danger from the Hanoverian forces. At Derby the decision was taken to retreat. Charles opposed it bitterly. (Since then, debate has never ceased as to what might have happened had their nerve held and they had made a dash for London.) Charles, having lost the argument, seems to have lost heart too. From being an inspiration on the march south, he now became a liability. He behaved like a spoiled child and regained his spirit only when all was irretrievably lost at Culloden. Then, during his five months' adventuring, he conducted himself with courage, composure and cheerfulness, but at the time of greatest danger for the men who had trusted themselves to him and risked all for his cause, he failed.

The rest of his life was an anticlimax. It could not fail to be. He suffered the penalty of the single-minded who fail in their object; caring for nothing but his cause, he could not even care for his own dignity. He was estranged from his father. He had no-one to love. His relations with his mistress Clementina Walkinshaw, herself possibly a Hanoverian spy, were tepid. They had a bond of common allegiance to what his brother Henry, Cardinal of York, called 'that nasty bottle', but eventually they drifted apart. His late marriage to Princess Louise of Stollberg, undertaken for dynastic reasons, was a dismal and squalid failure. She soon took a lover (the poet Alfieri) and abandoned her elderly husband, complaining of ill-treatment. Charles drank heavily; he had nothing else to do and nothing to care for. If he could not be king, he cared not what became of him. In his last years his natural daughter, Charlotte, brought him some comfort. He died in 1788 in the Palazzo Muti in Rome where he had been born. It is a mean palazzo, quite dwarfed by the great palaces belonging to the Colonna and the Odaleschi which stand in the same piazza. As he lay dying, a piper played 'Lochaber No More' in the courtyard.

Flora MacDonald
(1722–1790)

In Sir Walter Scott's collection at Abbotsford is the marriage contract of Flora MacDonald and Allan MacDonald of Kingsburgh. Its presence there is evidence of the hold on the imagination taken by one brief episode in Flora's life, which made her a heroine of Romance.

She was born on South Uist, the daughter of a tacksman to MacDonald of Clanranald. She belonged, therefore, to the Jacobite clan, and her father was a man of some means, for a Highlander at least. Clanranald was one of the first chiefs to adhere to the Prince when he arrived in Scotland in 1745, though like all the others he did so with some reluctance and much apprehension.

Her moment of glory came with the arrival of the Prince during his flight from Culloden. There was a price of £30000 on his head, but it never occurred to most of those with whom he came in contact that they should betray him, and Flora was no exception. Her precise feelings for the Prince are unknown, but it would be surprising if she did not feel tenderness as well as a sense of duty: he was young, handsome and in grave danger, and he was ready to trust himself to her. On the other hand, the circumstances of his journey from the Outer Hebrides to Skye were more ludicrous than romantic, for Charles was disguised as Flora's maidservant and called by the name of Betty Burke. Nor did he always seem aware of the danger of his situation, and he caused needless difficulty by stepping out of the character that he had assumed and showing himself more solicitous of her welfare than a maidservant would have been. Probably Flora was more weighed down by responsibility than buoyed up by any personal feeling for the Prince. Certainly on his side, he was grateful and courtly, and no more; it is hard to believe that Charles II would not have behaved more warmly towards Flora than the Prince. He took leave of Flora in pouring rain in Portree with the words, 'For all that has happened, I hope, Madam, we shall meet in St James's yet'. But she was never to see him again.

Nevertheless their association captured the imagination of all who heard the story, and Flora became and has remained a popular heroine. Many believe that she and Charles were lovers, and would be surprised to know how brief their association was. The popular instinct in these matters often errs, but rarely does so completely. It is in fact quite right to select Flora from all those who helped the Prince in his escape, because the association of this young woman, and the courage with which she faced danger, do serve to symbolise, as nothing else can, the wholly admirable way in which the Highlanders guarded and cared for the Prince who had been the cause of the disaster that had come on them. There was no repining, no recrimination. It is fitting that Flora should be commemorated in one of the two most famous of Jacobite songs, the Skye Boat Song, though that was not composed till almost a hundred years after her death; the interval proves the endurance of her appeal.

With the malice which the Hanoverians consistently displayed after Culloden, Flora was arrested for her part in the Prince's escape and imprisoned in London for several months, till she was released amidst a general amnesty of Jacobites. She returned to Skye where she married in 1750. Like most of the Highlanders she and her family accepted that the defeat at Culloden marked the end of Jacobitism, and accommodated themselves to the new ways. These, however, involved economic as well as social changes, and many Highlanders sought their fortune in the New World. Flora and her husband were among these, distressed by debt and emigrating to North Carolina in 1774. The outbreak of the War of the American Revolution displaced them again, for, perhaps overestimating the strength of the royal forces as a natural result of their own experience, perhaps feeling a genuine loyalty to the Crown which had after all eventually treated her with some generosity, they opposed the rebellion, and Allan MacDonald served in one of the loyalist or Tory regiments raised among the colonists. By 1778 their position had become untenable, and, like many other Tories, they fled to Canada. They were unable to settle there, and returned to Skye, where Flora died in 1790.

Flora demonstrated qualities of courage and loyalty much admired in Highland society. Her subsequent history is interesting because it shows how quickly and completely active devotion to the Stuarts withered, to be replaced by a sentimental attachment, in which she became a key figure. But in her real life, she showed an equally admirable ability to accept the fact of things, and to try to adapt herself to changed circumstances. In reading Flora Mac-

Donald's story one can see glimpses of a future in which the Highlanders, who had been the most dangerous opponents of the Hanoverians, became the staunchest defenders of the British Crown, and in which Highland regiments played so prominent a part in the defeat of Napoleon (though a Macdonald was among his marshals) and the expansion of the British Empire.

Robert Macqueen, Lord Braxfield
(1722–1799)

The prisoner in the dock, charged with sedition and accused of being a reformer, protested that 'Jesus Christ was a reformer too'. 'Muckle he made of that,' said the judge; 'he was hangit.' The speaker, presiding over the trial of those Friends of the People who wished to import the ideas of the French Revolution to Scotland, was Lord Braxfield, the Lord Justice-Clerk. His coarse vigour was to be condemned, yet immortalised, by Cockburn in his account of the Sedition Trials. He was also to be the model for Stevenson's Weir of Hermiston. Braxfield, like Sir Harry Lauder in a different and perhaps inferior context, is a test of Scottishness. Even those who shrink from him in disgust, as Cockburn did, are at the same time drawn to him by their recognition that they share a national identity with him. There is something in Braxfield that transcends judgement.

He is a reminder of how thin the veneer of the Enlightenment might be. He was born Robert Macqueen in Lanark in 1722, a Highlander well south of the Highland line. He became an advocate in 1744 and immersed himself in the dry matter of feudal law. He proved his skill early because after the Jacobite Rising, he was employed by the Crown in the cases of the forfeiture of Highland estates. He wrought well and harshly, to the satisfaction of his masters and the discomfiture of unfortunate Jacobites.

In 1776 he became a Lord of Session, and Lord Justice-Clerk in 1788. He was a judge of the heroic age of the Scottish Bench, a deep drinker who sat with a bottle of claret to hand. 'Bacchus', Cockburn said, 'never had an easy victory over Braxfield.' Yet the effect must have been cumulative, contributing to his narrow certainty and his inability to receive a new idea. He had all the self-assurance of the man who can deny the reality of what he has shut out. Wine contributed to this.

He would be forgotten but for the Sedition Trials. Now what was curious about the reaction of the Scottish Establishment to the Revolution in France was that there was nothing in the fundamental principles of Scottish Enlightenment philosophy or philosophical history to persuade men to resist the ideas of the Revolution – the whole tenor of the Enlightenment should have been favourable to the democratic base of the Revolution – and yet they shied away. The Friends of the People were proscribed and Braxfield was hired to judge them.

At the trial of Muir of Huntersfield, Braxfield was careful to pick a jury of known Government supporters. He told them that reform was intrinsically unconstitutional. Only the landed interest, said the old feudal lawyer, had the right to be represented in Government: 'As for the rabble who have nothing but personal property, what hold has the nation on them? What security for the payment of their taxes? They may pack up their property on their backs and leave the country in the twinking of an eye. But landed property cannot be removed.' As for the French, they were abruptly dismissed as 'monsters of human nature'.

The glee with which Braxfield meted out sentence disgusted even some of those who agreed with him. Lord Advocate Dundas deemed it wiser not to employ him in subsequent trials. Yet it is Braxfield who conquers posterity. Stevenson, looking at Raeburn's portrait of the upright old rogue, remarked that 'you may look in to that queer face of that portrait for as long as you will but you will not see any hole or corner for timidity to enter in'. It may be objected that there is no cause for the judge on the bench to feel timid, timidity being reserved for the dock, but it is Braxfield's rough certainty which appeals. 'Ye're a verry clever chiel,' he told one accused, 'but you'd be nane the waur of a hanging.' Such a sentiment from such a place is monstrous and disgusting. At the same time, however, there is a geniality, partly the result of the Scotch tongue, partly of Braxfield's native acceptance of the facts of life and death, that appeals. Cockburn called him 'the Jeffreys of Scotland' but Braxfield, for all his denial of political rights to any but men of property, has a certain democratic geniality which marks him out as different from the English judge. Perhaps his work in the sequestration of Jacobite estates had nurtured in him the understanding of how easily the turn of fortune's wheel could throw the judge himself into the dock.

Adam Smith
(1723–1790)

It was said of Edinburgh in the age of the Enlightenment that a man could stand by the Mercat Cross and 'in a few minutes, take fifty men of genius by the hand'. The hands of the surest genius would have belonged to David Hume and Adam Smith and, of the pair (who were good friends), Smith's genius has had the wider and more enduring influence.

He was a Fifer, born and raised in Kirkcaldy where his father, who came, however, from Aberdeenshire, was Comptroller of Customs. Smith was himself to be made Commissioner of Customs in 1778 and it is ironical that the Customs and Excise, that obstruction to the Free Trade which he recommended, should have played such an prominent part in his life.

At the age of fourteen he went to Glasgow University, where he studied under Francis Hutcheson. He proceeded to Balliol, Oxford, where he remained from 1740–6, then passed several years as a freelance lecturer in Edinburgh. In 1751 he was elected Professor of Moral Philosophy in Glasgow; his thirteen years there were, by his own account, the happiest of his life. In 1764 he became tutor to the 3rd Duke of Buccleuch and travelled with him in Europe. In France he met Voltaire and talked at length with the group of economists known as physiocrats, the leader of whom, Turgot, would become a Minister at the beginning of Louis XVI's reign and would attempt economic reforms which might, if continued, have averted the Revolution; however, his attack on the vested and sectional interests deplored by Smith failed. Returning to Scotland, Smith spent ten years working on his most important book, *An Inquiry into the Nature and Causes of the Wealth of Nations*. It was written in Kirkcaldy and published in 1776. From 1778 he lived in Edinburgh, at Panmure House in the Canongate, where his Sunday night suppers drew together the cream of Scotland's intellectual society.

Smith is most easily described as an economist, and the description is fair enough because the *Wealth of Nations* is one of the two most influential works of economic theory; the other is *Das Kapital*, and if Marx gains by passion, Smith has the advantage of sense. In our time economics has often seemed a narrow and technical subject, its practitioners more and more obsessed with feeding 'models' into computers, and Smith's most recent prominence has been as the originator of what is called 'monetarist' theory. This restriction obscures the scope and intent of his work, since his economics formed part of the Enlightenment's Theory of Man and was not conceived as a separate or distinct subject. There is in fact a logical progression from his essay in Moral Philosophy, *The Theory of Moral Sentiments*, to the *Wealth of Nations*. This first book, published in 1759, presents 'sympathy' as the means whereby Man, though essentially self-interested, yet limits his passions by the capacity for social affection. Here Smith develops the theories he had learned from Hutcheson and from Hume. The political value of his argument may be estimated by a comparison with the seventeenth-century theory of Hobbes. For Hobbes, Man's natural existence had been 'nasty, brutish and short'. Hobbesian Man was a driving egoist who could be controlled only by his fear of the same will to power exhibited by others. The Hobbesian view of Man's nature led logically to the acceptance of the absolutist State: Man, being mischievous and selfish, must submit to government, or his destructive passions would be loosed; rival egos would contend; and so, for Hobbes, anarchy and war were the natural condition of Man unless controlled by a strong authority outside himself. For Smith this was shallow philosophy. He saw instead that Man's habit of sympathetic association, his capacity for personal affection and for the pursuit of a rational and therefore self-limiting self-interest, did not require the trammels of absolutism. On the contrary indeed: in the *Wealth of Nations* he identified that absolutist State, which was determined to exercise control over natural activity, as an obstacle to human progress. It operated consciously over unconscious and therefore natural processes of human intercourse, and, in doing so, distorted and blocked development. The absolutist state could not be other than the expression of sectional interests; whereas 'enlightened self-interest', coupled with Man's 'propensity to truck, barter and exchange' would create a general prosperity in an expanding economy.

Smith is the true founder of classical economics and his work was developed but hardly revised for a hundred years. He offers among other riches a theory of wages and prices, of the nature of rent and profit; an economic history of Europe from the Roman Empire, and a sharp analysis of the dominant contemporary theory of mercantilism. He also reviews the State's necessary and unnecessary role in the economy. Most powerfully of all, perhaps, he reveals the economic basis of history and culture; Marx learned from him, even if he was not convinced by Smith's argument. Buckle, in his *History of Civilisation*, called it 'probably the most important book that has ever been written, whether we consider the amount of original thought which it contains or its practical influence'.

Smith's life was consistent with his work. He showed a great capacity for sympathetic friendship, well displayed by a famous letter on the death of Hume. This infuriated Dr Johnson, who could not bear to believe that an atheist like Hume should have died serenely. The dispute occasioned an exchange (described by Scott as 'a classic dialogue' between the 'two great moralists') when they met in Glasgow during Johnson's Scottish tour. It ended with Smith describing Johnson as 'a brute'. It appeared that Johnson had challenged the truth of Smith's account and bluntly called him a liar. 'What did you reply?' Smith was asked. 'I said, "You are a son of a bitch"'.

Robert Adam

(1728–1792)

There are three arts in which Scotsmen have excelled: literature, painting and architecture, and of these architecture is the least easy to escape. Yet, while everyone in Scotland has heard of Burns and Scott, the names of our great architects are far less celebrated. There are doubtless two reasons for this neglect: first, architecture is very simply there; buildings stand everywhere around us, and it requires a certain determined curiosity to inquire the name of their author: second, many buildings are the work of more than one hand, for the original design has frequently been re-modelled. Nevertheless the ignorance is curious.

In the case of Robert Adam there is a further curiosity. There is an 'Adam style', as there is a 'Mackintosh style', and it is quite probable that more people could give a fairly accurate description of an Adam fireplace, or could certainly recognise one, than could name any of his buildings. Yet the buildings are around us, in Edinburgh and other parts of Scotland, in London and the English countryside.

Of course, it is also true that Robert Adam was less an individual than a partner in a great family business. It is sometimes difficult to disentangle his peculiar responsibilities from those of his brothers; the introduction to *The Works in Architecture of Robert and James Adam*, for instance, was almost certainly written by James. Moreover, the mere fact that so great a part of his working life was spent in England, and so much of his great building done there, prejudices some against him. We are all familiar with the peculiarly Scottish habit of mind which will deny Scottishness to artists aware of other traditions, whose work does not have an exclusively Scottish focus. (There also exists of course an opposite tendency, which will claim Scottishness on the most tenuous basis; in his introduction to his study of Border warfare, *The Steel Bonnets*, George Macdonald Fraser dilates on the Scottishness of the American Presidents, Johnson and Nixon.) Yet no Scotsman built more nobly and impressively than Robert Adam, and none had a deeper influence on taste.

It was, as I have said, a family business. Robert's father William (1698–1748) was a master of the Baroque style, exemplified in

Hopetoun House and Floors Castle (though it was Playfair who gave Floors its delightful onion-domes). Robert's early work consisted of finishing buildings his father had designed. He also worked on the construction of the military post at Fort George, which taught him much about the necessary functional qualities of architecture.

With the financial support of his elder brother John, the manager of the family business, Robert set off on the Grand Tour in 1754. He was to spend four years abroad, mostly in Italy, especially Rome, and his time there formed the basis of his mind, taste and style. He studied under the French drawing-master Clérisseau, as his brother James did subsequently, and he was also influenced by the drawings and etchings of Piranesi. He formed a taste for the picturesque aspects of Antiquity, and this was powerfully reinforced by his examination of Diocletian's palace at Spalatro. His drawings of its ruins, published in 1764, after his return to London, established his reputation.

For some years he worked principally in London. His great patron was the Duke of Northumberland for whom he worked at Syon House, Alnwick Castle and Northumberland House. The last of these has long been destroyed by commercial vandalism, but the marvellous glass drawing-room can be seen in the Victoria and Albert Museum. Perhaps his English masterpiece was Kedleston in Derbyshire. The brothers' most ambitious enterprise – the Adelphi – was a failure, greatly to be regretted.

The building of the New Town of Edinburgh gave Adam a chance to work in Scotland. The Register House is his, and the north side of Charlotte Square, which has survived intact as a perfect expression of his taste and genius. Even more impressive, however, is the Old College of the university. The front is exposed to a street too narrow to allow its majestic and neoclassical monumentality to be seen to the fullest advantage.

Neoclassicism was the mode of expression most natural to him, but at Culzean Castle he combined it with a Gothic style. The two might seem hard to reconcile, but Adam brought it off. The resulting style has been called 'picturesque'; it is an architectural equivalent of the Romantic Classicism of Poussin and Claude; it points the way forward to a style of castle building which precedes Scottish Baronial and which is seen, for example, on a small scale at Abbotsford, and on a grander scale at Gillespie Graham's Drumtochy.

Adam's reputation sank after his death, and it took almost a hundred years for his full genius to be recognised. He himself had had no doubt of his genius: 'I think it not amiss for a man to have a little glisk of that infinite merit he is possessed of,' he wrote. The failure of some of the brothers' grand designs in town planning had left a whiff of financial chicanery behind, but Adam remains the outstanding architect and designer of a great age of building, a source of inspiration to his successors, who plundered his ideas while often denying their origins. In his work in Scotland he contrived to combine a distinctively Scottish note with architecture which was in the van of European taste.

James Ramsay
(1733–1789)

The philosophy of the Scottish Enlightenment was distinguished by the theory of Benevolence, adumbrated by Francis Hutcheson, developed by Adam Smith in his Theory of Moral Sentiments, and then by Thomas Reid and his pupils Dugald Stewart and Sir William Hamilton, the chief proponents of the 'Common Sense' School of Philosophy. They held that benevolence and the recognition of reciprocal obligations were essential to the existence of a just and moral society. This was a philosophy which could not fail to have practical consequences, for anyone schooled in it was likely to carry its teachings into a criticism of things as they were.

One such was James Ramsay. He was born in Fraserburgh and educated under Reid at King's College, Aberdeen. He was an Episcopalian, like many in the north-east – the part played by Episcopalians in the history of Scottish culture is too often disregarded, perhaps because of the mistaken popular description of the historic Episcopal Church of Scotland as 'the English Church', a designation that became common in the nineteenth century when an increasing number of Englishmen bought Scottish estates or simply holidayed in Scotland; until then, of course, despite its use of a modified form of the Anglican liturgy, the Episcopalians might more reasonably have been described as Scottish nationalists, for they had opposed the Union, which the Presbyterians, being Whigs, had supported, and most of them were Jacobites, as were James Ramsay's family. However, since he was only twelve at the time of the Rising, he belonged to a generation which accepted the Union *faute de mieux*, no reasonable alternative surviving, and he was himself commissioned in the Royal Navy. Leaving the navy, he was ordained a minister in the Church of England, and from 1762 to 1781 held benefices in the West Indian island of St Kitts.

Here he became convinced of the iniquity of slavery. Despite opposition from most of the whites there, who were economically tied to slavery, he devoted himself to the evangelisation and material welfare of the black slave majority. When he returned to England, he conducted a fierce campaign in the press, and by way of pamphlets, lectures and public controversy, against slavery. He met bitter and unscrupulous opposition; his character was attacked; he was threatened with assassination and challenged to duels; one of his opponents, the planter and Member of Parliament Edward Molyneux, claimed that he had brought about his death.

Ramsay was clearly a man of great courage and determination; of great humanity too. He was one of the first of a long line of Scots who worked against slavery, of whom Livingstone is chief. Most of his associates were English, though the Clapham Sect whom he influenced contained many who were of Scotch extraction like the Macaulays. It is also possible to see in Ramsay something of the English Tory tradition, exemplified by Dr Johnson, a fierce opponent of slavery. But this, of course, was not so very different from the Scotch Tory outlook, and indeed one of the key cases which established the illegality of slavery in these islands was Knight *v.* Wedderburn [1776] instigated or encouraged by the Lord Advocate Henry Dundas who, though from a Whig family, was to become the leader of the Scots Tories.

Indeed one can see in Ramsay's reasons for opposition to slavery the fruits of his education in Scotland. He was no radical, for, like anyone from a Tory and Jacobite background, he believed in a hierarchical society. But he also believed that the ranks of society must exercise reciprocal benevolence and confer reciprocal benefits. This was pure Hutchesonism. Furthermore, he had concluded that this was impossible in a slave society, for no benefit could compensate for the deprivation of liberty. He spoke from experience, for in his early years in St Kitts he had, like any other gentleman, owned slaves himself.

Moreover, Ramsay also drew on arguments employed by Adam Smith in *The Wealth of Nations*, to demonstrate that slavery was not only wrong in itself, but also inefficient. (These arguments were later to be deployed by many American abolitionists in the years before the American Civil War; for example, Frederick Olmsted, author of *The Cotton Kingdom*.) Slaves could never work as valuably as free labourers, for they possessed no interest in the success of the enterprise for which they worked; free men on the other hand might hope to be rewarded by a higher wage and improved standards of living. Reciprocal ties existed between employers and free workers, which could never be found between masters and slaves. It was in an employer's interest to treat free labourers well, but benevolent treatment of slaves depended entirely on the philanthropy of their masters; interest didn't enter into the affair, for there was always a fresh supply of slave labour. Indeed, as the greatest twentieth-century slave-master, Joseph Stalin, was to demonstrate, it might even be in the slave-master's interests to work his slaves to the death, and then replace them with fresh ones.

Ramsay then gave practical expression to the ideas of the Enlightenment. His combination of high thinking and practicality may be seen as characteristically Scotch; none the worse for that.

James Macpherson
(1736–1796)

In reputation in his own lifetime only Sir Walter Scott, among Scottish writers, was to surpass James Macpherson. James *who*? James Macpherson, author of 'Ossian', the most famous poem of the eighteenth century, which intoxicated the imagination of Europe but which was denounced by Dr Johnson (and others) as a forgery.

Macpherson was born in Kingussie and educated at Marischal College in Aberdeen. There he studied under Thomas Blackwell, who had written a *Life of Homer* in which he argued, with some justice, that the most sublime epic poetry was the product of a society emerging from barbarism to civilisation. The argument interested Macpherson, who regarded himself as a poet and whose Gaelic background offered to his youthful imagination just such a society as Blackwell posited. In 1758 he wrote and published a long poem called *The Highlander*. Though it has been described (probably correctly) as 'turgid', it drew on Gaelic legends and attracted some attention.

In October 1759 he visited Moffat in Dumfriesshire with a friend. There he met the poet and dramatist, John Home. The conversation turned to Gaelic poetry and Macpherson claimed to be in possession of some examples. He was persuaded to make translations, since Home had no Gaelic. Home was impressed and showed them first to Dr Hugh Blair, later Professor of Rhetoric and Belles Lettres in Edinburgh, and then to friends in London. All were admiring and excited. Macpherson dropped hints that these were but fragments of an epic poem 9000 lines long and was accordingly commissioned to go in search of it. An old man in Lochaber, he said, had it by heart but it would be desirable to find the manuscript.

After publishing *Fragments of Ancient Poetry collected in the Highlands* early in 1760, Macpherson set out on a tour to discover the manuscript. He visited Skye, North and South Uist, Benbecula and Mull. He travelled with his cousin, the Gaelic poet Ewan Macpherson, who would meet the deficiencies of his own Gaelic. In Benbecula he obtained some manuscripts from MacDonald of Clanranald (which he never returned) and also collected ballads recited to him. Then he returned to Edinburgh and set to work, collating, translating, adapting and inventing. In the autumn of the same year he published the result, *Fingal, an Epic*, created by Ossian, a third century bard who was also the son of Fingal, the Scottish counterpart of the Irish hero Finn.

The work appealed to the contemporary taste for the sublime and beautiful, in keeping with the cult for the natural savage which Rousseau made the starting-point of *Le Contrat Social*. The poem was hailed as the equal of Homer and Virgil. Doubts soon arose, however. Some were the natural result of the contemporary hostility to the Scots which had been stirred up by the ministry of the Earl of Bute, to whom the poem was dedicated. Others were more rationally based. David Hume, though at first impressed, soon told Dr Blair that Macpherson must submit his manuscripts or be branded an imposter. This proved impossible for Macpherson because, although he had drawn on Gaelic poetry and did possess some Gaelic manuscripts, his sources were not in the manuscripts that had been produced merely to lend verisimilitude to what was otherwise an unconvincing narrative. When eventually, after much blustering, he allowed Johnson's friend, William Shaw, to see his manuscripts, Shaw reported that the manuscript shown to him contained only Irish genealogies and an account of Montrose's wars. These had, unfortunately, taken place thirteen hundred years too late. Macpherson, on hearing Shaw's opinion, withdrew his offer and abused his critic. He had meanwhile published a second poem, *Temora*, which was more original and less successful.

That concluded his poetic career. He went into politics, first taking a post as secretary to the Governor of Florida, then receiving a more agreeable sinecure as 'Minister Plenipotentiary of His Highness the Nabob of the Carnatic to the Court of St James', which provided him with an income of at least £12 000 worth of pagodas a year. He sat in Parliament for a Cornish rotten borough and became active in the affairs of the East India Company. For a time, when he had schemed to make his kinsman, Sir John Macpherson, Governor-General in place of Warren Hastings, he even claimed to be 'the real ruler of India'. (Rather inconveniently at this time some Highland officers in India, proposed to finance the publication of the Gaelic text of Ossian, but Macpherson was able to divert their generosity.) Macpherson's affairs prospered. His investment company collapsed but he was able to buy up the property of his unfortunate clients. He bought an estate in his native Badenoch and commissioned Robert Adam to build him a house. Although reputedly unpopular with his neighbours, he could consider himself a success. He had never, he said, 'extended my view further than a perfect independence to which I have attained'.

Macpherson might have abandoned poetry but Europe clung to

Ossian. His works were widely translated. Goethe compared him to Shakespeare. Napoleon never travelled without Cesarotti's Italian version, which solaced him on the voyage to St Helena. The imperial apartments in Paris and Rome had been decorated with huge murals representing Ossianic scenes, including the bard welcoming the ghosts of Napoleon's soldiers.

Before then, however, the epic's lack of authenticity had been widely admitted. In an article in the *Edinburgh Review* in 1805, Walter Scott confessed that the case against Macpherson could not be refuted. All the same, he added: 'Our national vanity may be flattered by the fact that a remote and almost barbarous corner of Scotland produced . . . a bard . . . who gave a new tone to poetry throughout Europe.'

And even that is not the end of the story. Modern Gaelic scholars have found more that is authentic in 'Ossian' than earlier critics allowed. They have identified up to fifteen different ballads which contributed to the poem. Macpherson's difficulty was that he seems to have obtained these in oral form and then, with a duplicity which was habitual to him, pretended that he had found them in manuscript. Of course, it is probable that, if he had told the truth, his poem would have received far less attention. Its charm for many lay in its supposed authenticity. The upshot is that Macpherson received credit for a discovery he had never made and was consequently denied the reward for his ingenuity and originality.

This brings us to the final irony. Macpherson's 'Ossian' is a poem of enduring charm, even if its sentiments cannot fall on the modern ear in the way that they delighted its eighteemth-century readers. Nevertheless, Matthew Arnold, who knew that it was spurious and who wrote when its music might be thought to have staled, judged that there was 'still left in the book a residue with the very soul of the Celtic genius in it, and which has the proud distinction of having brought this soul of the Celtic genius into contact with the genius of the nations of modern Europe and enriched all our poetry by it. Woody Morven, and echoing Sora, and Selma with its silent halls! – we all owe them a debt of gratitude, and when we are unjust enough to forget it, may the Muse forget us. Choose any one of the better passages in Macpherson's "Ossian" and you can see even at this time of day what an apparition of newness and power such a strain must have been to the eighteenth century.

'"I have seen the walls of Balcutha, but they were desolate. The fox looked out from the windows, the rank grass of the wall waved round her head. Raise the song of mourning, O bards, over the land of strangers. They have but fallen before us, for one day we must fall.

Why dost thou build the hall, son of the winged days? Thou lookest from thy towers today; yet a few years, and the blast of the desert comes; it howls in thy empty court, and whistles round thy half-worn shield. Let the blast of the desert come! we shall be renowned in our day."'

'All Europe felt the power of that melancholy,' says Arnold, correctly. It is grand stuff. Perhaps Macpherson's sourness and spleen came from the knowledge that he had in fact done something remarkable. He could never acknowledge just what he had done and so was denied the praise that was his due.

James Watt
(1736–1819)

Every child used to be brought up on the story of the young James Watt being reproved by his aunt for indolence: 'I never saw such an idle boy as you; for the last hour you have not spoken one word, but taken the lid off that kettle and put it on again, holding now a cup and now a silver spoon over the steam, watching how it rises from the spout, catching and counting the drops it falls into.' This scene, in which the boy came, as if by magic, to an understanding of steam power and the law of thermodynamics, was captured in a famous painting by Buss, which reproduced in an engraving, adorned countless cottage and tenement walls in Scotland. Curiously enough, a similar story is told of the Cornishman Thomas Newcomen (1663–1729), Watt's precursor in the harnessing of steam power, but it is one of these stories which fairly attracts to itself the Italian tag: 'Se non è vero, è ben trovato' (if it's not true, it's well imagined).

The anecdote has this dramatic justification at least: Watt's steam engine was the single most important invention of the industrial revolution. It made heavy industry possible on an unprecedented scale. Though much of Watt's working life was spent in England, he belongs here for two reasons. First, he was the son of a Clydeside merchant and shipwright. He trained as an instrument-maker in Glasgow and he was encouraged and helped by Dr Joseph Black, the physicist and chemist, who first encountered him at Glasgow University where Watt was in charge of the maintenance of certain scientific instruments. Black (of whom Adam Smith observed 'no man has less nonsense in his head than Dr Black') had made the discovery of latent heat and, its corollary, the theory of specific heat, and not only gave Watt the benefit of his knowledge of theory, but financed his early experiments. Had it not been for Black, Watt's engine might never have advanced beyond the stage of possibility.

The second reason may be described as a metaphysical one. Watt's steam engine was not only a crucial development; it was also something peculiarly satisfying to the Scottish temperament. Kipling's chief engineer MacAndrew called for a Rabbie Burns 'to sing the song of steam' and, looking at his ship's engines, thought that 'John Calvin might have fashioned it', seeing 'predestination in the stroke of yon connecting-rod.' This was not fanciful. It explains why the romance of heavy industry was so potent a drug in Scotland, despite the hardships that accompanied it.

Newcomen's engine had been of limited utility. It could drive a pump, and that was all. Watt concluded that this was because the boiler was too small to operate the engine and the engine was, therefore, wasteful in the consumption of steam. He saw that an economical consumption of steam required that the temperature of the condensation chamber be kept low, while that of the cylinder remained high. He solved the problem by removing the condensation process from the cylinder of Newcomen's engine to another chamber; steam was exhausted into this and cooled with a constant flow of water, and there condensed. This process formed a vacuum without lowering the temperature of the cylinder. Watt then added an air pump to remove condensed steam, maintaining the vacuum.

This first engine was merely an improved version of Newcomen's, but very much improved. To make an engine capable of driving machinery Watt had to convert his engine from a reciprocating to a rotating instrument. He did this by what he called the 'sun and planet' method. A cogged wheel was attached to the crank connected to the piston. This wheel was then enmeshed with another which transmitted power to other machines. Both ends of the cylinder were kept in communication with the boiler which increased the speed and power of the engine. He developed the use of parallel motion, so that the piston-rod could both pull and push the centrifugal governor, which maintained constant speed of operation, and finally a steam pressure gauge.

Watt was primarily an inventor, but he was fortunate in finding partners capable of developing and exploiting his engines. The first of these was Dr Roebuck of the Carron Ironworks in Falkirk, the second Matthew Boulton, a Birmingham silversmith. Eventually a firm of Watt & Boulton was established. Boulton provided the capital, and also, from Birmingham, he supplied skilled workmen capable of manufacturing the parts of his engines.

Watt retired from business, a rich man, at the age of sixty-four. His firm continued to be the main producer of steam-engines for many years. He did not desist from inventions. In his eighty-third year, just before his death, he invented a machine for copying sculpture.

There is a memorial plaque to Watt in Westminster Abbey, a fair recognition of the importance of his work to Britain's century of industrial supremacy.

James Boswell
(1740–1795)

'If he had not been a great fool, he would never have been a great writer.' Macaulay's verdict on Boswell is famous, and many of Bozzy's admirers have expended vast stores of energy in attempting to prove Macaulay wrong. The effort is vain. Boswell had many admirable qualities: he had a rare talent for self-examination, he was affectionate and admiring; he was quick, he had a splendidly retentive memory, he had, evidently, charm, he was often capable of intelligence; but he was also a great fool. In one respect, however, Macaulay was mistaken; for all his rhetoric he fails to convince me that Bozzy's foolishness was the necessary condition of his success as a biographer; he underestimates the skill in arrangement which Boswell showed, and Macaulay's Boswell would have thrown material any-old-how into his biography of Johnson, whereas the material is artfully and designedly presented. In short, Macaulay was led astray by his love of dramatic contrast: he saw the greatness of the biography – 'Eclipse first and the rest nowhere', as he said – and he saw the foolishness of Boswell and yoked them together. Of course, Macaulay lacked the advantage that we have enjoyed, of reading the great Yale edition of Boswell's private papers, which has given us a better understanding of him. We know Boswell as he saw himself far better than Macaulay could, and we can see the goodness that lurked under his selfishness and thoughtlessness, and have learned to appreciate the surprising flashes of intelligence.

Boswell was certainly an eccentric but his eccentricity lay chiefly in his quite extraordinary appetite for life, and for all possible varieties of experience. He suffered from melancholia and hypochondria but he was also high-spirited and social. He was a patriotic Scot, who felt simultaneously inferior and superior in his consciousness of nationality and who was in love with London. (London represented freedom from responsibilities; Boswell was a good example of the truth of Chesterton's observation that a man may travel to escape life, not to experience it.) He was a loving and congenitally unfaithful husband. He loved refinement and revelled in the dirt. He quarrelled with his father and resented his attempts to influence his life, but he adopted a succession of alternative fathers to whom he enslaved himself willingly. His own robust father, Lord Auchinleck, took a cool view of this: 'Jamie's gaen clean gyte,' he said. 'He's done wi' Paoli; he's aff wi' the land-louping Corsican; and whase tail do you think he has pinned himself to now, man? A dominie, an auld dominie whae keepit a schule and caa'ed it an academy.' No wonder that, considering all these contradictions, T. H. Crawford has suggested that 'if there really is a "Caledonian antisyzygy", then Boswell was its living exemplar'.

Boswell craved attention. He was shameless in his approaches to great men and in his toadying of them when accosted. At the same time he was ready to think himself their equal. His visit to Corsica was enterprising; his championing of the islanders' cause generous and sincere. Yet he made himself, and it, ridiculous by his exhibitionism; he appeared at the theatre in Stratford wearing a hatband that read 'Corsican Boswell'. If he had lived today he would never have been out of the gossip columns, as he had a lust for unhealthy publicity.

His public life was by and large a failure. He had some success at the Scottish Bar but he had gone there with the utmost reluctance, when his father refused to purchase him a commission in the Guards, and was never content. In his middle forties he transferred to the English Bar and met with humiliating failure. He attached himself to the loathsome Earl of Lonsdale and swallowed any insult in the hope of preferment. Lonsdale declined to present him to any of the Parliamentary boroughs that were in his gift – Boswell had previously failed to persuade his fellow Ayrshire lairds to send him to Parliament as their representative – and all he got from Lonsdale was the appointment of Recorder of Carlisle which he held for only two years.

During these Lonsdale years his wife, Margaret Montgomerie, died. She was also his cousin and loved him with a sympathetic understanding that he both resented and required. He had depended on her more than he knew and he deteriorated when she was gone. He lived mostly in London, drinking far too much (he had always done so, but now he drank out of depression rather than sociability); yet it was in 1791, two years after Margaret's death, that his great *Life of Johnson* appeared.

Contrary to what Macaulay thought, the *Life of Johnson* shows

Boswell at his best. It is not only written with extraordinary art, apparent in the manipulation of mood and argument, but it reveals an admirable man as its author. Certainly he often shows himself to be vain and foolish but even this revelation rebounds to the credit of the artist. More important, however, is his attitude to Johnson.

That Johnson was a great man and a good one is evident; that he was awkward, uncivil, ill-tempered, frequently cruel, equally so. Boswell does not hide the black side of Johnson. He recognises and displays his faults. And yet he was capable of feeling a profound admiration, a touching reverence, for Johnson and is able to make his reader feel as he did. It is not always, I think, recognised how greatly Boswell's admiration of Johnson honours his own good sense and nature. Apart from his fame, what was there in Johnson to attract this thin-skinned, snobbish, self-conscious young Scot? Johnson was a difficult customer; he had no advantage of birth or manners. His uncouthness was a byword; so was his antipathy to the Scots. He was a stern moralist, all the more so because he had felt temptation strongly himself. Lord Auchinleck's view of him was by no means wide of the mark. A great many people were frightened of Johnson; others, like Horace Walpole, regarded him with disgust. He was perhaps the least likely hero a young man like Boswell might be expected to choose.

Yet Boswell did so, and stuck to him despite much discouragement from his father, his wife and even from Johnson himself. Why? There can be only one answer: that he recognised, and felt, Johnson's essential virtue and attached himself to it. Johnson appealed to the best that was in Boswell and Bozzy was a better man for it. Carlyle recognised this:

'Poor Bozzy . . . passes for a mean, inflated, gluttonous creature; and was so in many senses. Yet the fact of his reverence for Johnson will ever remain noteworthy. The foolish conceited Scotch Laird, the most conceited man of his time, approaching in such awestruck attitude the great dusty irascible pedagogue in his mean garret there; it is a genuine reverence for Excellence; a worship for Heroes, at a time when neither Heroes nor worship were surmised to exist.'

Henry Dundas, Viscount Melville
(1742–1811)

A huge column dominates St Andrew Square in the New Town of Edinburgh, but few can identify the figure on the top. Moreover, if they were told that it was Henry Dundas, Lord Melville, it is not likely that many would be much the wiser. For every person who has heard of Dundas, thousands know of Burns and Scott; such is the transience of political fame, especially when it does not chance to be associated with any great event or measure. No doubt it is usually just that politicians should be thus forgotten; they have their little hour of influence and self-gratification, and that's that. Yet Dundas was for more than thirty years the effective ruler of Scotland – he was even known as Harry the Ninth, which was nonsense, since no previous Henry has reigned north of the Border. There has hardly been a more important figure in the history of the Union, and he was also the first Scot to establish himself, for more than a brief moment, as a British politician of the first rank.

Politics wears an odd appearance in eighteenth-century Scotland. This intellectually active nation was politically passive. For most of the century, Scotland was left, as Scott put it, 'under the guardianship of her own institutions, to win her silent way to national wealth and consequence . . . But neglected as she was, and perhaps because she was neglected, Scotland has increased her prosperity in a ratio more than five times greater than that of England'. Scotland indeed remained, in the words of a modern historian, 'in a state of semi-independence, which allowed the Union settlement to work by providing a buffer between English government and assumptions, and Scottish institutions and society in general'. For this to be effective, however, the Government required a manager in Scotland. Duncan Forbes of Culloden did the job in the first half of the century, Henry Dundas for the last thirty years.

He came from a stoutly Whig family, attended Edinburgh University, and was admitted as an advocate in 1763. Ten years later he was solicitor-general, and the following year became MP for the County of Edinburgh; he was appointed Lord Advocate in 1775 and represented the City of Edinburgh from 1787 to 1802 when he was raised to the peerage. But Dundas differed from Forbes in that he became, as I say, a British politician too. In Lord North's generally incompetent government his was a rare and strong voice for common sense; he attacked the conduct of the war against the American colonies and demanded the resignation of the disastrous War Minister Lord George Germaine and the equally disastrous First Lord of the Admiralty, the Earl of Sandwich. He himself became Treasurer of the Navy in 1782, and as Pitt's right-hand man was successively Secretary of State for the Home Department and Secretary at War. In 1805, the year of Trafalgar, he was First Lord of the Admiralty.

Dundas was, therefore, a man of considerable administrative ability and common sense. That was one reason for his value to any Ministry. The other was that he was able to deliver the votes of Scottish Members of Parliament. He did so by the exercise of patronage. As Lord Advocate he controlled many posts directly, and more indirectly. His nominees governed both the Bank of Scotland and the Royal Bank. His influence in the Admiralty and the War Office could secure commissions for younger sons and brothers; he could appoint to numerous colonial sinecures.

Most of all, however, he employed the riches of the East in the management of Scotland. In 1784 he had become President of the Board of Control of the East India Company; this Board had been set up as a result of the India Act which Dundas himself had piloted through the House of Commons. As a result numerous appointments in the Company, which governed British India, and in the Army in India, in the Customs and judiciary, were virtually in Dundas's gift. Many of the Scottish gentry and nobility, particularly in the Highlands, were poor and prolific; there were sons to be provided for, and Dundas was the man to do it. Scots flourished in India in disproportionate numbers; wealth was repatriated, new families founded and new country houses built. Dundas sat in the centre of his web of influence, and gained power as he dispensed prosperity. Cockburn, who was his nephew, described him as 'the Pharos of Scotland. Who steered upon him was safe; who disregarded his light was wrecked'. As for the Town Council of Edinburgh, Cockburn wrote that 'the pleasure of Dundas was the sole rule for every one of them'.

Dundas's system withstood the French Revolution with its levelling tendencies. The Sedition Trials were his work; Braxfield was only his agent, to be discarded when he had served his turn. His patronage could transcend Party divisions; the young Cockburn adhered to the Whigs, but Dundas still had him appointed Advocate-Depute. Government was a matter of patronage, of the dispensation of loaves and fishes. Dundas bound men to him by gratitude and hope; fear came into it too, for sinecures could be lost and taken away. He was a benevolent *mafioso*.

Naturally he acquired enemies. He could hardly fail to do so. There were many in England who resented his promotion of his fellow Scots, and Dundas feared the emergence of a new Wilkes whose attacks on Lord Bute, George III's first choice as Prime Minister, and the beggarly Scots carried in his train had aroused violent anti-Caledonian feeling in London.

His fall came suddenly, and by one of those ironies in which history delights; he had himself forged the instrument which his enemies employed against him. In 1785 he had introduced a Bill which had prohibited Government ministers, especially the Treasurer of the Navy and the Paymaster-General, from appropriating money to their own temporary use; this had been a long-established custom, on which the great fortune of Henry Fox, the first Lord Holland, had been built. Now it was to be swept away as part of the Reform movement, instigated by Burke's Economical Reform Act of 1782, which was intended to reduce the power of the Crown by restricting its patronage.

Now in 1805 Dundas found himself hoist with his own petard. He was impeached on the charge of having done just what he had himself forbidden. Even before trial he was struck off the Privy Council. But when it came to the point, the case against him was impossible to make good, though his deputy, by name of Trotter, was found guilty. Dundas was acquitted and restored to the Privy Council, but not to office.

The Reform movement, checked by the fears aroused by the Revolution in France, gleamed on the horizon. The age of patronage and gentlemanly corruption, which Dundas represented, was waning, and would not revive till the expansion of the twentieth-century state opened a cornucopia of patronage besides which Dundas's efforts seem puny. Yet something of his work survived. He had oiled the wheels of the Union; he had established an imperial system in which the Scots found more than elbow-room. He had opened wide fields of opportunity to his fellow-countrymen, and it is right that he should stand serenely over the Edinburgh he had dominated, which was also in some degree his creation. It is appropriate that his statue should be visible from New St Andrew's House.

Sir Henry Raeburn
(1756–1823)

'Nothing ought to divert the eye from the principal object: the face.' That was the theory of portrait painting enunciated by Raeburn, Scotland's greatest master of the art. His faces are utterly expressive, and, if we feel we know Scotsmen of the late eighteenth and early nineteenth century better than those of any other time, Raeburn's paintings are partly responsible. A portrait painter is more than a mirror to the society of his day; he is a moral illuminater. All the strength and conscious rectitude of the Scotland of the Enlightenment is to be found in Raeburn's portraits. We can see there the *Romanitas*, the benevolent and public virtue on which Scotland prided itself.

Raeburn was an Edinburgh man, born in Stockbridge where his father owned a textile mill. It was in Stockbridge, or above Stockbridge, that late in life he designed Edinburgh's finest street of villas, Ann Street, which is the fullest expression of the picturesque desire for *rus in urbe*. He was educated at George Heriot's School and apprenticed to a goldsmith with whom he remained till he was in his middle twenties. At some time in the 1770s he began painting miniatures; his first full-scale oil has been dated 1776. In 1780 he married a widow of independent means and in 1784 left for Italy. No doubt the widow's funds made this possible, but Italy was then a necessary experience for an artist. On the way there he spent some months working in the studio of Sir Joshua Reynolds, from whom he doubtless learned much, but whom he was to surpass.

Little is known of his stay in Rome, which was presumably passed mostly in study. He knew James Byres of Tonly, a Scottish art-dealer and antiquarian who had made his home in the city; Byres gave him advice which he took as his guiding principle: 'never to copy any object from memory, but from the principle figure to the minutest accessory to have it placed before him'. It was perhaps this advice which encouraged Raeburn to dispense with preliminary studies. At a time when most painters, especially portrait ones, were accustomed to approach their painting by way of a number of sketches, Raeburn prefered to work directly on his canvas. Stevenson, in an admirable essay in *Virginibus Puerisque*, which probes Raeburn's genius, wrote that he could 'plunge at once through all the constraint and embarrassment of the sitter and present the face, clear, open and intelligent as at the most disengaged moments'. Raeburn paints character as well as features; this is one reason why he was most successful with those who had lived enough to let experience mark them. Looking at Raeburn's portraits, one might agree with Orwell that 'at forty, everyone has the face he deserves'.

Raeburn returned to Edinburgh in 1786, and was now in a position to establish himself as a professional portrait painter. The value of his Roman visit is apparent. Before that he was an apprentice; afterwards on his way to mastery. From the early 1790s he regularly exhibited in both London and Edinburgh. In Edinburgh he used part of his own house in York Place as a gallery, exhibiting other painters there as well as his own work.

He painted all the legal luminaries and the cream of Edinburgh society. He was particularly successful in his portraits of mature women. His series of Highland clan chiefs mark an important development in Romantic painting; they were the visual equivalent of *The Lady of the Lake* and *Waverley*, part of the same process of reconciliation between Gaelic and Lowland Scotland, as a result of which the tartan and Highland dress became acceptable as the national garb of Scotland.

He twice painted Scott himself, in 1808 and 1822. The first, which now hangs at Abbotsford, is the famous painting with the bull-terrier Camp and the deerhound. It was painted for Scott's publisher Constable, but at this first session Scott and Raeburn failed to establish friendly relations. That may add to the painting's power, not diluted by affection. The second, of which two half-length studies were made, was, in Scott's words, 'poor fellow, the last he ever painted, and certainly not his worst'.

Raeburn was knighted in 1822 during George IV's visit to Scotland, and also appointed King's Limner and Painter for Scotland. Unfortunately he died before he could execute a royal commission: George IV in Highland dress. A pity; it should have been a masterpiece.

Portrait painters are the eyes of their age, none more vivid and perceptive than Raeburn. Our sharp appreciation of his time depends on his lack of sentimentality. Yet there is no reproach or satirical intent in his work either. He shares the moral outlook of his sitters, measures them against the standards they had in common. He paints from within an agreed consensus. Cockburn's portraits in words do the same thing. Neither Raeburn nor Cockburn bring themselves, like Carlyle in his *Reminiscences*, to the point of questioning the whole ethos of the Enlightenment; yet their value might be diminished if they did. Raeburn was honest and yet conventional; he appraises, but he does not question fundamental assumptions. It is his assurance and solidarity with his sitters which gives his work its authority. His is Establishment painting at its finest.

Thomas Telford
(1757–1834)

Swift observed in *Gulliver's Travels* that the man who made two blades of grass or two ears of corn grow where only one grew before would deserve better of mankind that the whole race of projectors and politicians. This was an opinion full of common sense. It might be adapted to the man who eased the means of communication by building roads, bridges and canals. Few have been greater engineers of progress than Thomas Telford.

The son of a shepherd on Eskdalemuir, he served his apprenticeship as a stone-mason, engaged principally in the carving and inscribing of gravestones. It was a good apprenticeship: he learned the feel of his working material as modern civil engineers may never. He then worked for the Duke of Buccleuch who was busy re-housing his tenants, and in 1782 moved to London where he was given an introduction to Sir William Chambers, who employed him on the reconstruction of Somerset House. At this point it is possible that Telford might have become an architect, for he was following the road taken by many famous ones, but he turned aside to concentrate on civil engineering.

The early progress of the Industrial Revolution was hampered by vile communications, and at the same time opened opportunities to the more or less new profession of civil engineer. The increase in economic activity created a demand for new roads, and canals. In 1787 Telford was appointed Surveyor of Public Works in Shropshire and began building bridges over the Severn, still a formidable barrier between England and Wales. He was responsible for the construction of the Ellesmere Canal which, by connecting the Mersey, Severn and Dee, created a waterway between Liverpool and Bristol. He built the road from London to Holyhead, which improved communications with Ireland, and the great and beautiful Menai Suspension Bridge. In London he also worked in dockland: St Katherine's Docks, now converted into a leisure centre and tourist attraction, was his masterpiece there. He engineered the Gotha Canal in Sweden and was rewarded with a Swedish knighthood.

But his greatest work was reserved for his native country, and it is fair to say that there is hardly a river of importance which does not boast a bridge initially constructed by Telford. In 1803 he received the appointment of engineer to the Commissioners of Highland Roads and Bridges. Before this time there were few roads in Northern Scotland, and those which did exist had been built (mostly rather badly) by General Wade for purely military purposes. Under Telford's supervision 920 miles of road and 1,200 bridges were built in the Highlands, and Telford's work remains the basis for the road network of the Northern Counties to this day. It may be that his work, by opening up the hitherto impregnable glens, contributed to the subsequent exploitation and depopulation of the Highlands, but Telford is hardly to be held responsible for the use made of his roads.

In the Highlands he also cut the Caledonian Canal, linking east and west. As with all the canals its great utility was to be short-lived, for it would be superseded by the railway; nevertheless, as a feat of construction the Caledonian Canal must be accounted one of the masterpieces of the first Industrial Revolution.

Telford's best bridges combine grace and magnificence. Nothing in Edinburgh is more impressive than the bridge which he built across the valley of the Water of Leith, just downstream from the little village of Dean. It is one of the wonders of engineering in these islands: to stand beneath it and gaze upwards is to marvel. But Telford also showed himself capable of working with equal certainty and discrimination on a smaller scale: the bridge at Langholm or that across the Ettrick at Selkirk (the latter now re-modelled after a disastrous flood) are good examples; while the elegant bridge across the Tay at Dunkeld is perfectly positioned, offering noble vistas on either side.

Telford was one of the founders of the Institute of Civil Engineers in 1818, and did more than any other man to establish his profession. All the great railway architects, even Brunel, learned from Telford, and owed much to his solution of problems of stress and scale. In one of the happier of recorded puns the poet Southey called him 'the Colossus of Roads'. He was a man of wide interests and considerable culture, a friend of James Hogg, and one of the many who helped Hogg with money and advice, the former gift being accepted the more willingly. Civil engineering was to be one of Scotland's greatest contributions to nineteenth-century civilisation, and Telford was the Head of his profession. No man surely has made a greater mark on his country, and we are fortunate that he did so with such certainty of means and of taste.

Robert Burns
(1759–1796)

Burns's life has been mauled over, made the subject of biographies, novels, plays; sermons have been preached on his morals, in his own day and ever since. There is hardly a detail that is not known, hardly an encounter that has not been dissected. It is possible to make a cogent case against the weaknesses of his poetry, his poetic language and his influence, just as it has always been possible to make a case against his personal morality. It is all pointless. Burns is the national bard, and however false that phrase may ring – and it must ring false if only because the word 'bard' is not one that it has been possible to use without placing it in inverted commas for more than two hundred years – it nevertheless expresses the truth that Burns has been adopted by the Scottish people as 'our poet', in a way that has no equivalent anywhere in the English-speaking world. He is not only so regarded: he is read. You cannot find yourself in any gathering of Scots of any number more than a handful without encountering someone who can recite Burns by the screed. Burns is the true answer to the foolish boast 'Whaur's your Wullie Shakespeare noo?' yelled out at the first performance of Home's *Douglas*. He is not, of course, comparable to Shakespeare, for Shakespeare has a range and depth and a command of the language which Burns does not even approach. But he has one quality which is not found in Shakespeare or any English poet; and this is the ability to speak directly to the ordinary man and woman and become part of their experience, part of their life.

Two of the best judgements on Burns were made by the two greatest writers of the generation which succeeded his. (To avert argument, Scott belongs to a half-generation later than Burns.) Byron, in his *Journal*, noted, having been reading 'a quantity of Burns's unpublished, and never-to-be-published Letters': 'what an antithetical mind! – tenderness, roughness, delicacy, coarseness –

sentiment, sensuality – soaring and grovelling, dirt and deity – all mixed up in that one compound of inspired clay'. Carlyle, in his Lecture on the Hero as Man of Letters found Burns to be 'one of those men who reach down to the perennial Depths, who take rank with the heroic among men. . . . This Burns appeared under every disadvantage: uninstructed, poor, born only to hard manual toil; and writing, when it came to that, in a rustic special dialect, known only to a small province of the country he lived in'. Not quite right there: Burns's poetic language was more artful and artificial than Carlyle allowed. Likewise many will resist his next judgement: 'yes, I will say, here was a piece of the right Saxon stuff: strong as the Harz-rock, rooted in the depths of the world'. Well, few of us like to be reminded of the Anglo-Saxon roots of the Scots language, and many will put this judgement down to Carlyle's inveterate Teutonomania. But what comes next hardly brooks argument: 'rock, yet with wells of living softness in it! A wild impetuous whirlwind of passion and faculty slumbered quiet there; such heavenly melody dwelling in the heart of it. A noble rough genuineness; homely, rustic, honest; true simplicity of strength; with its lightning-fire, with its soft dewy pity'.

Lightning-fire, soft dewy pity, melody: do not phrases and words such as these go straight to the heart of Burns's appeal? Could any other poet have made a masterpiece of an address to a mouse? It requires a deep humanity to see tragedy in the plough's destruction of the mouse's nest, but it needs melody to rescue such a sentiment from bathos in verse.

Burns was a man of the resistance. There is, as I have insisted elsewhere, much that was noble and admirable in the rigours of the church of Scotland, but it was nevertheless a creed which at certain times and in certain places aspired to fix a straitjacket on errant human nature. Burns would have none of it. His mind could not soar into the loftiest philosophy; theology was, for all the sermons to which he was subjected, a closed book to him. This, incidentally, was no matter of class; Hogg, who had less formal education than Burns, could grapple with it. Burns was no thinker; feeling was all to him. That was why he could move easily from a lament for Jacobitism to an enthusiasm for the French Revolution. Both movements – politically antithetical though they were – appealed to his generous nature. His resistance was rooted in this same generosity; he could not deny the world of the senses or pretend that he did not find delight there. There is a sadness in his most moving songs, but delight is never absent. Again Carlyle rightly found a 'basis of mirth' in him, 'a primal-element of sunshine and joyfulness'.

Because there is no hypocrisy, there is no affectation in Burns. He never pretends to feelings he does not possess: if his feelings are different, even opposite, tomorrow, what does it matter? He catches the reality of the passing moment. He is the inspired poet of daily life. Here lies his superiority to Wordsworth (though in other respects Wordsworth may be a greater poet); Burns can find the same delight in a reaming tankard of ale as in the daisy.

It is this which makes him the poet of physical love. He renders the pleasure of the passing moment. In doing so he offers the authentic pastoral. Here is no poet pretending to be a shepherd, but a ploughman who was all the more a poet for being that. When he tells us of nights among the barley, we know that it is real barley which itches and scratches.

He is a poet capable of the most exquisite simplicity. 'O, my luve's like a red, red rose' is made up almost entirely of monosyllables. There is one three-syllable word: 'melodie'; and a handful of two-syllable ones: 'newly, sweetly, bonnie, again, thousand'. Out of this simplicity he makes the perfect expression of fidelity in passion: 'till a' the seas gang dry'. It cannot be bettered. Burns's taste is never shown to better advantage than in the old songs which he reworks, and always improves.

I have said he was no thinker. By that I do not mean he lacked penetration or intellectual grasp or even strength. I mean rather that he never formed, nor troubled to form, a coherent system for himself. Probably it was impossible that he should. He saw through some of the complacency which disfigured the fringes of the Enlightenment, for he saw (as many of the professors did not) that it led logically to a democracy which it was not ready to accept. But beyond a belief in the natural right of the individual man to liberty, Burns could hardly advance. No wonder: he was a representative of a world that was dying away, the world of the self-contained, self-sufficient country-side. He might have found it briefly in America – and he was on the point of emigrating thither when the success of the Kilmarnock edition stopped him – but even there the pastoral-poetic after which Cockburn also hankered was doomed.

Nevertheless Burns is great enough to transcend the limits of his condition. He affirms the goodness of life, and since he speaks out of a knowledge of guilt, frustration, poverty and hardship, his words have a solid and resonant significance which speak directly to all who hear them. He is aware of his contradictions, but he does not allow this knowledge to oppress him. On the contrary, his delight in the actual is so intense that he accepts these contradictions as the price of the human condition. He never pretends to eternity; even while he swears undying love, he is saying farewell. He knows that love and grief are never far separate, just as Tam O'Shanter's delight in the tavern ingle-nook is matched by his wife's displeasure.

Burns's life was difficult and chequered, but not, I think, unhappy. He struggled, but he knew the value of what he had achieved; of how, in his work for John Johnson's *Scots Musical Museum*, he had rescued a large part of our heritage, and added to it at the same time. He read widely and never ceased educating himself; he was rich too in friendship. He has himself been adopted as friend and guide by the Scottish people. He is that rarity: a truly popular poet who is also a great one.

Lady Nairne
(1766–1845)

How much of our sense of Scotland is given to us by our songs. 'Will ye no' come back again?' is a lament for what is lost and will never return that can bring tears to even a Campbell's eyes. It is easy to dismiss Jacobitism, after the failure of the Forty-Five, as sheer sentimentalism and easy to show too how fragile and uncertain was any devotion to the Stuarts. The fact remains that the Jacobite sentiment has never quite died, that Culloden is a word that falls on the ear with a dull and painful thud, and that the sense still survives that something noble died in the failure of the Prince's enterprise. That this is so is partly the consequence of the romance of the rising but it is also the result of its treatment in song, poetry and story. Yet this itself could only have been produced by the operation of the story on the imagination. It was Jacobitism which made Jacobite song and romance, and those songs and romances which kept Jacobitism vital.

This interplay is clearly shown in the life and work of Lady Nairne, the greatest of the Jacobite song-writers. She was born Carolina Oliphant of Gask, twenty years after Culloden. It was, therefore, some forty years distant when she was grown up. One might think it remote from her experience, and judge that her songs would be correspondingly second-hand, but she came from a Jacobite family. The Oliphant Lairds of Gask had been out in both the Fifteen and the Forty-Five and had suffered for their loyalty to the Stuart cause. They were, moreover, connections of the Murrays of Atholl, one of whom, Lord George Murray, had commanded the Prince's army. Carolina married (admittedly not until 1806) her cousin Lord Nairne, himself a Murray, whose estates had been attainted and whose title was not restored until 1824. His grandmother had seen her husband, son and four sons-in-law (who included Carolina Oliphant's father) fight for the Cause. All had suffered in fortune if in no other way. Clearly, an imaginative girl, growing up aware of this family background, knowing how much Jacobitism had cost her family, could hardly fail to see it as something unusually powerful and real; it was something she must either reject or embrace.

She interested herself early in song-writing, particularly in Burns's collections and reworkings and in other work brought together by James Johnson in the *Scots Musical Museum*. Her first songs were published under the pseudonym of Mrs Bogan of Bogan. In all, she was to write at least eighty-seven. Most were published in *The Scottish Minstrel*, a collection edited in Paisley by R. A. Smith.

Like Burns, and indeed Scott, she very often reworked traditional material. 'The Laird o' Cockpen', for instance, is founded on an older lyric, Lady Nairne's version was then added to by Susan Ferrier. Lady Nairne's peculiar gift was a directness and immediacy that generally stops short of an unpleasing sentimentality. A good example of this is offered by 'The Auld Hoose'. It expresses an emotion which everyone has felt and which, carried to extremes, topples over into a disgusting self-pity. In Lady Nairne's song it stops on the brink and the result is as charming and touching as it is memorable. Like all great song-writers, there is simplicity in her work: a song can carry only one emotion, though it may hint at others. She brings this off time and again: 'The Rowan Tree' is a good example. She had humour, as 'The Laird o' Cockpen' shows. It is a short story of the human comedy in eight verses. Yet this simplicity should not make anyone think her a naive writer: there is considerable art in the manner in which one song will echo another, and her concision is admirable.

Her masterpiece is 'Will ye no' come back again?' because it sums up the whole tragedy of Jacobitism in a few clear lines. Regret is there, but a pride in loyalty too. Through it all sounds this note of pride, that men should risk and lose all for an ideal and that they should submit to their misfortune without repining, because – and this is the extraordinary thing – there is no hint of self-pity in the song.

After Lord Nairne's death in 1830, she travelled on the Continent for a time before returning to Perthshire and to the new house of Gask, the auld one of the song having been pulled down. There she died exactly one hundred years after the rising, the spirit of which her songs had kept alive.

James Hogg
(1770–1835)

James Hogg, poet, novelist, man of letters and sheep-farmer, was born in the parish of Ettrick in Selkirkshire. His father was a shepherd and an assiduous reader of the Bible; his mother, also devout, had a great store of ballads, while his grandfather, Will o' the Phaup, was the last man known in Ettrick to have seen and conversed with the fairies. As a poet, Hogg called himself 'king of the mountain and fairy school'; his mind was formed by these influences in childhood in a remote and lonely valley where past and present intermingled. Consciousness of a parallel world of mystery, marching side by side with the world perceived by sense, was alive in Hogg.

He had at most a year's schooling during which he learned to read. If he also learned to write, he had forgotten how to do so by the time he grew up. He had to teach himself again by copying letters from a printed book. Contemporaries always stressed his lack of education. By the standards of his day, he was indeed uneducated. He knew neither Latin nor Greek and was ignorant of mathematics, logic and – in the formal sense – rhetoric (informally he was a master of it); his knowledge of History consisted only of the traditions alive in Ettrick. Nevertheless he was not uneducated as we might understand the term today. Whatever his deficiencies, there was no trash in his head. He had been brought up hearing the great poetry of the Ballads and listening to the Bible and long intense argument on Scriptural texts. One minister of Ettrick had been Thomas Boston, a famous preacher and Biblical scholar, who propounded the most extreme Calvinist doctrine with the utmost severity. The matter of Hogg's finest and most famous novel, *The True Confession of a Justified Sinner*, a penetrating study of the conviction that 'salvation was not contingent upon faith, but was the effect of justification, of grace', came directly from the arguments he had heard rehearsed by the fireside and in the kirk.

As a young man his enthusiasm for poetry and self-education knew no bounds. He would travel far to attend meetings of a literary society he had founded with some friends. He was recommended, as a man who might know old ballads, to Walter Scott, who was embarked in the research which would lead to the publication of the *Minstrelsy of the Scottish Border*. Hogg and Scott struck up a friendship which, despite ups and downs, endured till Scott's death, when Hogg described him as 'the best and most steady friend that I ever had to depend on'.

For some years Hogg's career swung between attempts to establish himself as a man of letters and as a farmer. In both he met with little success; he acquired a literary reputation but few of his publications made much money, while farming ventures in Harris and Dumfriesshire were even less successful. (Hogg had always the ambition to be a great sheepfarmer; among his publications is a treatise on diseases in sheep.) For a time he produced a magazine called *The Spy*, writing it all himself. When Scott asked him if he thought to rival Addison or Steele, he replied, 'I'll no be sae elegant maybe, but I'll be mair oreeginal.' *The Queen's Wake*, a collection of poems which includes the enchanting 'Kilmeny', revealed his quality to the discerning few. *The Poetic Mirror* displayed his ingenuity. He had thought to establish his fortunes by inviting poets to contribute to an anthology for his benefit; when most declined to do so, he produced a volume consisting of deft parodies and imitations of their work. In 1813 it seemed that his fortunes had taken a turn for the better when the Duke of Buccleuch presented him with the farm of Altrive in Yarrow, rent-free for life. Rashly, however, after his marriage in 1820, he took on another farm, Mount Benger. Without the capital to stock it, he embarrassed himself again.

In 1817 he had become associated with the group of clever young men, especially John Gibson Lockhart and John Wilson ('Christopher North'), who wrote for the new *Blackwood's Magazine*. Together they concocted the anonymously published *Chaldee Manuscript*, a high-spirited and, it was thought, scurrilous attack on the *Edinburgh Review* and the intellectual Whig establishment of the capital. Hogg's association with Blackwood's was to be ambiguous. On the one hand, it provided an outlet for his work, although, as the years passed, Blackwood showed himself increasingly reluctant to accept Hogg's best writing; on the other hand, it brought him celebrity, but of a damaging and often disagreeable sort. The chief feature of the magazine soon became the 'Noctes Ambrosianae', imaginary conversations (doubtless drawing on real ones) between the principal contributors to the magazine and conducted in Ambrose's Tavern in Picardy Place, Edinburgh. In these, Hogg was presented, in the persona of 'The Ettrick Shepherd'; as uncouth, boisterous and wild in opinion and humour. The pieces were an enormous popular success but hurt Hogg. 'I am neither a drunkard nor an idiot nor a monster of nature,' he wrote to Scott in protest. In allowing himself to be made into this sort of celebrity, Hogg destroyed nothing in himself but he made it more difficult for others to take him seriously as they should have.

Between 1818 and 1824 he published three remarkable novels, *The Brownie of Bodsbeck*, *The Three Perils of Man* and *The True Confession of a Justified Sinner*. The first is a tale of Covenanting times, drawing on local traditions. It irritated Scott because of its uncritical acceptance of Covenanting myths; he called it 'a false and unfair picture of the times'. Hogg replied that 'it is the picture I hae been bred up in the belief o' sin' ever I was born' and claimed that there was not one incident in the tale which he could not prove literally true, 'an' that's mair than you can say of your tale of *Auld Mortality*'. The second novel is a Romance of the Middle Ages, an astonishing medley of legend, witchcraft, diablerie and folk-lore which, if it is pre-modern, may also be seen as a precursor of much post-modernist fiction in its acceptance of an alternative or parallel reality. The last novel, structurally a work of astonishing subtlety, is, in the words of André Gide, 'an extraordinary achievement'. It has done more than anything to restore or indeed to make Hogg's reputation today and is widely regarded as one of the greatest Scottish novels. At the time of publication it received only one review, from the *Westminster Review*, which regretted that 'the author did not employ himself better than in uselessly and disgustingly abusing his imagination, to invent wicked tricks for a mongrel devil and blasphemous lucubrations for an insane fanatic'. Reviewers are advised to pin on their desks a copy of this notice as a warning.

Despite his misfortunes and lack of success, Hogg retained his naturally blithe disposition. In his autobiography he wrote that the reader might think 'that I must have worn out a life of misery and wretchedness; but the case has been quite the reverse . . . I never knew man or woman who has been so uniformly happy'. He delighted in his marriage, his family, his friends and field sports. At the age of fifty-eight he was still winning prizes at the St Ronan's Games and he said that his married life had been so happy that he could not 'distinguish one part from another, save by some remarkably good days of fishing, shooting and curling on the ice'. He could be vain, touchy and difficult but he was always a lovable man. His little book, *Anecdotes of the Domestic Manners and Private Life of Sir Walter Scott*, reveals much of Hogg's own character. It is quite charming and a credit to both men.

Mungo Park
(1771–1806)

It is extraordinary to reflect that Scott, Hogg, the philologist John Leyden and the explorer Mungo Park were all born within a few years of each other, and grew up within the same small area of the Borders. If it was true that you could not stand half an hour by the Mercat Cross in Edinburgh without encountering fifty men of genius (and the claim is possibly exaggerated) it seems also to have been the case that you couldn't, a little later, round a bend of the Tweed without the chance of meeting genius too. It is impossible to say why this should have been so, but the long tradition of independence of mind which prevailed in the Borders must have had something to do with it.

Mungo Park was born at the farm of Foulshiels some three miles out of Selkirk on the Yarrow road. A roofless building stands below the modern farm buildings and bears a plaque recording that it was his birthplace. (He is also commemorated by a splendid statue in Selkirk itself, where he stands surrounded by assorted Africans, one of who rather surprisingly is playing what looks like a ukelele.) There is a local saying 'A day oot o' Selkirk is a day wasted': Mungo Park does not seem to have agreed; yet he always retained a local piety, and it is fitting that he should be remembered in Selkirk.

He went to the local High School and was apprenticed to a doctor in the town called Thomas Anderson, whose son would later be one of his colleagues, and whose daughter he would marry. In 1788 he proceeded to university in Edinburgh, and there completed his training as a surgeon, though he did not trouble himself to take a degree. He became a ship's surgeon, and this was the most important single action in his life for it aroused in him a disinterested and scientific enthusiasm for exploration. When he returned to London he offered his services to the African Association which had been founded in 1788 to sponsor exploration of the continent which was then almost entirely unknown to Europeans. They had, of course, long been acquainted with its west coast, which served as a base for the slave trade, but the interior was unknown land. Great interest had, however, been aroused by the travels of James Bruce who had explored Abyssinia and reached the source of the Blue Nile. Many had received his reports with scepticism and the African Association was determined to put matters on a respectable footing.

In 1793, therefore, Park was appointed to lead an expedition to the Niger; it says much for his charm and powers of persuasion that so young and inexperienced a man should have been given such responsibility. He soon showed himself worthy of their confidence. His expedition lasted two and a half years and he reached the upper stretches of the river, mapping its course which was hitherto quite unknown. This was a remarkable feat, for the climate was unhealthy and Park was constantly compelled to improvise. In 1799 he published his account of *Travels in the Interior Districts of Africa, Performed in the years 1795, 1796 and 1797*, and this book, which is regarded as one of the classics of travel literature, had an importance which is quite distinct from his journey. Bruce's tone had been so vainglorious that it was easy and natural to cast doubt on his account; he, like many previous and subsequent travellers, had written to impress; Park wrote to inform. His modesty was evident, and the book justifies Carlyle's view that Park was 'one of the most unpretending and at the same time valuable specimens of humanity'.

Like many explorers Park found it difficult to settle on his return home; everything seemed flat after the Niger, at least once he had written his book. He married Alison Anderson in the same year, however. He considered emigrating to New South Wales, and his wife was willing, but instead in 1801 he set up as a doctor in Peebles. He remained there for three years, but the lure of Africa proved irresistible when he was asked to lead an expedition sponsored by the Government; the purpose was to trace the Niger to its source. Unfortunately he fell foul of the natives, and he and his party were ambushed and killed at Bousa in 1805.

Park is one of the most attractive of the great explorers. He was free of the neurotic impulses which have dominated some of them. His desire for fame was not excessive, as was shown by his willingness to try to settle with his wife and work as a doctor in a country town; he disliked the role of social lion in which some explorers have revelled. He had no inordinate desire for wealth. He seems indeed to have been driven by a pure spirit of scientific inquiry and a sense of adventure. Explorers have been castigated as the advance guard of imperialism, and no doubt Park cannot be acquitted of this charge, but he did not investigate African life in a spirit of hostility or condescension; his interest was real and sensitive. He was a likeable man and a very brave one, for the hardships he endured were extraordinary; one has to stretch one's imagination to appreciate the courage of venturing as he did into the unknown without any of the aids to communication which twentieth-century explorers possess. Moreover, his travels added to the sum of human knowledge, for even critics hostile to the Eurocentric attitudes of explorers have seen his work as 'a first, a genuine synthesis of knowledge', for not even the inhabitants of the regions of the Niger could have traced its course.

Sir Walter Scott
(1771–1832)

In May 1823 Byron, in the midst of his preparations for his Greek expedition, took the trouble to write to Henri Beyle (Stendhal), whom he had met in Milan seven years previously. After a few compliments, he came to the matter of his letter:

'There is one part of your observations in the pamphlet which I shall venture to remark upon; – it regards Walter Scott. You say that "his character is little worthy of enthusiasm", at the same time that you mention his productions in the manner they deserve. I have known Walter Scott long and well, and in occasional situations which call forth the *real* character – and I can assure you that his character *is* worthy of admiration – that of all men he is the most *open*, the most *honourable*, the most *amiable*. With his politics I have nothing to do: they differ from mine, which renders it difficult for me to speak of them. But he is *perfectly sincere* in them; and Sincerity may be humble, but she cannot be servile. I pray you therefore to correct or soften that passage. You may perhaps attribute this officiousness of mine to a false affectation of *candour*, as I happen to be a writer also. Attribute it to whatever motive you please, but *believe* the *truth*. I say that Walter Scott is as nearly a thorough good man as man can be, because I *know* it by experience to be the case.'

This letter does honour to both Byron and Scott. They had liked each other from their first meeting; their friendship was distinguished by a complete absence of jealousy, even though Byron had usurped Scott's position as the most popular poet of the day, and indeed turned him from poetry to novels. Scott had defended Byron when the world turned against him, and Byron was grateful: 'I owe to you far more than the usual obligation for the courtesies of literature and common friendship,' he had written to Scott in 1822 – 'for you went out of your way in 1817 – to do me a service when it required not merely kindness – but courage to do so'. He had not allowed his sense of obligation to corrode his feelings. He spoke his mind when he said Scott was 'as nearly a thorough good man as man can be'. The world, impressed by the courage with which Scott confronted the disaster of the financial crash of January 1826, and his resolve that he would work himself out of adversity by the efforts of 'my own right hand' has come to an agreement with Byron. A modern biographer, Hesketh Pearson, judged that 'Scott was the only person within my knowledge whose greatness as a writer was matched by his goodness as a man' and called him 'the noblest man of letters in history'. He was right to do so.

Scott was the greatest of Scottish writers, and the greatest of Scotsmen. We can see yoked in him the diversity of our national traits: an intense and Romantic attachment to place, persons and the past; a brooding sense of supernatural mystery alongside an innate scepticism; a reverence for rank and genius that was married to a powerful conviction of the worth of each individual man and woman; he had a sense of community that gave his work, despite his politics, a democratic basis, and yet also an awareness of his own isolation; history lived for him, and he did more than any other man to make history live for us, and yet he remained very much a man of his own times, with the prejudices, inclinations and hopes of his contemporaries; he had a wild and probing imagination, and a lucid and rational intellect; there is no poetry, Matthew Arnold suggested, sadder than Scott's, and yet there is no one who offers more robust common sense; he knew well the vanity of human wishes and the transience of all earthly things, and yet acquired land and built Abbotsford with the enthusiasm of a perfect materialist, and collected memorabilia with a magpie's lack of discrimination. The more of Scott's works you read, the more you read about Scott, the more you find yourself saying 'Why, this is Scotland; if I come really to know Scott I shall know all that is best and strangest about my country'. Only in one other European literature can you find an attachment to both the idea and the matter of the writer's native land comparable to Scott's, and that is the literature of Holy Russia.

He looked, in the midst of his disaster, with wonder on himself:

'What a life mine has been! – half-educated, almost wholly neglected or left to myself, stuffing my head with most nonsensical trash, and undervalued in society for a time by most of my companions, getting forward and held a bold and clever fellow, contrary to the opinion of all who thought me a mere dreamer, broken-hearted for two years, my heart handsomely pieced again, but the crack will remain to my dying day. Rich and poor four or five times, once on the verge of ruin, yet opened new sources of wealth almost overflowing. Now taken in my pitch of pride, and nearly winged (unless the good news hold), because London chooses to be in an uproar, and in the tumult of bulls and bears, a poor inoffensive lion like myself is pushed to the wall. And what is to be the end of it? God knows. And so ends the catechism.'

A man is to some extent explained by his heredity and the surroundings in which he grew up. Scott was a Borderer, even though born in Edinburgh, whither his father had removed to practise as a Writer to the Signet. They were Borderers on his mother's side too – Rutherfords, his grandfather having been Minister of Yarrow. He was conscious of his old tribal inheritance: the Duke of Buccleuch was more important to him than the king, though Scott of Harden was the head of his own branch of the family. Hogg, who thought 'Sir Walter's principal fault was his too great respect for rank' remembered how Scott used to say 'with a degree of exultation which I thought must have been astounding to everyone who heard it how he and his father before him and his grandfather before that always kept their Christmasses with Harden in acknowledgement of his vassalage'. He was instinct with that virtue which the Romans called *pietas*.

As a child he suffered a paralysis which left him lame (a bond with Byron) and debarred him from the military career after which he lusted – Scott was a soldier *manqué*. This accident meant that he passed the years between one and eight – those years when the imagination stores up memories so valuable to a writer – at his grandfather's farm of Sandyknowe by the gaunt tower of Smailholm overlooking the valley of the Tweed. Smailholm, and the surrounding scene, and all it conjured up, gave him a sense of the great march and broken romance of history. Looking far to 'the distant Cheviots blue', he realised in memory that:

> 'Yet was poetic impulse given
> By the green hill and clear blue heaven . . .
> Methought that still with tramp and clang
> The gateway's broken arches rang;
> Methought grim features, seamed with scars,
> Glared through the window's rusty bars,
> And ever, by the winter's hearth,
> Old tales I heard of woe or mirth,
> Of lovers' sleights, of ladies' charms,
> Of witches' spells, of warriors' arms:
> Of patriot battles won of old
> By Wallace wight and Bruce the bold;
> Of later fields of feud and flight,
> When pouring from the Highland height,
> The Scottish clans, in headlong sway,

Had swept the scarlet ranks away.
While stretched at length upon the floor,
Again I fought each combat o'er,
Pebbles and shells in order laid,
The mimic ranks of war displayed;
An onward still the Scottish Lion bore,
And still the scattered Southron fled before . . .'

All the ingredients of Walter Scott Romance – that new thing which fired the imagination of Europe and restored Scotland's consciousness of itself as an historic nation – are laid out in this galloping and yet poignant passage; and all came from his childhood beneath the walls of Smailholm, which offered him space, the line of the Cheviots and the sense of the past as a great procession.

Edinburgh, the Edinburgh of the Enlightenment and the philosophical historians, gave him other qualities: a discriminating historical sense, a moral balance and a knowledge of men and literature – Scott must have been the best-read of great novelists. The two fused to make the Waverley novels the richest body of fiction produced in these islands.

I cannot here expatiate on the wonders of the novels or deal with any in detail. I can only throw out a few reflections, which may encourage those who read this book to turn again or for the first time to the novels. Such encouragement is, alas, probably still needed, for many nurture a prejudice against Scott's fiction, bred by the suspicion that he is long-winded (which is not true, for he is the most rapid of writers, and the novels should be read at the gallop, as they were written) and nurtured by critics who failed to understand what he was doing, and either demanded what was not on offer, or misinterpreted what they found.

The stupidest of these critics was E. M. Forster, and perhaps the simplest way to give a brief exposition of Scott's genius is to offer Forster's judgement, and then demolish it.

This then is what Forster has to say: 'He is seen to have a trivial mind and a heavy style.' Read *Old Mortality* with its examination of the ebb and flow of historical consequence, its portrayal of political fanaticism which anticipates Joseph Conrad, and compare the justice and sympathetic under-standing displayed by Scott with Forster's own single essay in this sort of fiction, *A Passage to India*, which is disfigured by Forster's unwillingness to be just to those of whom he disapproves, and the charge of triviality rebounds on the critic. Read *Ivanhoe* and ask if this book 'where,' in A. N. Wilson's phrase 'the scenes are bright in English sunshine', which is, as John Buchan put it, 'a pageant so far-flung and glittering that, in spite of its artificiality, it captivates the fancy,' is written in 'a heavy style'.

Forster: 'he cannot construct'. Few novels are better or more subtly constructed than *Waverley* or *The Heart of Midlothian*. In both he rejects an obvious and dramatic structure to enable him to see events with a steady double focus, which, as A. O. L. Cockshut has said, 'is perhaps Scott's most important contribution to the novel of heroic action. Its successful use requires qualities of mind that are exceedingly rare'.

Forster: 'He has neither artistic detachment nor passion, and how can a writer who is devoid of both create characters who will move us deeply?' This is perhaps the most extraordinary of Forster's inane judgements: to deny artistic detachment to the creator of Jeanie Deans, and passion to the author of *The Bride of Lammermoor* and *Redgauntlet*. Would Scott, it is fair to ask, have been seized on by the makers of Italian opera if he had lacked passion, which these operas exist to exhibit? And is there a lack of passion in Redgauntlet's cry 'the privilege of free action belongs to no mortal – we are tied down by the fetters of duty – our mortal path is limited by the regulations of honour – our most indifferent actions are but meshes of the web of destiny by which we are all surrounded . . . the liberty of which the Englishman boasts gives as little freedom to its owner as the despotism of an eastern sultan permits to his slave. The usurper, William of Nassau, went forth to hunt, and thought, doubtless that it was an act of his own royal pleasure that the horse of his murdered victim was prepared for his kingly sport. But Heaven had other views; and before the sun was high, a stumble of that very animal over an obstacle as inconsiderable as a mole-hillock, cost the haught rider his life and his usurped crown. Do you think that an inclination of the rein could have avoided that trifling impediment? I tell you, it crossed his way as inevitably as the long chain of Caucasus could have done. Yes, young man, in doing and suffering, we play but the part allotted by Destiny, the manager of this strange drama. . . .' No passion there? Or in the exquisite simplicity of Redgauntlet's 'then is the cause lost indeed', when those preparing a Jacobite rising are simply and tolerantly dismissed to their homes by General Campbell? *Redgauntlet* is the most intricately and cunningly structured of novels ('he cannot construct'), but it throbs with passion, stirring rhetoric and an Ossianic sense of loss. The desolation which Matthew Arnold found in Celtic Literature is keen in *Redgauntlet*, but could not touch Forster's suburban soul. Enough, one might say, of Forster who condescendingly dismissed Scott's surging, unstable world of dark corners and warm sunshine, heroic enterprise and agonising defeat, and the man who could create in the same novel the warm and affectionate comedy of Jonathan Oldbuck and the terrible scene of lamentation in the fishermen's cottage where Steenie Mucklebackit's body awaits burial, with the judgement that 'he had only a temperate heart and gentlemanly feelings, and an intelligent affection for the countryside, and this is not basis enough for great novels'; words better applied to Forster's own fiction.

Scott was a complete writer because he was a complete man. His social and practical knowledge was wide, he had read voraciously, he had a fund of common sense, but he would also retire into the secret world of his imagination. The world of the Ballads meant more to him than the world of the *Edinburgh Review*. He was both sociable and a solitary.

Scott was a big man in every way – he stood more than six foot. He loved the open air and country sports. How he got through the quantity of work he achieved mystified visitors who did not know that he had risen first in the household, laid and lit his own fire, and written for several hours before they were up and about. He had a good sense of his own worth, but no vanity. When his daughter was asked her opinion of *The Lady of the Lake*, she confessed she had not read it, because 'Papa says there is nothing so bad for young people as reading bad poetry'.

This open-hearted and sensible man lived partly in a world of fantasy. His business dealings are almost incomprehensible, and suggest that he never really wanted to know how things stood. His imagination was out of kilter with the facts; his finances represent a degree of optimism not far short of the manic. He knew himself very well, but could not have said whence his deepest and truest strokes came.

Contradiction runs through everything one learns of Scott and yet no man was more coherent. He was a fervent Scottish patriot, jealous of any encroachment on the liberties of his country; no man did more to feed national pride, and yet no man did more to reconcile Scots to the Union with England. About that he could not be other than ambivalent: his reason assented to it; his sentiment rejected it.

Abbotsford supplies us with a key to understanding him, and yet Abbotsford has been misinterpreted. The house was no mad folly, though his purchases of land were in the circumstances unwise. Yet, in building Abbotsford, Scott did no more than any other prosperous lawyer of his time might: that is to say, he established himself in a country house. And Abbotsford represents Scott's mind too: it is no Gothic fantasy, but an essentially Georgian house with Gothic decorations. Its atmosphere is friendly: it is a house for living in, a home, not to be compared with Gothic extravaganzas like

Strawberry Hill and Fonthill. It looks serenely on the rolling Tweed. Yet it is also an odd house, with its medieval armour and its collection of curiosities: the oatcake taken from the sporran of a Highlander killed at Culloden, memorabilia of Mary Stuart, Montrose, Claverhouse, Bonnie Prince Charlie, Marie Antoinette and Napoleon. And Scott's little dark study somehow seems cut off from the airy lightness of the other rooms, just as the intensity of his imagination seems to belong to a different being from the genial laird and sensible lawyer.

One never comes to the end of Scott.

Francis Jeffrey
(1773–1850)

As one of the three founders of the *Edinburgh Review* and its editor from 1803 to 1829, when he became Dean of the Faculty of Advocates, Jeffrey was one of the most influential figures in what may be called the second stage of the Scottish Enlightenment; he was also a figure of the second class. His achievement was remarkable for he made the *Edinburgh* the most influential organ of opinion but he was not remarkable himself. He was very small, and Sydney Smith, who with Francis Horner was co-founder of the *Review*, used to refer to him as 'our diminutive editor'. Jeffrey was also a politician, long kept out of office by his adherence to the Whigs. He became Lord Advocate, however, in 1830 and was raised to the Bench four years later.

Jeffrey could recognise talent and promote it; he encouraged Carlyle and gave Macaulay his first chance. At the same time, his views on poetry were conventional and hardly advanced beyond what he had learned to like as a young man. Some critics remain with their immediate contemporaries and are unable to appreciate the work of younger men; Jeffrey was often blind to the merits of men of his own age. He attacked Scott's *Marmion*, which he saw merely as founded 'upon a tissue of incredible accidents . . . borrowed from the novels of Mrs Radcliffe and her imitators'. (This is an absurd verdict which wholly ignores the poem's remarkable sense of life and mastery of a new narrative technique.) He said of Wordsworth's *The Excursion*, 'this will never do'. His preference was for artificial diction and deliberate design, even though he could not always recognise design in a poem. However, he had great influence and encouraged his readers 'to adopt a style of literary and political criticism which was rooted, not in eternal principles, but in the ordinary experience of ordinary literate and responsible men living in a modern age'.

Carlyle indeed criticised him on this ground. In his view Jeffrey 'may be said to have begun the rash style of criticising everything in Heaven and Earth by appeal to Moliere's Maid: "Do you like it? Don't you like it?" – a style which in hands more and more inferior . . . has grown gradually to such insufferable lengths among us. . . . Democracy, the gradual uprise and rule in all things, of roaring, million-headed, unreflecting, darkly suffering, darkly sinning Demos come to call its old superiors to account, at its maddest of tribunals: nothing in my time has so forwarded this as Jeffrey and his once famous *Edinburgh Review*'. This is harsh and unanswerable criticism. It is made the more pointed by Carlyle's appreciation of Jeffrey's very real merits and by his sense of what he might have been. This, too, has a wider application than the immediate and personal. Carlyle's criticism of Jeffrey and his recognition of where Jeffrey failed was at the same time a criticism and a recognition of the weakness and loss of vitality in Scottish culture. Jeffrey, who had spent a year at Queen's College, Oxford, was careful to eradicate Scotticisms from his writing. (In this, of course, he followed Hume and other eighteenth-century *illuminati*.) But Carlyle found that, in conversation, Jeffrey clearly showed 'a finer talent than any he had evidenced in writing: this was chiefly when he got to speak Scotch, and gave me anecdotes of old Scotch Braxfields, and vernacular (often enough, but not always cynical) curiosities of that type'. And then Carlyle thought to himself: 'Here is a man whom they have kneaded into the shape of an Edinburgh Reviewer, and clothed the soul of in Whig formulas . . . but he might have been a beautiful Goldoni, too, or something better in that kind, and have given us beautiful comedies, and aerial pictures, true and poetic, of Human Life in a far other way'. Carlyle saw in him 'a potential Voltaire; say Scotch Voltaire', but also a man who was less than he might have been, who had in a sense wasted himself. 'He was not deep enough, pious or reverent enough to have been great in Literature' so, one might say, he fell back into literariness. Because he kept a large part of himself out of writing, and that part perhaps the best and most lively, Jeffrey seems to exemplify and go some way towards justifying Edwin Muir's judgement that Walter Scott had suffered from having lived 'most of his days in a hiatus, in a country, that is to say, which was neither a nation nor a province, but had instead of a centre, a blank, an Edinburgh in its midst'. That judgement – peculiar, and open to attack and detailed correction, though it is – nevertheless takes on a new authority when one reconsiders it in the light of what Jeffrey made of himself and might have done. The *Edinburgh Review* achieved a remarkable authority, but it diluted the distinctiveness of Scottish culture. Jeffrey, although he contributed to this, cannot be held wholly responsible. As his friend and biographer Cockburn said, 'the eighteenth century was the last purely Scotch age'. Yet Jeffrey was personally admirable. Carlyle called him 'a man intrinsically of veracity' and 'a beautiful little man'. It is sad to think that he might have been more.

Captain Robert Barclay of Ury
(1779–1848)

Captain Robert Barclay of Ury was a great eccentric. He came from an old family, long established in the north-east. An ancestor had fought alongside Robert the Bruce and the first Barclay of Ury had had a sword so heavy that no-one else could lift it. As was common among the gentry families of the north-east, many Barclays had gone to seek fortune abroad. The Russian marshal, Barclay de Tolly, who fought against Napoleon, was a cousin.

Like many of his neighbours in Kincardineshire such as Lords Monboddo and Gardenstone, Captain Barclay's father, also Robert Barclay, was an enthusiastic agricultural improver; he removed 100000 tons of stones from his fields. His son followed his example but he followed even more exactly in his footsteps. Robert Barclay senior had once walked the 510 miles from Ury to London in ten days. His son became the most famous pedestrian of that energetic age. He was also celebrated as a horseman, a scientific trainer of prize-fighters and an agriculturalist, but it was as a walker that he first made his name. In 1801 he walked 90 miles in 20 hours and 22 minutes; in 1802, 64 miles in 10 hours and, in one day, 72 miles between breakfast and dinner. In 1806 he walked 100 miles over bad roads in 19 hours and, the following year, 78 miles on hilly roads in 14 hours. That was just the beginning.

One morning in 1808 he rose at 5 am and walked some 30 miles while grouse-shooting. He dined at five in the afternoon and then set off to walk 60 miles to Ury. That took 11 hours. He spent the morning transacting estate business before strolling 16 miles to Laurencekirk, where a dance was being held. He danced through the night and then walked back to Ury, arriving there about seven in the morning, ready for a day's partridge-shooting. He had walked some 130 miles and had apparently gone for two days and three nights without sleep.

He had, however, theories about sleep. He had concluded 'on scientific principles' that it was harmful to sleep too long at a stretch. Accordingly, he arranged to have a servant interrupt his sleep every few hours. This practice stood him in good stead when he came to attempt the feat that made him most famous in his own day.

He made a wager that he would walk 1000 miles on Newmarket Heath (half a mile out from the Horse and Jockey and half a mile back) in 1000 consecutive hours. He accomplished it between 1 June and 12 July. In the last stages of the walk he had to employ John Gully, a famous prize-fighter, to keep the crowds at a distance. His average time for the mile varied from just under 15 minutes in the first week to just over 21 in the last. During the walk his weight dropped from 13st 4lb to 11 stone. However, he soon recovered and on 17 July set off for the Walcharen campaign as aide-de-camp to the Marquess of Huntly.

This famous walk was fully described by the Aberdeen historian, William Thom, in his *History of Pedestrianism*. 'The Captain moved with a sort of lounging gait, scarce raising his feet more than two or three inches above the ground. His dress was adapted to the changeable state of the weather. Sometimes he walked in a flannel jacket, sometimes in a loose, dark grey coat; he always used strong shoes and lamb-wool stockings.'

The Captain was famous for his strength as well as his endurance. As a young man he could lift half a ton. He had a party trick of lifting an 18-stone man from the floor to a table. The man stood on Barclay's right hand and was steadied by his left. In the winter of 1810/11 he would ride 51 miles twice a week in order to hunt, returning home the same night.

Naturally such a Corinthian took an interest in the prize-fight and was no mean performer himself. Promising professionals at Jackson's Rooms would be invited to spar a few rounds with the Captain. It is said that he used a special pair of half-stuffed gloves that gave him an advantage over his opponent who wore full-padded mufflers. When Black Molyneux came to spar with the Captain, he somehow managed to get the gloves exchanged and gave Barclay a hiding. The boxing journalist Thormanby observed that 'Barclay never forgave the nigger for thus beating him . . . and this was why he took such an interest in Cribb's second match'.

Certainly Barclay could claim credit for that victory of Cribb's at Thistleton Gap in September 1811. He had carried Cribb up to Scotland in July, at which date the London publican weighed 16 stone and 'from his mode of life, and the confinement of a crowded city, had become corpulent, big-bellied, full of gross humours and short-breathed', according to Thom. The Captan put him on a diet and a course of physic and made him walk up to 20 miles a day.

He led him up steep hills around Ury, chucking stones at him if he showed signs of stopping. After this treatment, he was able to bring Cribb into the ring weighing only 13½ stone. The famous

Leicestershire huntsman Dick Christian found him 'fine as a star, just like snow aside the black man. The black wur fat, that licked him as much as anything. Before the fight Barclay restricted his man to two boiled eggs, while Molyneux gobbled down a boiled fowl, an apple-pie and a tankard of stout'. Cribb remarked afterwards that he would rather repeat the fight than the Captain's training. Barclay won £10000 on him.

Barclay's scientific theories were also applied to horses, stock-rearing and crops. He farmed 600 acres at Ury himself, paying close attention to the quality of pasture and adhering to strict rotation: oats – barley – turnips (which the sheep were put in to eat) – barley – grass for hay – pasture. He had a flock of 1000 Leicesters which were sent to the London market by steam vessels from Aberdeen. His Shorthorn cattle went there too, his bull calves selling for £40 at six months. He reckoned he could bring his bullocks fat to market at two and a half years, against the three and a half then normal for Scotch cattle. He contributed greatly to the long, nineteenth-century supremacy of the Aberdeenshire Shorthorn. When his gambling debts forced him to sell his first herd, he started another within the month. His interest in agriculture was life long. In 1842 he published an account of an agricultural tour through the United States.

This robust eccentric had his weaknesses. He wasted time and money in various claims for the earldoms of Airth, and Strathearn and Menteith. Despite this silliness, he offers a striking example of the full-blooded vigour of our ancestors and was wholly character-istic of his age.

Henry, Lord Cockburn

(1779–1854)

Cockburn's name is commemorated in the Cockburn Association, a society devoted to preserving historic Edinburgh. It is a cause in which he interested himself, as he was an opponent of Edinburgh's expansion and was an early urban environmentalist. The appropriateness goes deeper, however, because Cockburn brooded all his life on the question of progress. He was able to be simultaneously a reformer and a sceptic, a man who loved the past, feared the future and yet knew that the present must give way to it.

He was born into the Scottish legal Establishment and remained there all his life. His father, Archibald Cockburn, was Sheriff of Midlothian and a Baron of the Court of Exchequer. He was also a first cousin to Henry Dundas, Viscount Melville, who was to be the Tory manager of Scotland throughout the long administration of Pitt the Younger. Although Henry Cockburn was to abandon his family's Toryism to become a Whig, he still profited from this connection. Dundas made him Advocate-Depute in 1807. Cockburn was still an insider, even if he was critical of the society to which he belonged.

He was a contributor from the first to the *Edinburgh Review* and a lifelong friend of its editor, Francis Jeffrey, whose biography he wrote. He recommended Parliamentary reform in its columns, though he did not support a wide extension of the franchise, and he feared democracy. He was an advocate of high repute and made his name as a defender in criminal cases. Among those he defended was Helen MacDougall, the associate of Burke and Hare. (It was Cockburn who remarked that 'except that he murdered, Burke was a gentlemanly fellow'.) When the Whigs came to power in 1830, he became Solicitor-General and was responsible for drafting the Scottish Reform Bill. In 1834 he was made a Lord of Session.

This was a career of useful public service. It is, however, as a writer that Cockburn is best remembered. His *Memorials of his Time*, posthumously published in 1856, is the fullest and liveliest account of Edinburgh towards the close of the Age of Enlightenment. It is supplemented by his Journals and by his *Circuit Journeys*, published in 1888, which is an account of his travels as a circuit judge and an invaluable mine for social historians. His *Examination of the Trials for Sedition*, also first published that year, is a lucid analysis of the effect of the Revolution in France on Scotland and Scottish politics.

That Revolution was the central event of Cockburn's life, although he was only ten when it broke out. He wrote that 'everything rung, or was connected with the Revolution in France; which for twenty years was, or was made, the all in all. Everything, not this or that thing, but literally everything was soaked in this one event'. A man of Cockburn's intelligence could not fail to see how the philosophic principles of the Scottish Enlightenment tended towards the ideas of the Revolution, and yet he shrank from the consequences. To him, democracy was a 'doom'. He reflected that 'that man must be very blind who does not see the shadow of the popular tree is enlarging and darkening; and he must see well who can tell us what its fruit will be'. It was not easy, he thought, to see 'how wealth and sense are to keep their feet'. He wondered whether 'we shall go on in this perpetual swelter. Or will manufactures be given up, and the pastoral-poetry state be recurred to?'

But if the future seemed dark and uncertain to Cockburn, the past could offer little comfort because it had vanished beyond hope of restoration. The eighteenth century, he thought, was 'the last purely Scotch age. Most of what had gone before had been turbulent and political. All that has come after has been English. The eighteenth century was the final Scotch century. We, whose youth tasted the close of that century and who lived far into the Southern influence, feel proud of a purely Edinburgh society which raised the reputation of our discrowned capital and graced the deathbed of our national manners'.

Caught between a future he feared and a national past he could only regret, Cockburn for all his vitality and robustness, his wit and common sense, is a curiously unhappy figure. Yet he is a significant one, for in his hesitations, regrets and foreboding we can see why the Scottish Enlightenment petered out or at least changed its direction away from grand general questions to a more narrow and utilitarian science. Cockburn resembles Sir Walter Scott in his reluctant acceptance of the Union and in his realisation that the weakening of a distinct identity and the loss of a separate history were part of an historical process which was unlikely to be reversed. He recognised the advantages of Union, just as he recognised the advances brought by industrialism; but he could love neither.

Thomas Chalmers
(1780–1847)

Thomas Chalmers was the most famous Church of Scotland minister of his day and, as such, one of the most influential men in the country. He was the leader of the party which walked out of the General Assembly of 1843 to form the Free Kirk of Scotland. He thus set in motion what is known as the Disruption, an event which divided Scotland.

The fact that it is necessary to begin a note on Chalmers with these flat statements indicates how he has faded from any general consciousness. His statue still stands in Edinburgh, but it is safe to guess that few who pass by it could tell you anything about him.

He came from Fife, his father being a merchant in Anstruther. He attended St Andrews University from the age of eleven and, after assisting the Professor of Mathematics there, became minister at Kilmany. Around 1810 he was converted to Evangelicalism. Evangelicals had a direct experience of salvation and a strong sense of missionary zeal. Chalmers, soon after his conversion, began to win a reputation as a preacher, which he never lost. Carlyle, in his *Reminiscences*, recalled that 'his tones, in preaching, would rise to the piercingly pathetic; no preacher ever went so into one's heart'. There is no art so evanescent as the orator's, unless it is an actor's – after all, the preacher requires and generally acquires something of the actor's talent – so we have to take Chalmers's preaching on trust. However, it secured him the ministry of the Tron Kirk in Glasgow, where he immediately enhanced his reputation as an active pastor. He was quick to see that the expanding population of the city, and the effects of industrialisation, were making new demands on the Church. He intended his ministry to be of social benefit as well as spiritual. Both at the Tron Kirk and at St John's, where he was minister from 1819 to 1823, he tried to find a new and wider role for the Church in a rapidly changing age. His ministry has been described as 'a social experiment which involved pastoral oversight of virtually every aspect of the life of the parish aimed at eliminating poor relief (except for the truly needy) by encouraging independence, self-reliance and self-help'. Sturdy individualism, within the care of the parochial structure and overseen by a pastor, seems to have been his message in answer to the indifference and poverty which were noticeable consequences of industrialisation and the new urban society.

Chalmers questioned neither the laws of classical, political economy nor the values of the middle-classes. He believed as firmly as any merchant or shopkeeper in the responsibility of the individual for his own material and spiritual condition. At the same time, however, he taught that wealth and power could not be justly enjoyed if their holders did not also practise philanthropy and understand that they had a responsibility towards their less fortunate and less successful fellow-citizens. Professor T. C. Smout in his book, *A Century of the Scottish People*, has observed that the fact 'that Victorian Scotland was as world-famous for serious philanthropists – like William Collins of the Temperance movement and William Quarrier of the children's homes – as it was for drunkenness and bad housing, was due in no small degree to Thomas Chalmers'. Yet, in the argument that is always waged by those who wish to reform the evils of society, between those who would ameliorate things as they are and those who advocate a fundamental change, Chalmers was firmly on the side of the ameliorists. That was why he was successful. He told his middle-class audience that they could enjoy the fruits of this earth and the Kingdom of Heaven as long as they were prepared to work to help their neighbours. This was perhaps a limitation. Carlyle certainly thought so. Among the encomia of Chalmers which are generally found, it is a shock to come on Carlyle's verdict: 'He was essentially a man of little culture, of narrow sphere all his life; such an intellect, professing to be educated and yet so ill-read, so ignorant in all that lay beyond the horizon in place or in time, I have almost nowhere met with.'

Carlyle did grant Chalmers 'capable of impetuous activity and blazing audacity, as his latter years showed'. That was in the crisis that led up to the Disruption. It was essentially a quarrel about Church patronage: the question was who should appoint the minister. Patrons, anathema to the old Covenanters, had been re-established by an Act of 1712. The patron was generally the Laird on whose ground the church stood. In 1834 the General Assembly, dominated by Chalmers and the Evangelicals, passed an act which gave congregations the right to reject the patron's nominee. The validity of this act was successfully challenged in the Court of Session. The quarrel simmered for the next decade until, in 1843, Chalmers led his exodus. Almost forty per cent of the ministers followed him and a third of the congregations. It was an astonishing display of resolution on the part of both the ministers, who lost their manses and stipends, and the congregations, who committed themselves to building new churches and financing their ministers.

It was a triumph for Chalmers, but a Pyrrhic one. Ironically it cut the ground from under his feet. One aspect of his message had been that the State should be ready to assist the Church in its work of social regeneration. Now his Free Church had separated itself from the Establishment. It had also condemned Presbyterian Scotland to a bitter and distracting division in which many of the issues raised by Chalmers were neglected.

Sir David Wilkie

(1785–1841)

In Chapter XXXI of *The Antiquary*, Scott pays a tribute to Wilkie's art: 'In the inside of the cottage was a scene which our Wilkie alone could have painted, with that exquisite feeling of nature that characterises his enchanting productions.' He then describes in the next paragraph the body of young Steenie Mucklebackit 'laid in its coffin within the wooden bedstead which the young fisher had occupied while alive. At a little distance stood the father, whose rugged weather-beaten countenance, shaded by his grizzled hair, had faced many a stormy night and night-like day ... His glance was directed sidelong toward the coffin, as to an object on which he could not steadfastly look, and yet from which he could not withdraw his eyes ... In another corner of the cottage, her face covered by her apron, which was flung over it, sat the mother – the nature of her grief sufficiently indicated by the wringing of her hands, and the convulsive agitation of her bosom, which the covering could not conceal. Two of her gossips, officiously whispering into her ear the commonplace topic of resignation under irremediable misfortune, seemed as if they were endeavouring to stun the grief which they could not console ... The sorrow of the children was mixed with wonder at the preparations they beheld around them, and at the unusual display of wheaten bread and wine ... But the figure of the old grandmother was the most remarkable of the sorrowing group. Seated on her accustomed chair, with her usual air of apathy and want of interest in what surrounded her, she seemed every now and then to resume the motion of twirling her spindle ... she would then cast her eyes about her, as if surprised at missing the usual implements of her industry, and appear struck by the black colour of the gown in which they had dressed her ... Then, finally, she would raise her head with a ghastly look, and fix her eyes upon the bed which contained the coffin of her grandson, as if she had at once and for the first time acquired sense to comprehend her inexpressible calamity'.

It is a remarkable piece of writing, of intense and unusual interest. What seems at first simply a graceful tribute from the novelist to the painter becomes, as we read, a realisation of a painting that was never made, but one which draws on the writer's knowledge of the painter's work. It is as if Scott was setting himself to visualise the painting Wilkie might have made, then giving directions to the painter, while at the same time the passage is a profound and sympathetic criticism of Wilkie's work. No examination in words of any of his actual paintings can make quite so strong an impression – or give so right a feeling for his work – as this account of a non-existent Wilkie.

Wilkie himself recognised the passage as laying him under 'a debt of obligation' as 'with an unseen hand in The Antiquary, you took me up, and claimed me, the humble painter of domestic sorrow, as your countryman'. This was fair enough; if you wanted to let a blind man have a sense of Wilkie's genius, that passage from the novel would supply it.

Wilkie is perhaps the most remarkable of Scottish painters. He was born in Fife, son of a parish minister, and as a young man moved to London to learn the art of portrait painting. As a portrait painter he is fine, though inferior to Raeburn. His true genius lay in what is often called genre painting: the depiction of domestic scenes. In this he revived a style largely absent from European painting since the days of Dutch painters like Cuyp. It is painting which is pictorially extremely satisfying, yet which also makes a social statement that is often moving. Wilkie, however, does not try to impart a message to his painting; the feeling is rather extracted from the composition. Hazlitt, the English critic, misunderstood him or missed the mark when he wrote: 'Hogarth never looks at any object but to find a moral or ludicrous effect; Wilkie never looks at any object but to see that it is there.' The criticism rebounds on its author, for in the blame he imputes he actually identifies the reason for Wilkie's superiority. 'Every painting,' Sickert was fond of saying, 'tells a story', and there is certainly a story to be read into any of Wilkie's; but it is a story, not a cautionary tale. Wilkie's art is on the same level as *The Antiquary*.

Wilkie eschews pretension. The portrait of Scott and his family, a masterpiece of domesticity, restraint and understanding, which hangs in the Scottish National Portrait Gallery, was condemned in England as 'a vulgar group' unworthy of 'an elegant poet'. Precisely: Scott himself would have been disgusted by the falsity of the appellation 'an elegant poet'.

Scott was not the only novelist whose work was sometimes close to Wilkie's. John Galt, author of *The Annals of the Parish*, was another, and his writing was influenced by Wilkie's painting. In both there is an utmost fidelity, a contempt for exaggeration. Burns, part of Scott, Galt and Wilkie provide us with an exact picture of pre-industrial Scotland, without sentimentality or distortion.

Wilkie succeeded Raeburn as King's Limner in Scotland in 1823, and was knighted in 1836. He seems to have suffered some sort of nervous breakdown in 1825, possibly brought on by the realisation that what he wanted to paint was not what appealed to his patrons in England. On his recovery he worked in the academic style, associated with Reynolds; not successfully. He did, however, try a Scottish Historical style as for example in his unfinished 'John Knox Preaching'. But he still achieved his best work when he returned to his old style; *The Cottar's Saturday Night* is a perfect expression of his enduring talent. Without Wilkie we would not be able to see rural Scotland as we do.

George Gordon, Lord Byron
(1788–1824)

What was there Scotch about Byron? Well, he gave an answer himself:

> But I am half a Scot by birth, and bred
> A whole one, and my heart flies to me head . . .
> I 'scotch'd not killed' the Scotchman in my blood,
> And love the land of mountain and the flood.

His lines on Lochnagar bear witness to this feeling, though it might be going too far to attribute Byron's celebration of the wildness and grandeur of Nature to his childhood holidays on Deeside.

His unfortunate mother was a Gordon of Gight, married by his scapegrace father for her little fortune. It was a small fortune indeed for one of his temper, and when he had run through all that he could lay his hands on, he discarded her. Mrs Byron retired to Aberdeen with her little crippled boy, and he spent his early years in mean lodgings there.

His mother's family provided him with a wild heredity, wilder even than the Byrons. There was, for instance, the 7th Laird of Gight, who buried a treasure in the Ythan to protect it from the Covenanters. After receiving a pardon in 1647, he sent down a diver to recover it. The diver found the devil sitting at table with the laird's silver before him, waiting for dead babies to be cooked for his supper. He returned, not surprisingly, to the surface, and refused to go back for the treasure till the laird persuaded him by pulling out his fingernails and sticking him with pins. 'Better the devil than the Laird of Gight,' he cried, and dived again. This time his quartered body surfaced with a knife impaling his still quivering heart. The 7th laird was an ancestor for any boy to boast of.

Byron lived mostly in Aberdeen till he was ten, at which age he inherited his title. It made sufficient impression on him at least for him to recall this period in his life in Ravenna in 1821 and note down a few memories. He learned to read there and studied Latin, and developed a passion for History. Is that Scotch? Hume called us 'the historical nation', and certainly a consciousness of History is generally greater among Scots than among English. Historical events cast long shadows here; few south of the Border. Byron remembered enough of Aberdeen to note that school was there pronounced 'squeel'.

He never saw Scotland again, and he seems never to have thought of returning here. When in Greece with his friend Hobhouse, it was Hobhouse (an Englishman) and not Byron who compared the Gulf seen from Nicepolis with Loch Lomond. Nevertheless, there are certain elements in Byron's character and work which may be thought essentially Scottish.

There was first his sense of fate. As a small boy he had been taught by his nursemaid the terrors of the Calvinist Hell. The sense that he was a spirit doomed to damnation never quite left him. At times he seems to have believed he was damned by his heredity; at others the victim of destiny; very often Byron seemed to himself like a spectator of his own drama. Though Walter Scott suggested to him that he might end in the Catholic Church, he was never to be quite free of the gloomy doctrines of extreme Calvinism, even when he saw himself as a cosmic rebel.

He had a passion for Liberty, which shone throughout his life and in his work; he involved himself in the attempt by Italians to free Italy from Austrian rule; he died in the cause of Greece. He was conscious of the dignity and worth of historic and oppressed nations. One consistent note which sounds throughout his poetry is his hatred of tyranny and contempt for tyrants. His lines on Greece sound a note which recalls the Declaration of Arbroath; his lines on Freedom echo Barbour's 'Brus'.

With this went an innate sense of decency which caused him to respect the individuality of all men, and hence to affirm their fundamental equality. In his daily life he was full of aristocratic prejudices – many who met him, such as Stendhal, found him far too conscious of his title – and it is easy to show that his idea of liberty was restricted to liberty for a limited caste. Certainly he was rarely free from social bias, mocking Leigh Hunt, for instance, for his Cockney manners, and he disliked radical agitators. (He thought that at Peterloo the troops should have cut down Orator Hunt.) Nevertheless, when it came down to particulars, from his maiden speech in the House of Lords in defence of the Nottinghamshire Luddites, to the deepest utterances of his poetry, Byron overcame these prejudices. Mazzini, the apostle of a free and United Italy, recognised this. He wrote that Byron 'by the implacable war he waged against the vices and absurdities of the privileged classes, and, indirectly, by investing his heroes with all the most brilliant qualities of the despot, and then dashing them to pieces as if in anger, combated aristocratic prejudices, and developed in men's minds the sentiment of equality'.

It may be objected that Scots have no lien on the ideas of liberty and equality, and, in the age of the French Revolution, this was evidently true. Nevertheless, these ideas are fundamental to the concept of the 'Democratic Intellect', which is itself fundamental to any understanding of the Scotch character and Scottish history, and only Burns among the poets has expressed them as forcibly as Byron.

Byron was Scottish too in his contradictions, and in his ability to contain and reconcile them in a coherent whole. He was a Romantic who despised Romanticism, an aristocrat who fought for liberty; a rhetorician capable of the purest sincerity; a debauchee who sighed for the comfort of domesticity; an enthusiast who was not deceived by his enthusiasm. Nothing makes this last clearer than his attitude to the Greeks and the cause of Greek Independence. He had no illusions about the Greeks. He had liked the Turks on his first visit to the East; he was doubtful if he could achieve anything for Greece. Yet, despite this, he was ready to devote himself to the Greeks' fight for Freedom, and indeed to offer his life for it.

Finally, Byron has no real precursor in English literature, but his tone is characteristically Scots; the poets he resembles most are Dunbar and Burns. Like Dunbar he could move easily from lofty rhetoric to direct conversational verse; from Childe Harold to Don Juan; and from one mode to the other within the same poem. Like Burns he could be coarse and delicate. Both are poets of physical love; both have an immediacy which cuts through the artificiality with which poets conventionally invested the subject. Don Juan, Byron's masterpiece, is like nothing else in English literature, but it is recognisably Scottish in its mixture of tones, its raciness, its tenderness, its freedom from flummery. It is perhaps the tragedy of our literature – well, one of the tragedies – that Byron's essential Scottishness has been insufficiently recognised (though T. S. Eliot drew attention to it), and so Byron has never been received into the mainstream and seen as a desirable model.

Archibald Simpson
(1790–1847)

Architects of talent are common enough (or were, at least, till Schools of Architecture were instituted) but architects of genius are as rare as genius in any other art and so Scotland can claim, I think, only three. Of these, Robert Adam and Charles Rennie Mackintosh have been widely celebrated but the third, and perhaps most remarkable, is still little recognised beyond his native city. Even there, there are many who know and admire and love his buildings but remain ignorant of their author. In a sense this is testimony to his greatness: his buildings have taken root and appear to be as natural an expression of their city as the churches and palaces of an Italian town are of theirs.

The city is Aberdeen and the architect Archibald Simpson. Simpson's genius is manifest in the copiousness and audacity of his imagination, the certainty of his execution, and his mastery of both brick and granite and of the Gothic and Classical styles.

He was born in Aberdeen, attended the Grammar School and Marischal College there, and had his first architectural training in the office of a local builder, James Massie; he began, that is to say, with practice and, having mastered that, moved on to theory. He learned how a building should stand before exploring styles. As a young man he visited Italy but he was in practice in Aberdeen by 1813 and remained there throughout his life.

Much of his work survives, as granite can be destroyed only by base intention, but one masterwork has gone. Since its destruction is perhaps the principal act of vandalism perpetrated in Aberdeen, we are fortunate to have from John Betjeman an appreciation of it which tells those who never saw it what they missed:

'My attention was held by a wall of granite, so bold, so simple in design, so colossal in its proportions that I stood puzzled. I have seen nothing like it before or since. Egyptian? Greek? Eighteenth-century? Modern? No, it couldn't be modern, for see the granite is weathered. This was the New Market built by Archibald Simpson in 1842. The magnificence of the entrance is designed to show the quality and strength of granite: the architect realised that there was no point in carving the unyielding material into delicate detail. Let the stone speak for itself, and then emphasise its scale and texture by a few strong mouldings and broad pilasters projecting only an inch or two from the face of the building. The inside of this covered market is worthy of its outside – colossal, simple, constructional. I seemed to be stepping into one of these many-vistaed engravings by Piranesi. Archibald Simpson was an architect of genius, a Soane, a Hawkesmoor, someone head and shoulder above the men of his time.'

Betjeman also admired Simpson's soaring octagonal brick spire above the Triple Kirks, which was based on St Elizabeth in Marburg but which he found 'so marvellous that only Salisbury is in my opinion its rival'. Significantly, he judged that Simpson was capable of 'creating in the Gothic style at a time when all other architects were only imitating'. Coming from an admirer of Pugin and Barry, that is praise indeed.

Simpson was, however, equally at ease, equally a master of proportion, in the Classical style. St Giles in Elgin is a masterpiece with a noble Doric portico. As if to show his range, the Castlegate in Aberdeen is framed by the Athenaeum, graced by elegant Ionic pillars, and the North of Scotland Bank, which curves with Corinthian sinuosity round the corner to King Street. Although ten years separate these buildings, they sit serenely against each other. Simpson's buildings always relate perfectly to their site; he had a master's eye for the use of space in the city.

Bon Accord Square and Crescent show that he could employ his genius to equal effect on domestic architecture. The sweep of the Crescent has been called 'one of the most striking essays in picturesque town planning in Scotland'.

Simpson is a reminder of the variety of Scotland. He was an architect who worked almost entirely in Aberdeen and the north-east and there produced work unequalled by any contemporary.

Thomas Carlyle
(1795–1881)

Carlyle was born in the same year as Keats; he died six years before Queen Victoria's Jubilee. That is to say, he was born into the second age of Romanticism and self-expression and survived into the age of scientific doubt. Throughout his life, but particularly in the 1830s and 1840s, he was the greatest moral force in Britain. For Scotsmen there is a peculiar and melancholy interest in his life: he was the first man of outstanding talent after the Enlightenment who found Scotland insufficient and removed to London.

He was born in Annandale, the son of a farming stonemason of whom he has left a vivid and tender account in his *Reminiscences*. He was brought up in the stern piety of the Burgher Secession Church and, though he abandoned its tenets, never shed the influence of its moral tenacity. No orthodox Christian, he believed that the time of Churches had passed and was yet imbued with a sense of the truth of revealed religion. His biographer, the historian J. A. Froude, wrote that for Carlyle 'God's existence was not an arguable possibility . . . but an awful reality to which the fate of nations, the fate of each individual man bore perpetual witness'.

In 1809 he went to Edinburgh University, having walked there from his home at Ecclefechan. He found that 'the young vacant mind was furnished with much talk about the Progress of the Species, Dark Ages, Prejudice, and the like'. The prevailing scepticism broke his childhood faith but he rejected what he saw as the complacency of the Enlightenment. He emerged, witness to the strong personality of Romanticism, radical and authoritarian, mystical yet practical and with a deep reverence for work. He was a man of the nineteenth century, the temper of which he did so much to form; preoccupied with social questions and with the revelation of divine justice in History.

In the 1820s he lived mostly in Edinburgh, working as a journalist and translator. He read deeply in German literature, especially Goethe. In 1826 he married the attractive, intelligent, but neurasthenic Jane Welsh, daughter of a Haddington doctor. Their marriage endured lovingly despite many strains; Carlyle owed much to her, which he came to appreciate fully only after her death in 1866. For a few years they lived on a farm that she had inherited in Dumfriesshire then, in 1833, they removed to London, where they were to remain for the rest of their lives.

In 1833/4 he published *Sartor Resartus.* This extraordinary fantasia, part social satire, part spiritual autobiography, made his name. It also revealed a remarkable, wholly individual style. Carlyle wrote like nobody else; the effect was to give his thoughts a startling novelty. Often grotesque, his writing was nevertheless always fresh and incomparably vivid. Carlyle never used words and expressions ready-made; he was a worker in language, new-minting his own coinage.

His history of *The French Revolution,* was published in 1837. There had been nothing like it before and there has been little since. Here was History presented not as an urbane record of events but as a passionate and moral drama. In his great scenes, Carlyle recreates the *possibility* of History, the sense that events happened as they did partly because of ineluctable consequence, partly because of the coincidence of particular impulses at a particular moment. For Carlyle, History becomes Theatre, but a Theatre of the utmost seriousness. He learned more from Shakespeare and Scott than from the formal historians of the eighteenth century. He never allows the reader to forget that historical personages could bleed, laugh, rejoice and weep.

The 1840s were Carlyle's decade. He embarked on a career as a public lecturer; the result was *Heroes and Hero-Worship.* He also wrote his masterpiece, *Past and Present,* which arose from his recognition that 'there is a deep-seated struggle in the whole fabric of society; a boundless grinding collision of the old and the new'. The book offers a penetrating critique of industrialism, individualism and the dominant utilitarian philosophy; these are contrasted with the organic society of the Middle Ages. This work spawned numerous novels dealing with the 'condition of England'. Significantly, there were none dealing in like manner with the 'condition of Scotland', because the principal consideration in Scotland at that time was not the new industrial society but the Disruption of the Church. It was this book, more than anything else, which led George Eliot to write in 1855 that 'there is hardly a superior or active mind of this generation that has not been modified by Carlyle's writings; there has hardly been an English book written for the last ten or twelve years that would not have been different if Carlyle had not lived'.

Carlyle remained thoroughly Scottish, however. His doctrine of personal responsibility, his insistence on moral consequence, even his attack on individualism delivered from a peculiarly individualistic standpoint – all had their roots in Scottish culture. Scotland honoured him, with honorary degrees and the Rectorship of Edinburgh University, but ignored his message. More and more, indeed, as he grew older, his message fell on deaf ears. His long biographies of Cromwell and especially of Frederick the Great were duller things than his early writings. His cult of the moral hero seemed submerged in a cult of the Great Man. There was something ironical in this master-ironist and preacher of essential morality selecting the amoral Frederick, a product of the despised Enlightenment, as his ultimate hero. Carlyle despaired of democracy in an age that was moving towards that form of government.

He lingered on till 1881. His *Reminiscences*, written in anguish after his wife's death, are nevertheless his most attractive book, offering a tender and restless intelligent picture of his early life. In Scotland Carlyle was a prophet without influence, although, by way of Nietzsche, his greatest disciple, his influence was to be felt later by Hugh MacDiarmid. The Scottish failure to respond to Carlyle is the clearest evidence of the intellectual withdrawal which marked the nineteenth century.

Thomas Babington Macaulay
1st Baron Macaulay of Rothley
(1800–1859)

'I wish I was as cocksure about anything as Macaulay is about everything,' said Lord Melbourne, who had just appointed Macaulay to his Cabinet. 'However,' Lord David Cecil assures us, 'he was not bored by Macaulay. On the contrary he sat listening to him "with an air of complacency and as if for instruction".' Since Melbourne was very easily bored, and Macaulay's conversation and oratory were both unusually copious and his delivery poor, this says much for its content.

Macaulay and Carlyle were the two great historians of the Victorian age and they could hardly have been more different. Carlyle was awkward, craggy, doom-laden and frequently pessimistic; Macaulay, sturdily optimistic and smooth, sought to make History as agreeable to read as a novel and was delighted to find that his *History of England* replaced fiction on the tables of young girls and ladies. There was something Panglossian in his view of History, because he was the foremost expositor of what has become known as 'the Whig interpretation of History'. This sees History as the story of human progress. Macaulay, devoted to antithesis, saw every conflict in History as a struggle between the forces of light, which were forward-looking and progressive, and the forces of darkness, which were reactionary and obscurantist. Fortunately the world was so well arranged that the forces of light always won. To put it like this is to simplify Macaulay's view of History and to do so even crudely; but he did just that to History itself.

Macaulay was a Scot only by heredity. He was born in Leicestershire and brought up in Clapham. He was educated privately and at Trinity College, Cambridge. Besides his ancestral links, however, he had close connections with Scotland, making his name by his review-essays (which might run to 30000 words) in the *Edinburgh Review* and sitting as a Member of Parliament for Edinburgh from 1839–47 and from 1852–6. Moreover, in his *History*, he gave due attention to Scotland (even though the book's title was the *History of England*); indeed his chapters on Scotland are among the most brilliant in his work. They are also, by his standards, fair-minded. He was also greatly influenced by the philosophical historians of the Scottish Enlightenment, even if his view of the historical process was less subtle than theirs. To some extent he may be thought of as a product of that movement.

His essay on Milton in the *Edinburgh Review* made his name in 1825 and was followed by an essay on Machiavelli which is still regarded in Italy as the finest introduction to that difficult moralist. Its peroration may be regarded as a fine example of Macaulay's style; it exhibits both his virtues – certainty of judgement and incomparable vitality, and his vice – of exaggeration for the sake of dramatic effect:

'In the Church of Santa Croce a monument was erected to his memory, which is contemplated with reverence by all who can distinguish a great mind through the corruptions of a degenerate age, and which will be approached with still deeper homage when the object to which his public life was devoted shall be attained, when the foreign yoke shall be broken, when a second Procida shall avenge the wrongs of Naples, when a happier Rienzi shall restore the good estate of Rome, when the streets of Florence and Bologna shall again resound with their ancient war-cry, 'Popolo, popolo; muiano i tiranni!'

It is grand stuff and reveals also his admirable and consistent support for the cause of liberty, at least for civilised men and those fit to enjoy it.

His literary work brought him to the notice of Holland House, the great Whig salon. His conversation, which was brilliant, made him a welcome guest there; and he was naturally found a seat in Parliament.

There he added to his reputation by his speeches in favour of reform, which held the attention of the House despite his bad manner of gabbling in a high-pitched monotone. When the Whigs came to power, he was rewarded with the office of Secretary of the Board of Control for India and in 1834 he went there as a Member of the Supreme Council. He was responsible for the codification of Indian criminal law. Even more momentous was his Minute on Indian Education, which argued (successfully) that this should be conducted in English and based on Western thought. It is easy to dismiss this as a piece of intolerable and ignorant patronage – Macaulay had no doubt that Europe was superior in every way to Asia – and yet it can be defended and it was certainly influential. The facts that Indian independence was eventually gained by men who had been educated in English schools and at English universities and the Inns of Court and that India is still, however uneasily, a parliamentary democracy, are the direct result of Macaulay's Minute on Indian Education. It is appropriate that the first and greatest Prime Minister of India, Jawarhal Nehru, should, like Macaulay, have been a product of Trinity College, Cambridge.

When Macaulay returned from India his interest in politics slackened, though he sat for Edinburgh and was Secretary of State for War from 1839–41. He published his *Collected Essays* in 1843 and the first volume of his *History* appeared in 1848. Edinburgh did in fact return him again in 1852 but, occupied with his *History*, he declined office. In 1857 he was created Baron Macaulay of Rothley.

The defects of Macaulay's *History* are obvious to any reader and this was true even in his own day. His political bias continually intrudes and his love of dramatic opposites renders many of his portraits as absurd as they are vivid. His optimism grates. He mocked the superstitions of the past but his own certainty of the transcendent virtues of the present was at least as uncritical as, for example, the faith in the efficacy of a saint's relics or the belief in witchcraft. It was characteristic of Macaulay that he was blind to the ravages of industrialism and the impoverishment of the human spirit that it might entail. But then it was also characteristic that he should perceive what might be hidden from more despondent spirits and be able to make a speech on 'the loveliness and intelligence of Leeds'.

The defects of his *History* are as nothing when compared with its positive qualities. It is intensely readable. The narrative is rapid, the prose vivid and the structure admirable. Macaulay has mastered a huge range of sources – there seems to have been hardly a pamphlet which he had not read and remembered. (His memory was astonishing; once, crossing the Irish Sea by night, he sat up on board and 'went through "Paradise Lost" in my head' and never enjoyed it more.) No doubt he was often led astray and, like many journalists, was inclined to ascribe too much importance to journalism; nevertheless much of the life of the *History* comes from the way he used this otherwise ephemeral literature, and this way was new.

He took a keen interest in social and economic history. His third chapter, in which he describes the condition in England in 1685, is not only a remarkable piece of writing but also an enduringly entertaining one; it is still the best survey of late seventeenth-century England that we possess.

His greatest virtue, however, was one that has often gone unnoticed, although Lord Dacre has drawn attention to it. No historian before him had understood the political process as Macaulay did and few have matched him since. He was perfectly suited to be the historian of a limited monarchy, where political power more and more resided in Parliament and where matters might be settled or altered by a debate in the House of Commons. He had been a Member of that Assembly himself; he knew how it worked and he had an imagination capable of throwing itself back a century and a half and realising the conflicts of that time. The ability to understand politics is a necessary quality of the historian, denied to many. It is unfortunate that he was unable to carry his *History* forward at least to the death of Queen Anne; one would give the work of many university departments for Macaulay's account of the Treaty of the Union and the great Parliamentary struggles of 1711–14. As it is, we have to content ourselves with the sketch given in his review article of Mahon's *History of the War of Succession in Spain*, written in 1833. This does, however, offer a reminder that Macaulay's party bias was not as consistent as sometimes assumed: 'It seems to us, then, that, on the great question which divided England during the last four years of the reign of Anne, the Tories were in the right, and the Whigs in the wrong.' That is an unequivocal judgement.

In fact, Macaulay's judgement was admirable whenever his passions and prejudices were not aroused. Nowhere is this better shown than in his review of Moore's *Life of Byron*. There is a certain priggishness but it is refreshingly free of cant.

Sir James Young Simpson

(1811–1870)

In 1870 the Prime Minister, Mr Gladstone, told the House of Commons: 'Sir James Simpson's death is a grievous loss to the nation; it is truly a national concern.' Westminster Abbey was proposed as his burial place, but his widow preferred the family grave in Warriston Churchyard, Edinburgh, where four of their children lay. All business in Edinburgh was suspended in the city: 'One road alone was crowded – it led but to the tomb.'

The nineteenth century was the heroic age of medical science. No country was more distinguished than Scotland, no city more than Edinburgh, and no man more than Simpson. An American doctor said on the occasion of his death: 'Prophet, philosopher, worker, and saint, they were gathered together in James Young Simpson.' Simpson himself liked to quote the words of the physician Menocrates to Philip of Macedon: 'It is your work to kill men; it is my work to save them,' and he said of Jenner, the discoverer of vaccination, that his 'lancet saved far more lives then the sword of Napoleon destroyed'. He had not only the highest view of his calling; he had also the lowest. The great researcher was not closeted in a laboratory; he was a working physician making his way through the stinking wynds and verminous closes of the Old Town of Edinburgh to care for the poorest of the sick.

Simpson was born in Bathgate. His father was a baker, the son of a peasant who practised the old rural superstition: when a murrain fell on his cattle, he buried a cow alive to frustrate the Devil. Simpson recorded in an antiquarian paper written in 1861 that 'another near relative of mine bought a farm not many years ago. Among his first acts after taking possession was the enclosing of a small triangular corner of one of the fields within a stone wall. The corner cut off – which remains to this day in the same state – was the "Goodman's Croft"'. The leap from superstition to science might be a long one, but it was made quickly.

His mother's family were of Huguenot stock, and Simpson's daughter, Eve Blantyre Simpson, who wrote a charming little biography of her father in 1896, full of delightful anecdote and the spirit of nineteenth-century Edinburgh, liked to think that 'from the Jervays' French extraction many traits in James Simpson's character are traceable'. This is a hazardous task, but portraits of Simpson have a square and angular French look.

Be that as it may, the family were poor. Simpson depended on the support and generosity of his father and then of his brothers for his education. He was a lad of pairts, but like many another such, his rise owed much to the self-denial and practical help and encouragement of less brilliant members of his family. Simpson went to Edinburgh University at the age of fourteen and began his medical studies two years later. How these records of the early maturing of our ancestors make us question the prolonged adolescence we impose today. Nor were his studies or reading narrow. He studied Greek and Latin and read Byron and Scott. Among the lecturers he attended was the famous Dr Knox, the anatomist and patron of Burke and Hare. He was a Member of the Royal College of Surgeons before he was out of his teens. By 1839 he was married and Professor of Midwifery, still very conscious of 'that frightful load of debt he owed his brothers' for his education and start in life.

It is for his work in obstetrics and his contribution to the alleviation of pain that Simpson is famous. Early in his student days he had been so sickened by the suffering he saw in an operating theatre than he had all but thrown up medicine and turned to law. The question of pain occupied him. In 1836, when house-surgeon at the Lying-In Hospital at Leith, he had asked: 'Cannot something be done to render the patient unconscious while under acute pain, without interfering with the free and healthy play of the natural functions?' He experimented with mesmerism, as others had, and of course he was not alone in exploring the question: medical pioneers never are. In 1846 ether was first tried in America, news which stimulated Simpson, who was quick to try it. (He always reminded his students that the search for a means of relieving pain had a long history, from the time when the Lord cast Adam into a deep sleep in order to remove his rib, and he paid tribute to Sir Humphry Davy's experiments with nitrous oxide.) Sulphuric ether, however, had certain inconveniences – 'its disagreeable and persistent smell, the occasional tendency to irritation of the bronchi during its first inspirations, and the large quantity of it required to be used (more especially in protracted cases of labour)'. He therefore cast round for something better, and, with his assistants Drs Keith and Duncan tried various narcotic drugs. A certain Mr Waldie from Linlithgow suggested 'perchloride of formyle', and on 14 November Simpson wrote to him from his house in Queen Street: 'I had the chloroform for several days in the house before trying it, as, after seeing it such a heavy unvolatile-like liquid, I despaired of it, and went on dreaming of others. The first night we took it Dr Duncan, Dr Keith and I all tried it simultaneously, and were all "under the table" in a minute or two.'

The breakthrough had been made. In a footnote to the same letter, Simpson, anticipating opposition, wrote, 'The true moral question is: "Is a practitioner justified by any principle of humanity in not using it?" I believe every operation without it is just a piece of the most deliberate and cold-blooded cruelty.'

That was his position, and he stuck to it. 'Is it not against nature to take away the pangs of labour?' an Irish lady asked. 'Is it not against nature unnatural for you to be have been carried over from Ireland in a steamboat against wind and tide?' Simpson answered. The fight was bitter, but Simpson was able gradually to show the effectiveness of his discovery. Full respectability was ensured when Queen Victoria in 1853 submitted to chloroform for the birth of Prince Leopold. 'Her majesty was greatly pleased with the effect, and she certainly never has had a better recovery,' one of her physicians wrote to Simpson. Incidentally the first child born under the drug, the daughter of one of his colleagues, was christened Anaesthesia. When she was seventeen she sent her photograph to Simpson who hung it over his desk.

Simpson achieved other improvements in obstetrics. He introduced acupressure (a new method of binding arteries), he contributed to the eradication of zymotic diseases, he foresaw X-rays in a paper in which he wrote: 'Possibly even by the concentration of electrical and other lights, we may render many parts of the body, if not the whole body, sufficient diaphanous for the inspection of the practised eye of the physician or surgeon.' He worked for hospital reform, being a keen supporter of cottage hospitals; but his main contribution to humanity was the elimination of pain during operations.

Honours were showered on him. Queen Victoria made him a baronet. He was made a foreign Associate of the Academy of Medicine in Paris, and the French Academy of Sciences awarded him a prize for 'most important benefits done to Humanity', but all his life he remained a hard-working doctor, known to all classes in Edinburgh for the quality of his care. He was not only a great man, but a good one.

David Livingstone
(1813–1873)

Explorers were nineteenth-century heroes, opening up what Conrad called 'the dark places of the earth'. Travelling with the Bible in one hand, and a compass in the other (with a breech-loading rifle slung across the back), they exemplified Western Man's sense of his civilising destiny. Those hostile to imperialism have found it easy to denigrate their achievement. At the simplest level it has been suggested that the concept of 'discovery' was often merely an expression of European arrogance: the lands discovered were already well known to their inhabitants. This is a futile argument: they were not known to the explorers, who therefore discovered them for themselves and their compatriots. More importantly, their relation to other lands was not known; they were, at best, indifferently mapped, and usually not mapped at all. The second criticism is directed at the explorers as 'exploiters': they opened up parts of the world to pillage; they destroyed native cultures which they did not trouble to understand; they displayed arrogance and insensitivity; their civilising mission was a fraud, and their assumption of superior moral standards intolerable. This is a curious argument, for it depends on the assumption that morality is relative, and there is no possibilty of any real moral superiority; yet of course the very act of criticism directed at the Victorian explorers is itself an expression of the critic's sense of his own moral superiority to them. If a sub-Marxist professor can claim, without any awareness of his own absurdity, to be morally superior to David Livingstone, then it follows that Livingstone can hardly be condemned if he felt similarly assured of his own moral superiority to Arab slave-traders.

Livingstone was a hero simply because he was a man of quite unusual courage, imagination, tenacity and faith; he was also, which is not rare among great men of action, a man of real sensitivity and depth of understanding. He was driven by a daemon, and the drive intensified as he aged. We can watch him lose all tentative doubt, even as his faith in the practical effects of his missionary work weakened. It has been said mockingly that he made no lasting converts to the Christian faith he carried into the heart of Africa, but, if he did not, then his successors did, as the enduring influence of the Church of Scotland in Malawi, Zimbabwe, Zambia and Tanzania shows. Moreover, he caught the imagination of his contemporaries; he opened up a knowledge of Africa previously hidden from Europeans, and, as I say, established the facts of relations between different parts of the Continent. Most important, he did more than any other individual to reveal the iniquities of the slave-trade practised by Arabs, assisted by African chiefs, for centuries.

He was born in Blantyre, Lanarkshire, where his father was a shopkeeper. At the age of ten, he was put to work in a cotton mill. He pursued a course of self-education, and at the age of twenty-three was admitted to Anderson's College, Glasgow, to train as a medical missionary. The following year he joined the London Missionary Society, and in 1841 was sent to South Africa. He saw the whole of the first half of his life as a preparation for the work God had entrusted to him.

His first journeys took him across the Kalahari desert. In 1849 he discovered Lake Ngami and two years later arrived at the Zambesi river. He had already married, in 1844, Mary Moffat, daughter of a Scots missionary: 'She is not romantic,' he wrote, 'but a matter-of-fact lady, a little, thick, black-haired girl, sturdy and all I want.' She would have to submit herself to the rigours of life with a man whose whole aim was directed towards difficult and dangerous tasks. (As to the danger, about the time of his marriage, his left arm was damaged by a lion, which 'shook me as a terrier does a rat'.)

Between 1852 and 1856 Livingstone made the journey which made him famous. Setting out with twenty-seven men of the Makololo tribe, he crossed the continent from North Bechuanaland to the Angolan coast at San Paolo de Loanda. His equipment would seem ridiculously inadequate to later travellers. 'To avoid the discouragement which would naturally be felt on meeting any obstacles if my companions were obliged to carry any heavy loads, I took only a few biscuits, a few pounds of tea and sugar and about twenty of coffee, which, as the Arabs find, though used without milk or sugar, is a most refreshing beverage after fatigue or exposure to the sun.' He would rely on three muskets and two rifles to supply them with meat. He took a spare set of clothes and some medicines, a compass, sextant and 'artificial horizon thermometer'. His books were a nautical almanac, Thomson's logarithm tables and the Bible. He also took 'a magic lantern, which we found of much use'. Fever, hostile chiefs, the threat of mutiny, all assailed him, but he made his destination in just under two years. Then, refusing a passage to England, he retraced his steps: he had promised to restore his Makololo men to their own country. Besides, he said: 'I feel that the work to which I set myself is only half accomplished.' Arrived back in the Makololo territory, he then proceeded, with new men, down the Zambesi. It was on this journey that he discovered the Victoria Falls.

Back in England, he published an account of his travels. They show his respect for African tribal life. He was now one of the most celebrated men of the age, on whom honours were showered. 'I cannot pretend to a single note of triumph,' he said. 'A man may boast when he is pulling off his armour, but I am just putting mine on.' He was accused of having abandoned his missionary service (and in fact resigned from the London Missionary Society in 1858) but defended himself by saying 'my views of what is missionary duty are not so contracted as those whose ideal is a dumpy sort of man with a Bible under his arm . . . I feel that I am not "my own".' He had, by God's help, 'got information which I hope will lead to more abundant blessing being bestowed on Africa than heretofore'. That was justification enough.

His second Zambesi expedition was a failure at first owing to quarrels with his companions. However, he discovered and explored Lake Nyasa and was then confronted with the horrors of the Waiyau slave raids. The extirpation of slavery became a motivating force. Livingstone was remarkably honest about the difficulties: the very Arab slave traders whom he opposed often treated him with kindness. When he fell ill after discovering Lake Banwuelu in 1868, it was a party of Arabs who nursed him back to health. He was aware, too, of the problem of confronting a culture with quite different standards of right and wrong. 'They think that rhyming over "God is great" etc., all sin is forgiven. A slave of Thani bin Suelim of Ujiji named Yahood boasted in my hearing of having with his colleagues killed one hundred people and burned nine villages – all for a single string of red beads which a Manyema man tried in vain to steal. I said to him, "You were sent to trade, not to murder". He replied, "We are sent to kill people, that is our work".'

That was on his third expedition when he set out to try to find the tributaries of the Nile. It was near disaster. He suffered constantly from fever and dysentery and took little heed of his health. He lost his stores and was attacked by hostile tribes. Only his faith and his sense of humour restrained him from despair. He was reported lost. Two relief expeditions were despatched. At Ujiji he was discovered by the journalist H. M. Stanley. The celebrated encounter, as recorded by

Stanley, need not be repeated. Stanley wanted to bring him home, but Livingstone refused to leave Africa. He would discover the source of the Nile or die; he was by now a man possessed. He could hardly stand; even sitting in a canoe was difficult. He reached Ilala on the shores of the Molilamo. 'Knocked up quite . . . and remain . . . recover . . . sent to buy milch goats. . . .' he noted in his last journal entry. When he died, his servants, with great courage and perseverance, dried his body and carried it, with his papers and instruments, more than a thousand miles to the coast. He was buried in Westminster Abbey, but his heart remained in Africa.

All the benefits of his work were indirect, except one: this was the example he set of courage, endurance and devotion. There is much to be said for an age which found its hero in Livingstone.

Queen Victoria
(1819–1901)

When George IV visited Edinburgh in August 1822, he was the first reigning monarch to be seen in Scotland since Charles II had led his army south to Worcester in 1651. (If you were a Jacobite, of course, you might count James VIII and III's brief participation in the '15 Rising.) There was much that was absurd in the King's visit, but it is nevertheless possible to date the modern monarchy from his decision to show himself to his subjects. It was George IV too, who made the first gesture of reconciliation to the exiled Stuarts, commissioning Canova to erect the great monument to Jacobus III, Carolus III and Henricus IX which may be found in St Peter's in Rome. But George was too old, too indolent, too selfish, too dissipated and too unpopular to do more than point the way that the monarchy was to travel in order to survive in the dawning age of democracy, and it was his niece, Queen Victoria, who reconciled the Scots to the Crown, and established the Royal Family in Scotland.

She was, of course, far more German than Scottish or English, for the Hanoverians had always chosen their brides from among the numerous royal or princely families of Germany; yet she gloried in her descent from James VI, proclaimed herself a Stuart, and wrote of Mary Stuart as 'poor Queen Mary', while her love for Scotland was sincere and exuberant.

She first visited Scotland in 1842, and found Edinburgh 'quite beautiful; totally unlike anything else I have seen; and what is even more, Albert, who has seen so much, says it is unlike anything *he* ever saw'. She found 'the people very friendly and kind', and that was to be her abiding opinion. 'The country and the people have a quite different character from England and the English,' she at once decided, and the next day 'tasted the oatmeal porridge, which I think very good, and also some of the "Finnan haddies".' On that first visit they travelled north to Perthshire, and at Scone signed 'a curious old book in which the last signatures are those of James I (of England) and Charles I'. They stayed at Taymouth Castle where Prince Albert shot his first stag, and where an old woman told the Queen that her people were delighted to see her in Scotland. Victoria was equally delighted to be there, all the more so because Albert kept finding points of comparison with the landscape of Thuringia and Switzerland. As they sailed south, she vowed that she would never forget her tour.

Naturally she came back, in 1844 and 1848, and naturally she and Albert decided they should have a house of their own in Scotland. One says naturally, because reading the Queen's journal and letters it seems the most natural and inevitable thing that they should so decide, but of course it was not. It was an unprecedented, and, as it turned out, revolutionary decision. When they leased the little estate of Balmoral in 1848, and then four years later, started to build a castle there (to Prince Albert's design), they were doing something more than establishing a holiday retreat for themselves.

Much has been written about Balmorality or rather against it. It has been argued that it imposed a false vision on Scotland, and a false vision of Scotland on the world. There is, of course, some truth in this. For all the Queen's real love for the Highlands and for the Highlanders, she could never really be part of Scottish life. There was always an element of comic opera make-believe about her sojourns at Balmoral. Balmoral helped to turn the Highlands into a sporting playground for the Victorian aristocracy and newly rich industrialists. The Highlands became a place where they came for a few weeks in the year to catch fish and shoot deer. With Queen Victoria at Balmoral, we are but a small step from the false romanticism which sees the Highlands as 'Brigadoon'. And so on.

Yet there is another side to the matter. We have only to ask what might have become of the Highlands in the nineteenth century without this development to realise that their condition would have been very much worse. The castles and shooting-lodges at least provided some employment and, in the modern phrase, injected some money into the local economy. Throughout the nineteenth century, agriculture declined even in the most fertile parts of Britain; it did so more thoroughly in the Highlands. But for the fashion Queen Victoria set, the depopulation of the north of Scotland would have been even worse.

The Queen's establishment at Balmoral did not set the tourist industry in motion; Sir Walter Scott had done that with 'The Lady of the Lake' and 'Waverley'. But it encouraged it. The Queen herself was a tireless and enthusiastic sightseer, and when she published

'Leaves from the Journal of our Life in the Highlands' in 1868, she invited her subjects to share her enjoyment of Scotland. They flocked north to do so. No tourist authority, had one existed then, could have wished for a better advertisement.

There was another consequence of the Queen's love for Scotland. Her eager association with the country and its history – she and Albert decked themselves in Royal Stuart tartan and she proclaimed herself a Jacobite – attached many Scots, who were hitherto indifferent to the Monarchy, to the Crown. In doing so she helped to cement the Union. Her evident love for Scotland and for her Scottish subjects contributed to the feeling which was already developing in the country that Scotland was a proud constituent part of the Empire. Scots were pleased to learn that the Queen was much happier at Balmoral than anywhere else. It confirmed them in their 'guid conceit' of themselves. They adopted the Queen as the honorary Scot she proclaimed herself to be. They were amused and pleased – where the English were offended – by her warm regard for John Brown, who had been the Prince's manservant and became hers. In Ireland the Crown remained remote, and foreign. Thanks to Queen Victoria the Scottish experience was quite different.

Sir Charles Tennant

(1823–1906)

Sir Charles Tennant was the very model of a Victorian entrepreneur. He revealed the daring that made Britain the greatest industrial and commercial power in the world; yet in the last twenty years of his life he made certain errors of judgement that may be regarded as examples of how Britain was to be surpassed by Germany. At the same time his political course, following that other noted entrepreneur, Joseph Chamberlain, into the campaign for Tariff Reform displayed a defensiveness characteristic of neither man in his prime, yet symptomatic of a new and feebler attitude to be found in British industrialists. Tennant is also an emblematic Scottish figure. While he did much to forge links between the City of London and manufacuring industry in Scotland and the north of England, he was one of the first, great West of Scotland industrialists to remove himself from his home base, set up as a country gentlemen and enter, as if by right, metropolitan society.

His daughter, Margot, who married the Liberal Prime Minister H. H. Asquith, liked to give the impression that Tennant (known to his family as 'the Bart') was a wholly self-made man. This was not quite accurate. The Tennants had been bonnet lairds in Ayrshire for generations. The Bart's great-grandfather, John Tennant of Glenconner, was a friend of Burns (a witness indeed at his wedding) and celebrated by him in the lines: 'My heart-warm love to guid auld Glen,/ The ace an' wale of honest men'. John's son, Charles, known as 'Wabster Charlie', started a bleachfield in Paisley, producing a solution of chloride of lime which was an effective bleaching agent. Later he established the St Rollox Chemical Works in Glasgow, where one of his partners was Charles Mackintosh FRS, the inventor of the waterproof. Wabster Charlie's son, John, expanded the business. (The famous 'Tennant's Stalk', the chimney which pierced the Glasgow skyline, dates from his time.) When he died in 1878, he left nearly £80000.

Long before then, however, his son Charles had surpassed and eclipsed him. John Tennant was a great Glasgow businessman; the Bart was an imperial figure. He was a man of rare qualities. 'My father', Margot wrote in her autobiography, 'was a man whose vitality, irritability, energy and impressionability amounted to genius.' He was small and neat in appearance, fond of solitude yet a loving father and warm friend, unfailingly generous to his family and acquaintances. He was charitable, both publicly and privately. Every begging letter, we are told, 'would receive a favourable response'. On the other hand, in 1879 the Tennant chemical works paid the average worker only £40 a year.

His great quality, however, was his daring. His education, at Ayr Academy, was completed by the age of fourteen. He then worked for some years in the office of a Liverpool merchant where, an unconfirmed story tells, he made his first fortune by cornering the market in cochineal. Thence he proceeded to London, where he founded the trading firm of Tennants, Knox & Co., which also acted as agent for Charles Tennant & Son. He borrowed boldly for investment purposes. In 1848 a venture in an Australian Land Company brought him a profit of £80000. Four years later, still not yet thirty, he bought Glen Estate in Peeblesshire and built a house there in the Scottish baronial style. This alarmed his father who asked him how much money he had. 'About £90000.' 'The devil you have,' was the surprised reply.

His great venture, however, was the purchase of the pyrite mines of Tharsis in Southern Spain. This was a logical enterprise, as it linked with the family's chemical interests. Pyrites, being some 48% sulphur, was of evident interest to alkali-makers. Its other components included copper and gold. In 1862 the Tharsis Copper and Sulphur Company was incorporated in Edinburgh. The Bart was now deeply involved in the technology of metallurgy. He bought gold mines at Mysore in India. The investment stumbled at first. Some shareholders grew disgruntled. The Bart showed his mastery of chairmanship by offering to purchase their shares at par value. Most were reassured. A few sold and lived to regret it; between 1896 and 1905 the dividend paid on shares in the Mysore Gold Mining Company never fell below 100%.

Expansion and diversification proceeded. A new process for extracting gold from pyrites was patented by three of his employees. One of Tennant's companies bought the patent and was able to charge a royalty on its use. Tharsis became a great copper company. In an attempt to use the quantities of iron also contained in pyrites, the Bart formed the Steel Company of Scotland. This enterprise was initially less successful but eventually, working Scottish pig iron instead, it contributed to the shipbuilding industry on the Clyde. The Bart also formed the British company, Nobel's Explosives Ltd, with headquarters in Glasgow to exploit Nobel's patents.

The first sixty years of his life saw a record of unbroken success. Then, in 1884, his health broke, but he recovered. (He later married for a second time in 1898 and fathered four more children, the last when he was eighty-one. He had sixteen children altogether.) The Depression of the 1880s brought difficulties too. Most important, Tennants retained faith in the Leblanc process for alkali manufacture, despite the appearance of the new, technically superior Solvay method. This would eventually lead to the Germans outstripping British chemical firms. Then Tennant's gold patents were challenged in the courts and declared void in 1896. The same year a decision was made not to open a new plant in Germany, which was mistaken. Meanwhile the Scottish Steel Company had run into trouble and had to be restructured. Probably the Bart was not quite the man he had been, which is hardly surprising. Nevertheless, his own fortune was far too great, too widely spread and too well-founded to be severely shaken. When he died in 1906 his personal estate in Great Britain alone was valued at more than £3 million.

He lavished his wealth on his beloved Glen and on his collection of paintings, rare books and other works of art. His collection included Gainsboroughs, Raeburns, Turners, Constables and Cotmans. There is a touching story in Margot Asquith's autobiography of the old man going round his London house by night, viewing his paintings lovingly by candlelight. He had political interests too. He represented Peebles and Selkirk as a Liberal; it was Gladstone who made him a baronet. He held with Gladstone when the Liberals broke up over Irish Home Rule but, in the next decade, Harcourt's introduction of Death Duties began his disillusionment with the party. He lifted his own family from the world of provincial business to the heart of political and social life. His sons were sent to Eton, his daughters were glittering members of the social group known as the Souls. His eldest son was made Lord Glenconner. He served as Lord High Commissioner to the General Assembly of the Church of Scotland and gave Dryburgh Abbey to the nation. One of his descendants is the novelist Emma Tennant. One of the Bart's daughters by his second marriage married the Tory politician Walter Elliot. She became one of the first Life Peers, as Baroness Elliot of Harwood, in 1958. She must be one of the few people alive in 1987 whose father was born in the reign of George IV.

William Thomson, Lord Kelvin
(1824–1907)

In 1896 the University of Glasgow staged a celebratory exhibition to honour the jubilee of its Professor of Mathematics and Natural Philosophy. The library was filled with a display of his inventions. Two thousand guests, including representatives of the principal learned societies of the world, attended. A telegram of congratulations was despatched to him from the library. Travelling by way of Newfoundland and New York to the coast of California and back across the Atlantic, it returned to him in seven and a half minutes. It was the great man himself who had invented the submarine cable; this telegram was lively proof of the practicality of his genius.

The recipient of the telegram was William Thomson, who had been knighted in 1866 and created Lord Kelvin of Largs in 1892. Only Clerk Maxwell was his rival as the greatest natural scientist of the great Victorian Age of British Science. Strictly speaking, Kelvin was an Ulsterman but he was brought to Glasgow at the age of eight, when his father was appointed to the Chair of Mathematics at Glasgow, and he always regarded himself as a Scot. This was fair enough for, like so many Ulster families, the Thomsons had Scottish roots.

His mathematical genius manifested itself early, as is normal. He matriculated at Glasgow when he was ten. At the age of sixteen he won the University Medal for an essay *On the Figure of the Earth*. (Notes on the manuscript reveal that he still thought it worth pondering over even in the year of his death.) The following year he proceeded to Cambridge, where he found time to row for his college and to win a sculling competition. All his life Kelvin loved water and the sea. Even in old age he kept a yacht in the bay off Largs.

After work in Paris with Professor Regnault, who was researching the thermal properties of steam, Kelvin was appointed to his

Chair at Glasgow at the age of twenty-two. He retained it till 1899, more than once refusing offers of a Chair at Cambridge. From now on he specialised in Physics. His astonishingly acute and fertile mind not only evolved important physical laws but also threw out suggestions on which were later based many of the profoundest researches of other physicists.

His work in pure theory would by itself ensure his reputation. In two lectures to the Royal Society of Edinburgh, in 1851 and 1854, he expounded the two laws of thermodynamics, those of equivalence and transformation or conservation of energy. The latter states that the earth retains the heat it receives from the sun, transforming it into other forms of energy. He demonstrated this with examples from all the branches of physics – mechanics, heat, magnetism and electrostatics.

Kelvin, however, was not only a pure scientist. He believed that 'the life and soul of science is its practical application' and he was ready to take an active part in this. He not only invented the submarine cable and the mirror galvanometer, which overcame the difficulty experienced hitherto by the long-distance telegraph (namely, the longer the cable, the slower the transmission), but he himself superintended the laying of the first Atlantic cable. While doing this he took the opportunity to improve the ships' compass.

Realising that the practical application of science depended on the quality of the instruments available, he devoted much of his life to the invention of instruments. The first electric meter was his work. (His was the first house in Britain to be lit by electric light). He involved himself in business too. Kelvin may indeed be seen as a precursor of the Science Parks that are found in modern universities. He went into partnership with James White, a maker of optical instruments, and the firm of Kelvin and White manufactured and marketed instruments and devices for electrical and optical measuring, telegraph transmitting and navigational aids. In the 1890s the firm employed 200 skilled technicians. Kelvin, according to Professor Sydney Checkland, thus 'presided over the largest and most complete electrical laboratory in Britain'.

He also took out patents in connection with his submarine cables and formed another company to handle this business. In 1879 the telegraph patents earned him £5500, at least five times his salary as a professor. None of this prevented a stream of theoretical work. During his life he wrote more than 300 scientific papers.

One sees in Kelvin a peculiarly Scottish practicality and it is impossible not to speculate on how much happier the industrial history of twentieth-century Britain might have been had science not subsequently experienced an unhappy divorce between its pure and applied branches, something which would have made no sense to him. It may be that the increasing specialisation forced on Scottish universities, in order to have them conform to the English model of Oxford and Cambridge, contributed to this divorce by weakening the links between science, philosophy and the humanities. The consequences of this specialisation have been analysed in two masterly books by Dr George Davie: *The Democratic Intellect* and *The Crisis of the Democratic Intellect*. Kelvin himself believed that he had derived benefit from his studies of the Classics. At the age of twelve he had won a prize for his translation of Lucian's *Dialogue of the Gods*.

Kelvin seems to have been attractive, kindly and unaffected by his fame. According to the German physicist, von Helmholtz, 'he far exceeds all the great men of science with whom I have made personal acquaintance in intelligence, lucidity and nobility of thought, so that sometimes I felt quite wooden beside him.' Kelvin married twice. Both marriages were happy, though childless. His second wife, whom he met and married in Madeira, was Frances Blandy, a member of one of the families which dominated the trade in Madeira wine.

Unlike some Victorian men of science, Kelvin's discoveries fortified, rather than shook, his religious faith. He declared that he was 'a great believer in design' and his researches revealed design in the management of the physical world. Although at his home in Largs he attended the Free Kirk, he was buried in Westminster Abbey, next to Sir Isaac Newton.

Sir Robert Pullar
(1828–1912)

The Industrial Revolution has left deep scars on Scotland, and the scars are both physical and moral. Perhaps it is time we saw it in perspective and realised that no country, and no sort of society, has achieved industrialisation without much suffering. The hideous slums of Central Scotland and the stunted and deprived lives of early factory workers are foul to contemplate, but they can be matched in New York or Chicago and hardly approach the horrors perpetrated in the Soviet Union, where Stalin showed us that planned industrialisation can surpass the unplanned in brutality and that the commissar can outdo the capitalist in ruthlessness.

From the start of the Industrial Revolution in Scotland there were employers who were aware of the cost of the process which made them rich. Robert Owen, a visionary, had tried to correct it by turning his factory towns into model societies; others were more empirical, and perhaps for that reason more successful. One such was Sir Robert Pullar.

He belonged to the second generation of industrialists. His father, John Pullar, had started a small dyeing business in Perth in 1824, which, despite difficulties over pollution, was employing more than twenty people within a few years. Robert Pullar was apprenticed to his father in 1841 at the age of thirteen. He was, therefore, as he always claimed, 'a working dyer'. He grew up in the worst decade of the century, 'the Hungry Forties'. The experience made him a Free-Trade Liberal, and convinced him of an employer's moral duty towards his workforce.

The coming of the railway to Perth at the end of the decade opened great opportunities. The firm of John Pullar & Son was founded in 1848, and thereafter expansion was rapid. They were forward-looking and enterprising, sending samples of their work to the Great Exhibition in 1851 for instance, and being rewarded with the title 'Dyers to the Queen' the following year. Robert Pullar was exploring the possibilities of synthetic dyes by the middle of the fifties. He employed chemists to do research, and in 1865 created a modern factory for his 500 workers. They formed a German connection – Robert's younger brother marrying the daughter of

Germany's leading dyer – and Robert was ready to send workers to France and Germany to master new skills. By the end of the century Pullar's was a huge firm. They employed 2400 workers themselves, and had 4000 agencies for their dry-cleaning and dyeing.

Care for their workers was paramount. As early as 1872 the working week had been reduced to fifty-one hours. Staff were soon given annual holidays with pay. Their health was cared for. All the managers had risen from the shop floor, and Robert Pullar could boast that they had never had a strike. As time passed his paternal care extended further. He provided his workers with electrically lit houses, savings banks, skating rinks, bowling greens, allotments, bands – free entertainment which he hoped would keep them out of the pubs, for he was a keen Baptist and temperance advocate – pensions, and, most important perhaps, security of employment; he tried to avoid lay-offs in poor times and refused to cut wages as was then normal. It all sounds rather like a modern Japanese factory, or perhaps like Fiat in Italy. Reading of Pullar and Pullar's of Perth one wonders that British industry did not follow his direction.

He was a public man too. He touched on national politics, being a friend of Gladstone and Campbell-Bannerman, and was indeed elected Member of Parliament for Perth at the age of seventy-nine, making him perhaps 'the oldest new member in history'. But his main efforts were directed towards his own city of Perth. Here his generosity was remarkable. He built an opera house, provided different parts of the city with public halls, spent £8500 on a public wash-house, caused a free library to be built (and probably paid for most of the cost), paid for hospitals, soup kitchens for the unemployed, gave money to education and numerous charitable societies. He was rewarded with the Freedom of the City and was known as 'Perth's Prince of Industry'.

The philosophers of the Scottish Enlightenment had stressed the power of benevolence as a motivating force in human affairs. Few have exemplified this so greatly as Sir Robert Pullar (he was knighted at Windsor Castle in 1895). It is clear that his moral code and religious beliefs were at the heart of his philanthropy, but one can also see at this distance what an advantage it might be to have a business actually owned by the man who ran it, with no responsibility to shareholders other than his immediate family, and so no calls for 'rationalisation' in time of difficulty. One can see too the advantage to be found in such a business having a strong local identity. Pullar's was of Perth, and Pullar's was Perth. The loss of autonomy experienced by businesses in the twentieth century has destroyed all this. If Pullar's had been part of a conglomerate, it is inconceivable that Perth could have benefited from the firm as it did from Sir Robert Pullar. Something valuable was lost when paternalism came under attack.

James Clerk Maxwell
(1831–1879)

James Clerk Maxwell is to Scottish scientists as David Hume to philosophers and Sir Walter Scott to novelists: *facile princeps*. The two comparisons are useful, for they make it at once apparent that he is closer to Hume than to Scott. The application of science affects us all and there is no one living today whose life has not been influenced by Maxwell's work; yet he is remote from common experience as Hume is remote and Scott is not. Pure science is as abstruse as philosophy, as difficult for the layman to make anything of. We have to take so much for granted; we are indeed unable even to appreciate the beauty of the mind which is at work. Consequently, Scott is a household name, for literature can speak directly to a wide range of humankind, while Hume and Maxwell are scarcely known beyond the doors of Faculty departments.

We rely on the authority of experts to let us appreciate Maxwell's work. It is accepted by his fellow scientists that he ranks with Newton and Einstein, and Einstein himself on the occasion of Maxwell's centenary called the change in the conception of physics which resulted from Maxwell's research 'the most profound and the most fruitful that physics had experienced since the time of Newton'.

He was born in Edinburgh where his father practised as a lawyer, and attended the Edinburgh Academy (where he published his first scientific paper) and Edinburgh University; but the family also owned the estate of Glenlair in Dumfriesshire, and he spent much of his youth there, delighting in country life and pursuits. He was always a country laird as well as a scholar.

From Edinburgh (where he published two more scientific papers) he proceeded to Trinity College, Cambridge, Newton's college, which in the twentieth century has produced more Nobel Prize winners than any other seat of learning. His tutor there, by name of Hopkins, famous as a mathematical coach, pronounced him 'the most extraordinary man he had met with in the whole of his experience': this was not a bad testimonial since Hopkins had also taught Lord Kelvin. 'It seemed impossible,' he added, 'for him to think wrongly on any physical subject', though – perhaps Hopkins felt he must maintain his own critical credit – 'in analysis he was far more deficient'.

He was offered a Fellowship at Trinity, but declined because he wished to live in Scotland. In 1858 he was appointed Professor of Natural Philosophy at Marischal College, Aberdeen. He married the Principal's daughter, which might be thought likely to secure his position; yet when in 1860 the two colleges of Marischal and King's were amalgamated to form the University of Aberdeen, Maxwell found himself out of a job. Few, even among university selection committees, can have made such a blunder. He was immediately appointed Professor at King's College, London. In the following year he was elected to the Royal Society, but in 1865 resigned his chair in order to return to Glenlair and pursue his researches there, free of the burden of teaching. In 1871, however, he was lured back to Cambridge by the offer of the new Cavendish Professorship there.

In 1873 he published his most important work: 'A Treatise on Electricity and Magnetism'. This showed how Faraday's physical ideas might be converted into mathematical laws. He concluded that he could 'scarcely avoid the inference that light consists in the transverse undulations of the same medium which is the cause of electric and magnetic phenomena'. He suggested that electro-magnetic waves could be generated in a laboratory. Eight years after his death the German physicist Hertz demonstrated that this could indeed be done. The development of radio thus had its origins in Maxwell's publication.

His field equations which were themselves based on Faraday's observations of the electric and magnetic lines of force, paved the way for Einstein's Theory of Relativity, which established the equivalence of mass and energy. It was also Maxwell's description of electromagnetic radiation which eventually led to the development, as a result of the work of Max Planck, of what is called the 'Quantum Hypothesis'. This is the theory that radiant-heat energy is given out only in finite amounts which are called quanta. Maxwell's work thus played a central role in the twentieth-century development of the theory of the structure of atoms and molecules.

He was not restricted to his work in the field of electro-magnetic theory. He published papers on the viscosity of gases; he demonstrated colour photography, rather charmingly, by demonstrating a photograph of tartan ribbon to the Royal Institution of Great Britain as early as 1861. His hypothetical intelligent being known as 'Maxwell's demon' was a stage in the development of information theory, and his analysis of speed governors is regarded as a foundation of cybernetics. More immediately remarkable to the lay mind, or perhaps a clearer testimony of his genius, is the work he did on the rings surrounding the planet Saturn. By pure mathematical speculation he established to his own satisfaction that these consisted of masses of matter which were not mutually coherent; he was proved right more than a hundred years later when the first Voyager space probe reached Saturn.

Andrew Carnegie
(1835–1919)

Andrew Carnegie, aged seventeen, wrote to his uncle from the Pittsburgh Telegraph Office: 'Although I sometimes think I would like to be back in Dunfermline, I am sure it is far better for me that I came here. If I had been in Dunfermline working at the loom it is very likely I would have been a poor weaver all my days, but here I can surely do something better than that, if I don't it will be my own fault for anyone can get along in this country.' Forty-nine years later he retired from business, selling his company to John P. Morgan's United States Steel Corporation for $500 million.

Carnegie was perhaps the supreme example of the Protestant work ethic; he was the poor boy who made good and did good. He acquired enormous wealth and dispensed it widely; he declared in 'The Gospel of Wealth' that it was the duty of a rich man to distribute his surplus wealth for the general welfare'. At the same time he had been a tough and ruthless boss; a characteristic figure of the great age of what has been called 'robber-capitalism'; during the 1892 Depression armed police bloodily suppressed a strike in his Homestead mills.

He left Scotland as a boy, worked first in a cotton factory, then as an engine tender, and then as a telegraph operator and messenger. From 1853–65 he was employed by the Pennsylvania Railroad Company; he became General Manager and introduced sleeping cars. In 1864 he bought Storey Farm, in Oil Creek, Pennsylvania, and, as the name suggests, struck oil there. He went into the iron industry, and then steel, forming the Keystone Bridge Company in 1873. By 1888 he owned an extensive plant served by its own tributary coal and iron fields, by a private railway more than 400 miles long, and by its own fleet of lake steamships. He was fortunate, of course, that his career coincided with the great expansion of

American industry in the decades after the Civil War; on the other hand there were numerous entrepreneurs who failed in the same period. Carnegie was exceptional in his acumen and devotion to industry; he was an embodiment of the principle of hard work.

He was exceptional also in the use he made of his wealth. Other millionaires might be philanthropists; none on Carnegie's scale, and none, it is safe to say, with such a degree of principled commitment. Moreover, if he could be a tough and unscrupulous employer, he was also a pioneer in the establishment of pension funds for his workers.

The list of his benefactions is extraordinary. He believed, with an almost religious faith, in the value of education. Hadn't he proved it in his own life? He left a monument in the Free Library movement. In all he built and endowed more than 2500 libraries in the USA, Scotland, England and Canada. He also set up the Carnegie Foundation for the Advancement of Teaching which provided pensions for college lecturers. He funded the Negro College in Tuskegee, Alabama, which had been set up by Booker T. Washington. In 1903 he established the Temple of Peace at The Hague, and in 1911 the Carnegie Corporation of New York which was dedicated to 'the advancement of civilisation'. The Carnegie Foundation was to be the model for subsequent American grant-giving bodies such as the Rockefeller, Ford and Mellon Foundations. It is estimated that Carnegie gave more than £70 000 000 directly and indirectly. This was benefaction on an unprecedented scale.

He retained a love for Scotland and for his native town of Dunfermline. In 1901 he bought Skibo Castle in Sutherland as the home for his retirement. Two years later he informed the Liberal politician and biographer of Gladstone, John Morley, of 'the greatest event in my life. I am Laird of Pittencrieff, the biggest of all titles to me. King Edward not in it! It's part of the Abbey and Palace ruins at Dunfermline. The Glen, King Malcolm's Tower, St Margaret's Shrine, all mine! Ask Mr Shaw – he'll explain my transports. He feels it, every Dunfermline child must feel it'. Characteristically he had no thought of keeping it to himself. 'I'm going to make it a public park and present it to Dunfermline . . . It's the most sacred spot to me on earth.' He employed Patrick Geddes to lay out the park.

Those who talk of the iniquities of capitalism find Carnegie a stumbling-block. His benevolence was in no sense what is called conscience-money. He believed in the civilising influence of wealth. Money in his hands could be creative. He was the opposite to the gold-hoarding miser of legend; money was a fructifying influence, something benign. He himself had been a poor boy who had become rich by his own efforts and the exercise of his talents; he would employ what he had gained to make the lives of other poor people richer.

Sir James Murray

(1837–1915)

The little village of Denholm, half a dozen miles from Hawick, is the birthplace of two of Scotland's greatest scholars: John Leyden and James Murray. Both were exceptional linguists; Murray used to teach himself a new language by studying translations of the Bible. He was the son of a tailor and was educated locally at Minto School but was apparently too poor to proceed to university. Inevitably he became a schoolteacher himself. At the age of twenty he was headmaster of Hawick Union School. His passion for language had already evinced itself. When the Hungarian patriot Kossuth was given a civic reception on a visit to Hawick, the High Street was decorated with a banner inscribed in Magyar: 'Jojjon-el a' te orszagod', meaning 'Thy kingdom come'. It is unlikely that any small town in Scotland could now produce a local citizen who knows the Lord's Prayer in Magyar.

Murray removed to London to work in a bank but three years later was teaching again at Mill Hill School which had been founded as a Dissenting Academy as a rival to the great Anglican public schools. There he became a member of the Philological Society and began editing texts for the Early English Texts Society. His attitude to language was modern. Partly because he had been brought up speaking the broad Scots of the Borders, he had no time for notions of the correctness of some standard English. To him, a philologist's job was to observe and record how words were actually used. Dialects could not be classed as 'incorrect' speech; they were survivals of other and earlier forms of languages. He laid emphasis on the importance of sound and attended lectures given by Alexander Melville Bell, who had invented a system that he called Visible Speech. At the same time Murray gave lessons in electricity to Bell's son, Alexander Graham, who was later to invent the telephone.

In 1873 Murray published *The Dialect of the Southern Counties of Scotland*. In 1879 he was appointed editor of the Philological Society's proposed *Dictionary of the English Language*. This had in fact been under way for some twenty years. It was originally to be published by Harper in New York and Macmillan in London. The publishers thought of a book of some 2000 pages; the Philological Society imagined it might run to 6000. The publishers' feet cooled.

The Delegates of the Oxford University Press took over the project. The result was the *Oxford English Dictionary*. It was to occupy the rest of Murray's life, though he had reached only the letter T when he died. The *OED* may be compared to a medieval cathedral, always in the making and never assuming a final form; but its architect was not anonymous. This monument to philological and historical scholarship is also Murray's memorial.

He began the project in his garden at Mill Hill, where he was still teaching. He set up an iron shed there which he called the Scriptorium. He lined it with pigeonholes for word-slips. This was the idea of the project's first editor, Herbert Coleridge. Coleridge had thought that fifty-four pigeonholes might suffice; Murray soon had a thousand. He received two tons of paper slips, the fruit of the work of the past two decades. They were chaotic and largely useless. Organisation had been slapdash; the slips came from all over the place. Some of *Pa* was discovered in a stable in County Cavan, but most of the slips had been used to light fires.

In effect Murray had to start all over again. He sought volunteers wherever English was spoken. His children were conscripted as slip-sorters. That was how they earned their pocket-money. (Eventually he had eleven children, mostly with Anglo-Saxon names though the youngest was called Jowett, as a tribute both to the Master of Balliol and, humorously, to the Patriarch.) Murray himself was responsible for the definitions, for indicating pronunciation (by a system still employed by the Supplements to the *OED*) and for choosing the historical citations which help to display how words are actually used.

He was scientific in his approach: a dictionary recorded words as they were used and moral judgements did not apply. (The Delegates of the Press did not agree and so swear-words and words with unpleasant meanings or connotations were excluded.) Murray was so admirable that it is pleasant to note that he was not entirely consistent: 'Browning', he observed, 'continually used words without regard to their proper meaning. He has added greatly to the difficulties of the Dictionary' but Browning's usages could become part of the words' meaning.

The first part of the Dictionary was published in 1884, only five years after Murray's appointment. He removed to Oxford to be near the Press. Devoted though he was to his work, it did not occupy him exclusively. On seaside holidays with his children he would teach them about marine biology and would construct models of Grendel (the monster in *Beowulf*) out of sand.

He had not attended university, though he had taken an external degree at London. Doctorates descended on him, however, as his work proceeded. When Edinburgh awarded him one, he was so pleased that he wore his Doctor's Cap at meals. He was knighted in 1908 and was anxious lest tradesmen respond by raising their prices. He was recognised as a great man and besieged by would-be biographers. He would have none of it and replied, 'I am a nobody – if you have anything to say about the Dictionary, there it is at your will – but treat me as a solar myth, or an echo, or an irrational quantity, or ignore me altogether.'

Fortunately, some sixty years after his death, his grand-daughter, K. M. E. Murray, disregarded this wish and wrote an admirable biography, *Caught in a Web of Words: James A. H. Murray and the Oxford English Dictionary*. Despite the title, Murray was no fly caught in the web; he was rather the spider that spun it, a great man who brought honour to his age and his country.

Alexander Graham Bell
(1847–1922)

If necessity is the mother of invention, then Scotland may claim to be its midwife. Actually, no necessity dictated Alexander Graham Bell's career as an inventor; habit and curiosity seem to have been the motivating forces. He is an interesting, if not so very uncommon (see Galton's *Hereditary Genius*), example of inherited talent. His father Alexander Melville Bell taught elocution in Edinburgh, and invented what he called 'visible speech', a system of teaching lip-reading to deaf-mutes.

Graham Bell was born and brought up in Edinburgh, where he attended the Royal High School and the University. He proceeded to further study in London and at Würzburg in Germany, where he obtained a Ph.D. Doubt was later to be cast on Bell's achievements, so it is as well to stress that, though neither a trained electrician nor physicist, his academic attainments were high.

He emigrated to America as a young man, apparently because he had some weakness of the lungs, thought it seems unlikely that the eastern seaboard of the United States offered a healthier climate than the east coast of Scotland for those threatened by tuberculosis. He became Professor of Vocal Physiology and Elocution at Boston, where he continued his father's work. There was an urgent personal reason: he had fallen in love with a deaf girl (whom he later married) and was trying to construct a machine which would enable the deaf to hear. The girl, whose name was Mabel Hubbard, persuaded him however that lip-reading was more practicable than any machine.

However, Bell's researches had put him on an interesting track. 'If I could make a current of electricity vary in intensity precisely as the air varies in density,' he wrote, 'during the production of sound, I should be able to transmit speech telegraphically'. Progress seemed slow and uncertain, and he consulted Professor Joseph Henry, the

Secretary of the Smithsonian Institute in Washington; he explained to him his conception of undulating current, how he had studied the working of the ear (examining that of a dead man, which was not, of course, actually working), and how he had obtained sound response from an empty coil. Henry, Graham Bell wrote to his parents, 'said that he thought it "the germ of a great invention" . . . I said I recognised the fact that there were mechanical difficulties. . . I added that I felt I had not the electrical knowledge necessary to overcome the difficulties. His laconic answer was "Get it".' Much encouraged by this response he proceeded to do just that.

There were other scientists working in the same field, and when Bell filed his patent for an improvement in telegraphy in February 1876 he was just a couple of hours before one of his rivals; another, not far behind, was Edison, and so close was the competition that eventually Bell had to defend his right to the invention in numerous law-suits, all of which he won.

He conducted his experiments with one assistant, by the name of Watson, in Boston. On 10 March 1876, less than a month after he had filed his application for a patent, Watson was in the basement with the receiving instrument against his ear; he heard clearly the sentence, 'Mr Watson, come here, please; I want you.' These were the first words to be spoken over the telephone, which has been summoning people ever since.

He exhibited his apparatus at the Centennial Exposition that year in Philadelphia. (It was celebrating the Declaration of Independence.) There he held a conversation on the machine with the Emperor of Brazil. Bell recited Hamlet's soliloquy, 'To be or not to be.' The words may have been wasted on the Emperor, but their effect was clear and astonishing enough.

Bell left the exploitation of his invention to his partners in the company he had formed, and settled down in a country house in Nova Scotia, where he amused himself by experiments, few of which were very successful. However, he did also invent a photophone and a graphophone, which was rather like Edison's more successful gramophone. He dabbled in aeronautics, invented a universal language, World English (a forerunner of Basic English), set himself to improve fertility in sheep, and tried to teach animals to speak. This last venture was not a success. Little has been heard either (to my knowledge at least) of his apparatus for distilling the moisture from the breath, which would, he thought, be useful to those travelling through deserts.

But he had no doubt about the merits of his principal invention. 'The great advantage it possesses over other electrical apparatus,' he told investors in his British company, 'is that it requires no skill to operate.' This is undeniable, but more remarkably, Bell saw the commercial utility of his invention. He saw that cables of telephonic wires might be 'laid underground or suspended overhead communicating by branch wires with private dwellings', and that this could have more than a local range, so that 'a man in one part of the country may communicate by word of mouth with another in a distant place'. The ease with which we now dial directly from continent to continent would probably not have surprised this remarkable visionary.

His invention changed the world. Personally, he didn't think much of it, being accustomed to stuff his own telephone bell with paper. 'I never use the beast,' he once said. Millions, cursing the blessing he bestowed on them, must agree with his description.

Archibald Primrose, 5th Earl of Rosebery
(1847–1929)

When Rosebery came to write of Napoleon, he chose to deal with his 'Last Phase', the exile on St Helena. That was characteristic. Although Rosebery had fulfilled his three youthful ambitions, to marry an heiress, win the Derby and become Prime Minister, his attitude to success had never been whole-hearted. Despite all the advantages of birth, great wealth, high intelligence, good looks, charm and oratorical skills, his Premiership lasted only eighteen months and ended in confusion and dismay. He never again held office after his resignation at the age of forty-seven.

There has always been something mysterious about Rosebery. It was partly a matter of temperament; no one could ever be sure just what he wanted, which way he would move. In 1897 it was revealed that one of his Eton schoolmasters, the poet William Johnson Cory, had said of him: 'He is one of those who like the palm without the dust.' Johnson (as he was then known) suggested that the boy was unwilling to work hard enough for success. That may have been as untrue of the boy as of the grown man, but the phrase also implies a dislike for struggle. There was in Rosebery a fastidiousness which caused him to recoil from the murkier side of politics. He had high principles and clear ideas. He would be taken on his own terms or not at all. As Foreign Secretary in Gladstone's last Government, for instance, he demanded to be free from interference from either the Prime Minister or the Cabinet.

The Primrose family fortunes had originated in the seventeenth century with Sir Archibald Primrose, who had fought alongside Montrose and was taken prisoner at Philiphaugh. He survived till the Reformation and then flourished. Bishop Burnet reported that 'he thought that the chief thing that a great man ought to do was to raise his family and his kindred, who naturally stick to him; for he had seen so much of the world that he did not depend much on friends, and so took no care in making any.' He contrived to hand down to his descendants the estate of Dalmeny on the Firth of Forth and other properties in the Lothians. His son became the first Earl in 1703. The Roseberys were Scottish nobility of the second class but the 4th Earl raised their consequence by marrying Lady Wilhemina Stanhope.

She was a member of one of the great Whig families and a connection of William Pitt. This gave their son entry to the most exclusive political circle. He himself married Hannah Rothschild of the great banking family. It was a happy marriage. He mocked her and her relations ('To your tents, O Israel,' he would say as he wished them good-night) but she understood and soothed his difficult and nervous temperament. She was also probably the greatest heiress of the age. Rosebery would inherit the Rothschild palace of Mentmore. Before his marriage his gross annual income was about £30000; after it about £140000. It may be recalled that some forty years earlier, the Radical Earl of Durham had said 'a man can jog along on £40000 a year'. After his marriage, Rosebery jogged easily.

For a young man entering politics in the early 1870s, the choice lay between attachment to Gladstone or to Disraeli. The Whigs and Radicals were still in the process of coalescing into the Liberal Party of which Gladstone, once a Tory, was now leader. Rosebery's family connections made him a Whig and he responded also to Gladstone's high seriousness. On the other hand, Disraeli could not fail to appeal to a young man of Rosebery's sensitivity, literary interests and imagination. He had first met Disraeli when he was eighteen and had been enchanted by him. He continued to collect information about him throughout his life but he refused an invitation from the Trustees of Disraeli's estate to write his biography, despite being offered £20000 to do so. In one respect he was better suited to Disraeli and the Conservative Party than to Gladstone and the Liberals; he was struck by the glamour of the British Empire and all his life believed in the imperial mission. Nevertheless, though it is possible to argue that his political career would have been happier had he joined the other party, all his connections drew him to Gladstone. Also, he had a romantic concept of the radical aristocrat championing the cause of the poor and the oppressed. Finally Scotland was Whig, Liberal and Radical, and Rosebery was always a Scottish patriot. As early as 1880 he was urging that the office of Secretary of State for Scotland be revived. Indeed the Scottish Office today may be seen as the result of Rosebery's prolonged advocacy of the need to have a separate department of government for Scotland.

In 1879, however, he had stood by Gladstone's side during the Midlothian campaign, acting indeed as Gladstone's host. It had a profound and lasting effect on him. He referred to it as 'a chivalrous adventure'. J. M. Barrie wrote that 'during the first Midlothian campaign Mr Gladstone and Lord Rosebery were the father and son of the Scottish people. Lord Rosebery rode into fame on the top of that wave, and has kept his place in the hearts of the people, and in oleographs on their walls, ever since.'

Six years later, in 1886, he became Foreign Secretary. He was not yet forty. No-one, except Gladstone, had a higher reputation in Scotland and he was clearly the coming man of the Liberal Party. That year the Party split over the Irish Home Rule Bill. Most of the old Whig families opposed it. Rosebery remained loyal. He had few illusions about it. He doubted whether Home Rule would cure Ireland's ills but he considered it was the only alternative to eventual separation and should therefore be attempted. That Government lasted only a few months but Rosebery was Foreign Secretary again when Gladstone returned to office in 1892. Two years later, when the Old Man was at last persuaded to retire, Rosebery became Prime Minister after a bitter quarrel (which he found distasteful) with Sir William Harcourt, the Chancellor of the Exchequer.

His elevation could not have come at a worse time for him. His tenure of office was miserable. His wife had died in November 1890 and he had never recovered from his grief. He always observed a fast on the anniversary of her death. His best biographer, Robert Rhodes James, considers that 'her death drastically accentuated the gloomy – indeed, almost morbid – side of Rosebery's nature'. From then on he suffered from severe insomnia. He would often have his horses harnessed and drive through the night hours round the roads of his estates. He was also being persecuted by the unbalanced Marquess of Queensberry, who resented Rosebery's influence over his older son, Lord Drumlanrig, who was Rosebery's under-secretary at the Foreign Office. Rosebery tried to laugh this off. 'It is a material & unpleasant addition to the labours of Your Majesty's service to be pursued by a pugilist of unsound mind,' he told Queen Victoria, but the hostility and scandalous allegations that Queensberry spread, particularly after Drumlanrig's death in a shooting accident, unsettled him. Of more immediate import, he received little loyalty from his colleagues. Harcourt indeed conducted a vicious campaign against him. Finally, the position of a Liberal Prime Minister based in the House of Lords, where the Conservatives had a big majority, was intolerable. After eighteen wretched months, he had had enough; the Ministry resigned. A few weeks later he wrote to the Liberal Chief Whip to say that, as far as he was concerned, the Liberal leadership was vacant. He sent a copy of the letter to the newspapers and made a valedictory address to a great crowd in Edinburgh.

For three years he played almost no part in politics. He spent much of the time at his villa on the Bay of Naples. He had adored the city and its surroundings since his first visit at the age of twenty. He worked on *Napoleon: The Last Phase* and most of his public addresses were on literature rather than politics. His glamour grew with his retirement. Elsewhere in this book he is quoted as saying, 'every Scot is a Jacobite at heart'; he had put himself in the position of a Pretender, a King in exile, and his home became a sort of St Germains or Palazzo Muti.

The South African War brought him back to politics. He was associated with Grey, Haldane and Asquith as Liberal Imperialists and was their leader. They were in a difficult position. They supported the war but were ready to advocate a negotiated peace. They were at odds with most of their party. In 1902 the Liberal League was formed, which was intended to give unity and cohesion to the Liberal Imperialists and to encourage the Party to jettison policies such as Home Rule for Ireland, in which Rosebery had ceased to believe. It was his last fling but a half-hearted one. When the next Liberal Government was formed under Sir Henry Campbell-Bannerman in 1906 there was no place for Rosebery, though Grey, Asquith and Haldane were all included.

Rosebery lingered for another two decades, increasingly marginal, increasingly reactionary, devoting himself to his books, his estates and his racehorses. He continued to fascinate all who met him. The young Winston Churchill fell under his spell and considered Rosebery's misfortune to be that he 'flourished in an age of great men and small events'.

He was a failure, a dilettante in politics, who nevertheless made a greater mark on men's imagination than most so-called successes. As a social reformer he was very much the benevolent aristocrat, as his surprising chairmanship of the London County Council showed. He had a real feeling for Scotland's history and heritage, an admiration for the Calvinist virtues that was already a little old-fashioned, but very little understanding of Scotland's present difficulties. He believed in the civilising influence of the British Empire and could not see how soon it would be rejected by its beneficiaries. But he did win the Derby twice while Prime Minister, and it is safe to guess that no one will do that again.

Robert Louis Stevenson
(1850–1894)

'The truth is,' Stevenson wrote towards the end of his life, 'I am nearly hopeless at literature.' If true, this would have been unfortunate, for Stevenson is the most literary of our great writers. By this I mean that Stevenson was a writer or he was nothing. He might, like most Scottish writers, have moments when he feared that scribbling words on paper was something less than what became a man, and might sigh for a life of action. But it was no good: Stevenson was so constituted that he could not make a holiday trip without seeing in it material for a little essay; he could hardly read a book without wishing to write about it. The truth was, that he came perilously close to being too good at literature. His very literary talent was forever endangering his genius.

He was, of course, an invalid throughout his life, and that was frustrating for a man whose imaginings were all of action. He was as a child and young man both indulged and controlled. He kept something in him of the child – no one has written better verse for children – and something of the rebellious young man too. He suffered, as a result, a long immaturity. His early work is self-conscious and precious; he had all the airs and graces; the temptation to turn into a little literary man, the darling of the Savile Club, was strong.

His first achievement was to resist this. There was something of the adventurer in Stevenson which made it impossible that he should be satisfied with the tame existence of drawing-rooms and studies which sufficed timid Civil Servant souls like his friends Gosse and Colvin. Even more important, beneath the graces – the velvet jackets, the long hair, the pose of a dandy-aesthete – there was granite. Stevenson was that rarity, the graceful but inexorable moralist. The Scotch Presbyterian was the truest strain in his character, however he might jib at the self-satisfied ethics of middle-class Edinburgh.

His life has been portrayed as a search for health; and so it was. It was also, like many lives, a journey away from, and then back to, his father. Relations between father and son were to be dodged till his last unfinished novel, *Weir of Hermiston*, and there, though the idealism and morality of young Archie Weir may seem Stevenson's, it is his father, rough, crude, brutal Hermiston who wins the reader: there is an essential decency hidden under his harshness. He has standards to which he is loyal, whereas Archie has only inclinations.

Stevenson's marriage showed him a man seeking responsibility. Not only was there a stepson ready-made (to whom he was devoted) but Fanny Osborne, as she then was, was difficult, demanding, possessive, lacking in self-confidence, somewhat neurotic. She was nevertheless the woman Stevenson wanted, and it is a misinterpretation to suggest that he chose her because he wanted someone to mother him – she was older than he was. No doubt he sought a wife who would in a way stand between him and the world, but it was also true that he had to stand between the world and Fanny. It was an odd match, but not one he regretted. He loved her, was amused by her and knew she needed him.

He had a long apprenticeship. There were too many projects, too many false starts. His writing was cursed with the dangerous quality of charm. He knew too well how to please the reader. The early essays, however hard-worked, read with a cloying facility; one suspects, at a distance, that one is being called on to admire the writer. Stevenson sensed this himself; hence his recurrent dissatisfaction. He had a very clear idea of what he wanted to do; few novelists have thought more deeply about their art. He found his personality obstructing him.

There were two solutions. The first was to make use of his defect, and to give fantasy and fancy full rein. This resulted in *The New Arabian Nights* and later *The Wrong Box*, both masterpieces of artificiality, light champagne writing, buoyant as Rossini. No one has done this sort of thing better, not even Max Beerbohm.

He arrived at his other solution by way of writing children's stories, in which there was no place for the aesthete author. *Treasure Island* was his first masterpiece, and all that needs be said of this piece of writing for boys is that every scene strikes fresh and true at each new reading. It taught him perhaps that he could get outside himself, and away from himself, by finding another and simpler voice: Jim Hawkins here, David Balfour in *Kidnapped*.

Kidnapped is a test of the Stevenson reader; it is a test of the twentieth-century intelligence too. Here Stevenson achieves something quite extraordinary in the portrayal of Alan Breck, soldier of fortune, principled mercenary, with his fixed and twisted loyalties, his vanity and courage, his pique and tenacity. There is nothing literary about Alan, for Stevenson has struck out every conventional feature we might expect, and Alan is as full of surprises as life itself. Of *Kidnapped*, Henry James, who once gave a book to Stevenson as 'the only Anglo-Saxon capable of understanding how well it is written', wrote 'the art is so ripe that it lifts even the subject into the general air; the execution is so serious that the idea (the idea of a boy's romantic adventures) becomes a matter of universal relations'. Moreover, in the relations between David Balfour and Alan Breck, Stevenson gives a new turn to the opposition between Knox and Mary, Covenanter and Cavalier, Rationalist and Romantic.

Weir of Hermiston is no more than a fragment, mutilated by the haemorrhage that killed its author; but in its sense of life, its firm characterisation and the justice with which each character is placed, joined to a feeling for the movements of a whole society, it comes closer than anything in English or Scottish Literature to Tolstoy. *Weir* is an unfinished cathedral, made of granite. There is hardly a sentence which could be improved on.

Stevenson, as *Dr Jekyll and Mr Hyde* shows, knew the dark side of his nature and of Scotland's. (The two aspects are portrayed also in *The Master of Ballantrae*, where they lose force by being split between the two brothers.) There was an impulse of cruelty there, and he knew the temptations of surrender to the evil in man. He was saved because he never had any doubt what was evil and what good. He was a moralist, and his morality was taken from the faith of his fathers. 'The world must some day return to the word duty and be done with the word reward. There are no rewards and plenty duties,' he wrote from Vailima. That certainty is the key to understanding him. His revolt against his father never went very deep. He knew from an early age that a man could only keep his self-respect by doing his duty: 'Fear of the Lord is the beginning of wisdom.' In an early essay on Villon he wrote, 'For a man who is greedy of all pleasures and provided with little money and less dignity of character, we may prophesy a safe and speedy voyage downward.' The last phrase has a smug Edinburgh ring to it, such as he would lose as the granite in his character came through; but he would never deviate far from that trust in 'the dignity of character'. Without that, there was no guard against self-indulgence and self-destruction.

Arthur James Balfour,
later 1st Earl of Balfour
(1848–1930)

'Balfour', Lord Beaverbrook told A. J. P. Taylor, 'was a hermaphrodite. No-one ever saw him naked.' This was not so. On one occasion his private secretary, Sir Sidney Lee, brought a despatch to him in his bathroom and found him 'in native majesty like Milton's Adam.' There are no means, of course, of proving whether anyone else saw him naked, but Beaverbrook's assertion would seem to have been unfounded. Yet the fact that he made it reveals something of Balfour (as well, of course, as of Beaverbrook). There was a remote sexless quality about him. He never married, and yet there was no scandal attached to him, though at Eton he had been known as 'pretty Fanny'; he seemed to many to be a disembodied intelligence. It was once reported that he intended to marry Margot Tennant, later Asquith; he scotched the rumour by saying that he was 'thinking of having a career of his own'. He was not actually disembodied; he enjoyed playing golf and lawn tennis into old age.

Balfour was an East Lothian Scot on his father's side; a Cecil on his mother's. It was an interesting heredity: he combined a Covenanting strictness and restraint with the sinuosity of an English courtier. He was an avid politician who was believed to be a reluctant one. He was an intellectual who wrote works of philosophy and who lacked the common touch. His weakness as a politician was that he could not pretend to a moral indignation which he did not feel and his scepticism prevented him from indignation.

In the manner to which his class was growing accustomed, he was educated in England, at Eton and Cambridge. The Cecil influence soon secured him a seat in Parliament, where he amused himself by co-operating with Lord Randolph Churchill in harassing their Party Leader, the unfortunate Sir Stafford Northcote. Balfour's uncle, Lord Salisbury, who became Prime Minister in 1886, saw that his abilities were suited to Government and, to everyone's surprise, made him Chief Secretary in Ireland. The choice of this apparently languid and conceited aristocrat was derided but those who scorned soon found their mistake, when Balfour proved the toughest and most tenacious Minister Ireland had known.

Balfour was essentially a man of Government. Fortunately, since despite his debating skill, he was easily bored in opposition, he had plenty of opportunity. He held Cabinet rank for twenty-seven years, longer than Churchill, Gladstone, Pitt or even Palmerston. His only lengthy period out of office was during the Liberal administration that began in 1906; even then he served on the Committee of Imperial Defence (his own creation) or its sub-committees. When the War Council was formed in November 1914, he became a member even though he held no Government post and was a former leader of the Opposition. He was, in fact, temperamentally averse to party politics, which perhaps explained his failure as Prime Minister, but his attachment to the Conservative Party was never doubted.

His long involvement in Government led to a curious intellectual development. He was by instinct a sceptic, who believed that legislation and Government activity could do little to ameliorate social conditions, and certainly always less than it claimed to do. In the best Conservative tradition he distrusted the efficacy of reasoning: 'a force', he observed, 'most apt to divide and disintegrate; and though division and disintegration may often be the necessary preliminaries of social development, still more necessary are the forces that bind and stiffen, without which there would be no society to develop.' His interest in science and economics (in 1885 he had already read Marx) and his experience of Government, particularly during the Great War, led him to revise his views in the 1920s. He was then instrumental in creating a body which was intended to be the civil counterpart of the Committee for Imperial Defence. This implied a non-party basis, and a permanent structure, for long-term planning.

In a curious way Balfour was a very modern politician. Even his views have often a modern ring. In 1904, for instance, when a Labour-sponsored Trade Union Bill was being debated, he explained his objections to the King thus: 'It has to be observed that "peaceful picketing" is, or may be, a most serious form of intimidation; and, as such, can scarcely be permitted unless surrounded by precautions which the bill does not contain. As regards Trade Union funds, it may be perfectly right that the portion of these funds which is devoted to charitable purposes (pensions and so forth) should not be liable to seizure; but it can hardly be right that the funds employed in promoting strikes should possess privileges which no other corporate funds in the Kingdom are allowed to enjoy.'

Lucidity and logic were the features of his mind and, for all his philosophical interests, he combined them with a distrust of abstraction. The ding-dong of party argument bored him. During debates on Tariff Reform, for example, he deplored 'the manner in which political economy is treated in this House and on public platforms. It is not treated as a science, or as a subject which people ought to approach impartially with a view to discovering what the truth is, either from theory or experience. Not at all. They find some formula in a book of authority and throw it at their opponents' heads. They bandy the old watchwords backwards and forwards; they rouse old bitternesses, wholly alien, as far as I can see, to any modern question; and our controversies are apt to alternate between outworn formulae imperfectly remembered and modern doctrines imperfectly understood.' It is a verdict which might usefully have been delivered in the House of Commons at any time in the last eighty years.

Balfour remained a man of Government to the end. His charm and courtesy could not disguise his ruthlessness. Although Asquith was a friend and relied on him as his prop, Balfour ditched him for Lloyd George in 1916 without compunction. His affections were tepid, but he would never allow affection or personal loyalty to infringe on his public duty. There was something of the Roman Republican, of the best and least sympathetic stamp, about Balfour.

Robert Cunninghame Graham
(1852–1936)

He was known as 'Don Roberto' and 'the uncrowned King of Scots'. He was indeed descended from Robert the Bruce and, through the dormant Earldom of Menteith, had a claim to the throne of Scotland. He was famous as a traveller, politician and writer. His grandmother was a Spanish aristocrat and he grew a beard that gave him a seventeenth-century look, as if he had walked out of a canvas by Van Dyck. Unhappy at Harrow, he was removed at the age of fifteen and then spent much of the next decade in South America. He later had a spell as a rancher in Texas and Mexico and travelled widely in Spain and Morocco. He was a brilliant and eccentric figure whose admirers found hyperbole inadequate to describe him.

The critic William Power called him in 1935 'perhaps the finest literary artist alive in Europe today', which was nonsense. Mac-Diarmid called him the only Scotsman of his generation 'to win the second rank as an imaginative artist'. Since Stevenson was only two years older than Cunninghame Graham, this opinion too was nonsense unless MacDiarmid was prepared to put Stevenson in the first rank, which is unlikely. Even Maurice Lindsay, by no means overwhelmed by Graham, considers that he put his experience of travel 'to better literary use' than Burton and Doughty, which is odd since Graham wrote nothing that approaches the magnificence of Doughty's *Travels in Arabia Deserts*.

But it is not surprising that Cunninghame Graham made such an impression. He was clearly a remarkable man in himself. He was also, as MacDiarmid put it, 'the damned aristo who embraced the cause of the People' and, finally, he devoted his old age to the cause of Scottish Nationalism.

His orthodox political career was brief. He was Liberal MP for North-West Lanarkshire from 1886–92. He had a sympathy with oppressed labour and advocated reduction of the working-day. In 1887 he was prominent in the Trafalgar Square riots, when the Government had tried to ban a mass demonstration on behalf of the unemployed; he was jailed for six weeks in Pentonville for unlawful assembly. This prison sentence established his radical credentials. The following year, his friend, Keir Hardie, invited him to become the first President of the Scottish Labour Party. He left Parliament on the grounds that he was 'no longer able to endure the concentrated idiocy of the Asylum for Imbeciles at Westminster', a sentiment which endeared him to many.

He supported the Independent Labour Party and, after the First World War (in which, despite being over sixty, he had tried to take part as a Rough Rider), joined the Scottish Home Rule Association. He became President of the National Party of Scotland in 1928 and, four years later, when it had amalgamated with the Scottish Party, President of the new Scottish National Party. Cunninghame Graham was an excellent figurehead but, even earlier in his life, was an unsatisfactory politician. He had too many interests. He would make a brilliant speech, dominate a committee meeting, and then depart on his travels. The routine of political action was never to his taste.

He was far more a professional writer than a professional politician. He published a book a year for at least half a century. He was a friend and associate of writers of unquestionable genius such as Conrad and W. H. Hudson, both of whom admired him in turn. Shaw was another friend, who used Graham as a model for *Captain Brassbound's Conversion*. There is much that is surprising about his writing, not least its restraint and the absence of panache. Far from being the gifted amateur who could dash off something, his writing was painstaking and contrived. He was essentially a miniaturist; he excelled in catching the feeling of a place, a way of life, a particular man or woman. He had a feeling for old-established cultures, especially at the moment when they were threatened with dissolution. So he catches and admires the traditional Arab culture of North Africa or the old pastoral Scotland that industrialism had destroyed or was destroying. His good taste saved him from the vulgarities of the Kailyard, which indeed he despised and deplored. He complained that 'the douce pawky three-per centing of the Kailyard has quite eclipsed the pre-Culloden type'. Yet this phrase reveals a weakness in his own view of things because, if he was not deceived by the sentimentalities of the Kailyard, his own pre-Culloden type was itself a nostalgic conception. All of his best writing about Scotland was backward-looking. This is why his sketches and stories are always a little less then they promise to be.

He was perhaps a great figure rather than a great anything else; but what a figure he was. And there was one aspect of his emblematic importance which was very valuable: he was, in his own person and in his own assumptions, an assurance of Scotland's historical continuity and of the community of interests of all Scots.

Sir Hector Macdonald
(1853–1903)

On 25 March 1903, Major-General Sir Hector Macdonald shot himself in Room 105 of the Hotel Regina, in the Rue de Rivoli, Paris. Five days later he was buried at dawn in the Dean Cemetery in Edinburgh. In the course of that day some 30000 people visited the grave to pay their respects. The wretched death and mean burial on the one hand and the public homage on the other are the two poles of Macdonald's tragedy.

Macdonald had all the qualifications to be a Scottish hero. In the first place he was a Highlander. In the latter half of the nineteenth century, a strange combination of guilt and admiration made the Highlander seem the ideal representative of the Scottish nation and the kilt, which no Lowlander had worn, was adopted as the national dress. Second, Macdonald was a crofter's son who had risen to command armies, and so he appealed to the Scottish democratic ideal; he was a martial lad o' pairts. Third, he was also a symbol of Scotland's place in the expansion of the British Empire; it was this expansion, and Scotland's prominent part in it, that reconciled Scots to the loss of separate nationhood. It is important that it was always the 'British Empire' and never the English one; the century between the developing consciousness of the greatness of that Empire and its dissolution was the only securely 'British' century in our history. Only the Empire, it seems, made a British patriotism possible. Scots traders spread the Empire and Scots merchants profited from it. Scots missionaries carried the Christian message; Scots administrators brought law and education to savage peoples; Scots regiments conquered new territory and guarded the frontiers. In all of this, Scots were disproportionately prominent.

Hector Macdonald was completely an imperial soldier. He served in the Gordon Highlanders, first in the ranks and then was commissioned into the same regiment as a result of bravery on the field of battle and the leadership he had shown. All of his service was on the imperial frontier; in India, the Sudan and South Africa. He was personally heroic and was imperturbable on the battlefield. He was popular with the troops and a masterly commander of native auxiliaries. His coolness at Omdurman made him, in many people's

217

eyes, the true hero of that battle. One reporter observed that 'a non-combatant general officer who witnessed the scene declared that one might see 500 battles and never such able handling of men in the presence of the enemy'. Macdonald commanded the Highland Brigade in the South African War and restored its morale after early disasters. At the end of the war he was knighted.

In Scotland he was a popular hero, known as 'Fighting Mac'. The Highland Society of London gave him a banquet. The Clan Macdonald Society presented him with a sword of honour. His native town of Dingwall gave him the Freedom of the Burgh, Glasgow University an honorary doctorate. He was an ADC to both Queen Victoria and Edward VII.

In January 1902 he was made commander of the military establishment in Ceylon. It was the sort of post a General Officer might be expected to hold briefly. Macdonald was not yet fifty but he was already sufficiently senior to be hard to employ, especially at a time when the Empire was at peace. He had just made a successful tour of Australia and New Zealand and he had been wounded in South Africa; and the Ceylon post was clearly an interim appointment. Macdonald had made himself unpopular in some quarters by advocating conscription but that can hardly have harmed him in the army, where the same policy was supported by the Commander-in-Chief, Lord Roberts.

Ceylon was therefore in no sense an exile but it was the end of his career. He was accused – the details and exact nature of the charge are uncertain – of sexual offences with schoolboys. The Governor of the Colony, Sir Joseph West Ridgeway, was naturally reluctant to make the charges public. He suggested to Macdonald that he should take extended leave, return to England to consult with his superiors at the War Office and either secure an appointment elsewhere or send in his papers. 'His immediate departure is essential', Ridgeway informed the Colonial Office, 'to save grave public scandal which I cannot explain by telegraph.'

Roberts, however, insisted in an interview with Macdonald, that he could not remain in the army unless he cleared himself of the charge and therefore advised him to return to Ceylon to face a court-martial. 'He protests his innocence', he wrote to Lord Kitchener, 'but if he is innocent, why on earth did he not insist on having the matter cleared up?'

Macdonald crossed over to Paris, whence he could travel to Marseilles to catch ship to the East. He booked into the Hotel Regina in his own name but without revealing his rank. On 25 March, four days after his arrival, his story was on the front page of the *New York Herald*. He went up to his room and shot himself.

The matter was hushed up as far as possible. Nobody wanted a scandal involving an imperial hero. This in turn gave rise to wild and persistent rumours, the strangest of which, surfacing during the First World War, had Macdonald entering the service of the German Emperor and assuming the personality of the officer who became Field-Marshal von Mackeson. Others believed that MacDonald had been framed and was the victim of jealousy. An American millionaire, believed to have been Andrew Carnegie, financed a Committee to prove Macdonald innocent and this committee obligingly found 'not the slightest particle of truth in foundation of any crime'.

Yet the truth can hardly be doubted. Macdonald, like many of an intense masculinity, was attracted to boys. He had lived in the East where such tastes were common and not regarded as reprehensible among warrior castes. He had spent all his life in a closed male community. His own marriage, which was secret, had played little part in his life. He had reached a dangerous point of middle age when inhibitions frequently lose their power to control. There can be little surprise at his conduct. He was discovered and preferred death to exposure. In another age and another army he would have had nothing to fear.

Patrick Geddes
(1854–1932)

Scotland has always produced polymaths, and found it hard to employ them. This is, of course, usually in part their own fault, for their interests may be erratic as well as many, and their concentration is often fitful; they can rarely match the duller and more plodding talents for persistence. One such polymath was Sir Patrick Geddes, botanist, town planner, social reformer and economic theorist; and if it is difficult to believe that his talents were not to some degree wasted, it is hard to deny that he was himself much to blame.

Geddes was born in Ballater and first worked in a bank. However, before he was twenty, he went to study in London under T. H. Huxley, the master of biological and botanical sciences, and one of the greatest controversialists of the day. Geddes learned much from him in all these fields. This was to be the only part of his life which Geddes lived in London, and he learned to resent London's influence; he set himself to rescue Scotland 'from the intellecutal thraldom of London'. He returned to Scotland in 1880 after spending some time in Mexico, but was unable to get an academic appointment till 1888 when he became Professor of Botany at University College, Dundee, then part of the University of St Andrews. This was to be his base for thirty years, but his interests soon showed that they extended far beyond botany.

Geddes was a man who came more and more to resent and distrust the tendency of modern life to demarcate experience; he believed it was more important to retain a conception of the whole. Life could not be confined in separate compartments, since by definition each such compartment was contained within something bigger, and could not therefore be evaluated only from within itself. In Edinburgh he became active in a body known as the Edinburgh Social Union, which was primarily concerned to rehabilitate the decayed properties, and deprived or stunted lives they housed, of Edinburgh's Royal Mile. Here was a clear opportunity to give practical expression to Geddes's burgeoning theories: Edinburgh had once been a whole city; then it had become a divided one, with the division being unusually clearly expressed in the crossing of the valley that lay between the Old Town and the New. He took up residence himself in James Court, and then sought to lure the middle classes back to the area by building Ramsay Gardens just below the castle. He converted the old observatory on Castle Hill into the Outlook Tower, where the *camera obscura* was used to survey the whole city and demonstrate the relationships between landscape, economy and people. Geddes was essentially a teacher, rather than a man of action, but a teacher who distrusted absolute reliance on the printed word, even though he was himself the author of almost twenty books.

Many of these were written in collaboration, but a mere list of their titles will show the range of Geddes's interests. *John Ruskin; An Analysis of Economics; Every Man his own Art Critic; The Evolution of Sex; City Development; Cities as Applied Sociology; Cities in Evolution; On Universities in Europe; The Making of the Future; Education in Return to Life.* They give the impression, correctly, that Geddes was one of those gurus with whom we have become more familiar in the second half of our century, whose particular self-appointed task has been the recreation of a coherent view of life and the restoration of a broken order. He shared certain failings common to the genre, one of which was a tendency to commit the very errors he upbraided. So, for instance, in economics he held that resources were more important than finance, which is doubtless true, but he seemed blind to the difficulty in an advanced economy of effecting a separation between them. The result was that his economic theories, which to some extent prefigure C. H. Douglas's *Social Credit*, can appeal only to the economically naïve who refuse to understand the working of money, and its role in developing resources.

Geddes's practical achievements are slight in comparison with his claims. Ramsay Gardens is an agreeable piece of work, but it could not play the part he assigned to it, and it might have been designed by an architect with fewer pretensions; his plans for Pittencrieff Park in Dunfermline were pleasing, but no more so than many public parks laid out by city and borough gardeners. The failure of his precise plans was often due to their inappropriateness, often to the manner in which he advocated them. For, as a propagandist Geddes not only claimed too much for himself, but displayed one incapacitating defect: he was a bore.

He was then important as an influence, rather than as a practical man. Here undoubtedly he contributed to the thinking of the next generation of sociologists and planners. To that extent he helped shape the world we live in. Many who, with reason, think it ill-shaped may reproach him; and yet unfairly, for his disciples often worked in accordance with the letter of his advice rather than its spirit. Yet it was in the spirit that the chief value of Geddes's teaching lay: in particular in his insistence on the need for a humanist view of urban life. His idea of the future was built on an understanding of the past, and it was unfortunate that many who honoured his name should have tried to plan the future by eradicating the past.

Sir J. M. (James Matthew) Barrie
(1860–1937)

Asked who was the greatest French poet, André Gide replied: 'Victor Hugo, hélas'. Similarly, the Scottish response to the question, 'Who was Scotland's greatest dramatist?' might be: 'Barrie, I'm afraid'. Barrie, caught in a curious time-warp, disfigured by sentimentality, infantilism, self-regard, and charm, was nevertheless not only the most cunning contriver of plots but also possessed of a remarkable quality of imaginative penetration. When everything else has been said against Barrie, one fact stands forth unavoidably: *Peter Pan* is the most complete theatrical success that any Scottish writer has achieved. Uncanny in its working, it overcomes time and again whatever preconceived resistance one brings to it.

Barrie was born in Kirriemuir, a weaving town in Angus. He was the son of a weaver. Driven on by his formidable mother, Margaret Ogilvy, he became an archetypal 'lad o' pairts', going on to Glasgow Academy and Edinburgh University before settling into a career as a journalist. He made use of his birthplace, which he called 'Thrums' in his fiction, in a series of sketches and novels that appealed to a powerful nostalgia for a simpler and vanishing culture of the small town and countryside. He even exploited his mother's last months, chronicling them with what has been called 'a deplorable lack of taste'. It was precisely the lack of taste that gave the book its peculiar and irresistible flavour. It was at the same time cloyingly sentimental and cruelly honest, a combination which proved commercially successful. Barrie, like many best-sellers and successful dramatists, such as Tennessee Williams, was consumed with a self-pity that he was able simultaneously to dissect and exploit.

His is a success story, on the worldly level at least. In 1898 he dramatised his novel, *The Little Minister*, and the stage production eventually earned him £80000. It established him as one of the leading dramatists of the Edwardian period and introduced him to Society, which eagerly adopted him as a literary lion. In 1913 he was made a baronet, the first Scottish writer to be so honoured since Scott. In 1922 he received the Order of Merit; the universities of Edinburgh, St Andrews, Oxford and Cambridge showered honorary degrees on him. Plays, such as *What Every Woman Knows, Mary*

Rose, Dear Brutus and *The Admirable Crichton*, were triumphant successes. Their mixture of whimsy, sentiment and wit and their cunning craftmanship delighted audiences. Barrie was as entertaining as Shaw without offering Shaw's disturbing intellectual challenge.

Meanwhile his private life was odd. Probably he never escaped his mother's influence. Part of him certainly wanted to remain the adored small boy. His marriage to the actress Mary Austell was probably never consummated and ended in divorce. He found his chief delight in acting as friend and guardian to the children of a lawyer friend, Llewellyn Davies, especially after their father's death. *Peter Pan* was written for and about the Llewellyn Davies boys. In this magical play Barrie constructs, explores and exploits a myth of perpetual childhood, a world where the adults are inadequate and hostile and where the children revel free. His subtlety is shown by his knowledge that the myth is doomed; Peter may survive to live untrammelled but the other children must return to adopt their adult roles. Wendy will become the mother that her performance as Little Mother foreshadowed, and her brothers will doubtless follow their father into the City. *Peter Pan* belongs, with the Alice books and Kenneth Grahame's *The Wind in the Willows*, to a world of enchanted childhood which can never quite deny the grim logic of adult demands that brood over its freest moments. The magic and astonishing rightness of *Peter Pan* is the result of Barrie's ability, revealed here as nowhere else, to transform into an objective art his own weaknesses and his longing to escape the responsibility imposed on him by Margaret Ogilvy that at the same time denied him the liberty to be fully himself. The play may be criticised or used to dissect Barrie's peculiar and complex nature but it nevertheless remains, like nothing else in his work, something which exists completely apart from himself. It is a piece of theatre that delights even those who have never heard of its author because, like the highest art, it escapes from him to stand independent in its own right.

Two or three of Barrie's other plays can still hold the stage but his novels are now hardly readable by anyone but literary critics and historians. He was of course the most skilful of the Kailyard School, which does not deserve quite all the obloquy cast on it. There is still some charm and interest in his work but his fiction consistently falsifies life, presenting a picture of Scotland in which the Land of Cakes is covered with syrup. *Peter Pan*, on the other hand, transforms life, which is a different matter altogether.

Douglas Haig, 1st Earl Haig of Bemersyde
(1861–1928)

A story is told of a First World War private who ran away from the trenches. His flight was halted by a bevy of officers from the General Staff. 'Jings,' he said, 'I didna ken I was that far back.' Many would be ready to believe this obviously apocryphal story. The popular image of the commanders in the Great War, as expressed for instance in the repellent musical play and film *Oh, What a Lovely War*, is of callous, indifferent, incompetent and above all remote figures, who sent wave after wave of men to their death while obstinately refusing to change their calamitous strategy. It is a calumny but it sticks.

Haig, as Commander-in-Chief of the British Army from 1915 to the end of the War, has suffered most criticism. His reputation stood high in 1918, when he was rewarded for his part in the victory with an Earldom. It was tarnished when Lloyd George began to publish his unreliable memoirs and blackened still further when the true cost of the war was realised and a revulsion against the methods that had obtained that terrible victory grew stronger. The judgement that the British Army was composed of 'lions led by donkeys' found popular favour. (The enduring vitality of the phrase was illustrated recently when it was applied by another Trade Union leader to the National Union of Mineworkers and their President, Arthur Scargill.) Even the shine on Haig's top-boots seemed offensive, while the devotion with which he worked for the wounded survivors of the war was cruelly misinterpreted. No attempt to rehabilitate Haig has fully succeeded. The official biography by Duff Cooper, a gallant effort by one who had fought as a Guards Officer in the last year of the war, had no chance in the atmosphere of the 1930s. Later, John Terraine, in *Haig: The Educated Soldier*, argued the case for him powerfully; his arguments were disregarded rather than answered.

Haig's detractors could not deny two facts, though they were able to pervert both. First, in the face of a moral and physical challenge for which there was little precedent in the history of warfare, Haig's nerve and confidence in ultimate victory never failed. (This was interpreted as indifference to heavy losses.) Second, the war ended in total victory with the British Army advancing along its whole front. (This triumph was variously attributed to the Americans, to the

French or to the economic and political collapse of Germany. The last was, in fact, the consequence of defeat in the field.)

Haig was born in Edinburgh and brought up in Fife but belonged first and last to the Borders. His family had been settled at Bemersyde, near Dryburgh Abbey, since the Middle Ages: 'Come wind, come rain, whate'er betide/ Haig shall be Haig of Bemersyde' as the old rhyme puts it. John Buchan noticed that under the stress of war Haig 'spoke with a broader accent – of the Borders, oddly enough, instead of his native Fife'. When he was ennobled, he took his title from Bemersyde rather than from one of the great battles of the war as his predecessor, Sir John French, had done and as most of the generals of the Second War were to do. During the war he found a faith in his destiny that recalled the spirit of a seventeenth-century Covenanter.

Unlike most of the soldiers of his time, he had had a university education. He had attended Brasenose College, Oxford. He commanded cavalry in the Boer War but, like all the other British generals, he had no experience of handling large bodies of troops in action until war broke out in 1914. A soldier's life is curious in this respect: he spends years preparing for a trial which may never come and for which in fact there may never be adequate preparation. Moreover the First War had certain unprecedented features. Never before had the defensive weapons attained so great a superiority over the offensive. It took the generals of all armies on the Western Front a long time to learn this. If the German commanders seem to have grasped this truth earlier, it was because German strategy required them, after their initial thrust has been contained, to do no more than hold the line in the West while they tried to destroy the Russian Empire in the East.

Haig must bear the responsibility for the two most appalling battles in British history: the Somme and Passchendaele. In both, it is argued, his initial tactics were mistaken. The effect of the great artillery barrage was far less than it was expected to be and he persisted long after any chance of a decisive breakthrough had been lost. Perhaps the second battle may be defended on the grounds that, by continuing it, Haig diminished the effects of the mutinies and collapsed morale in the French Army that threatened to lose the war. He had difficulties with his allies and with the politicians. Lloyd George schemed to undermine his authority and denied him necessary reinforcements. Haig persisted, perhaps too long, in a style of fighting which was unjustified by success. But he learned slowly. In 1918, when he broke through the Hindenberg Line, he did so in defiance of the doubts expressed by the Cabinet; an example of high moral courage. His whole command was distinguished by fortitude.

He lacked charm and communicated poorly to the troops but, in contrast to what was later said, they came to revere and trust him. He was too unimaginative to count among the great commanders of History but Buchan is surely right when he claims that 'the losses [of the British Army] would have been greater under a brilliant empiric like Nivelle or Henry Wilson'.

(James) Ramsay MacDonald
(1866–1937)

The first Labour Prime Minister of Great Britain decreed that his Cabinet colleagues should present themselves at Court in formal morning dress. (Two years earlier, the wild Fascist leader and ex-Socialist, Benito Mussolini, had answered King Victor Emmanuel's invitation to form a Government by appearing in morning-coat, top-hat and spats.) The Prime Minister's decision disgusted some, appeased more; it was absolutely characteristic of Ramsay Mac-Donald and, like almost everything in MacDonald's life, puzzled many. MacDonald was perhaps the strangest and most interesting Prime Minister of modern times. He was a man easy to misunder-stand and, being misunderstood, to despise. Some called him a snob, others a class traitor; some found him vague and woolly; Winston Churchill once compared him to a 'boneless wonder' that he had been forbidden, when a child, to view at a fair. There was some substance in all of these charges but they give quite the wrong impression of MacDonald.

Perhaps the most important fact about MacDonald was that he had the temperament of an artist rather than of a politician. (Of course politics may be fairly described as an art, even if an impure and inferior one.) MacDonald's dominant quality was his imagination. He was governed by his imaginative sympathies, which led him always to exaggerate the part he played and this made him distrusted. He was at the same time sincere and yet playing a part. That part might be the wild socialist orator, the noble pacifist, the dignified leader of the nation, the champion of the underdog, the courteous friend of duchesses. For him, politics was the tune he played; others were exasperated by his changes of key and lack of consistent purpose. Only one politician fully understood him. That was Stanley Baldwin, who for eight years led the Conservative opposition to MacDonald's Labour Party and then for six years collaborated with him in Government. Baldwin understood him because they resembled each other: unusually among politicians, both feared and disliked power; both worked intuitively; neither was a master of detail. They also had ideals in common: the preservation of peace abroad and the easing of class conflict at home. Each had a sense of the nation as an organism. Curiously, Baldwin was himself a MacDonald on his mother's side.

MacDonald's life was a romance which ended sadly, in the manner of Celtic romance. He was born illegitimate, the son of a plough-boy and serving-girl. He grew up with a touchy pride that never left him. Naturally he became a Socialist, though his was hardly the socialism of Marx and he quite lacked dialectical skills or the capacity to understand economics. His was a socialism of sympathy: there were the poor, hideously oppressed in the midst of a society of unprecedented wealth; he would make himself their champion. He spent years speaking at street corners and in chill meeting-halls. In his youth he was an inspiring orator. In old age his rhetoric became empty. He was one of the makers of the Labour Party but he had little real feeling for trade unionism and the Party's middle-class intellectuals despised him. Beatrice Webb, who failed to understand him, said he was the best substitute for a leader they could find.

In 1914 he had advanced to the fringe of respectable politics. He threw away his position by denouncing the war hysteria and opposing the war. He showed a fierce courage in these years, when his meetings were broken up and he was vilified in the Press. Meanwhile his sedate Labour colleague, Arthur Henderson, proceeded to a seat in the War Cabinet. Nevertheless it was probably MacDonald's opposition to the war that brought him the leadership of the Parliamentary Party. He was elected principally by the efforts and votes of the Clydesiders.

He was twice Labour Prime Minister, on both occasions heading a minority Government dependent on Liberal support. Neither Government achieved much, nor could this have been expected. MacDonald, however, made Labour a respectable party, a part of the normal political process. Probably nothing could have stopped Labour from supplanting the Liberal Party but MacDonald made the transition smooth. He also took the Foreign Secretaryship, a position that suited his gifts far more than the leadership. His imagination allowed him to understand how other nations felt.

His second administration had to cope with an unprecedented economic crisis. Within two years, unemployment rose from one to three million. The pound, foolishly restored to the Gold Standard by Winston Churchill (whose understanding of economics was equal to

MacDonald's), came under pressure. The crisis climaxed in 1931. There were calls for a Coalition. The king, who liked MacDonald and enjoyed good relations with him, urged him in this direction. A splendid role opened before MacDonald: he could be the Saviour of the Nation. Only a far less imaginative and histrionic man could have resisted the temptation or the challenge. MacDonald decided to form a National Government.

Most of his Party refused to follow him. He found himself leader of a Government with few of his own supporters in the House of Commons. He had become the prisoner or the figurehead of what was essentially a Conservative administration. To Labour he was a traitor. He saw it differently, of course. To him, abandoning office in 1931 would have been an act of cowardice. He, and Labour, had presided over the crisis; they should not shrink from what was necessary to repair it. His retention of the office of Prime Minister was an ill-requited act of personal and political courage.

For some years he retained his vigour. He still devoted himself principally to foreign affairs, attempting to secure disarmament in Europe and to work through the League of Nations. He failed to understand the new forces rising in Germany, although he had the imagination to understand the nature of German grievances. He though that perhaps they could be appeased but he did not realise that the economic disasters that Germany had suffered had unbalanced the nation.

His last years were dismal. His faculties decayed and he became an object of mockery to those who hardly knew him, an object of embarrassment to those who did. In 1935 he resigned the Premiership in favour of Baldwin but remained in the Cabinet as Lord President of the Council. That year he lost his seat at Seaham to Shinwell, once his protégé. He was subsequently returned as Member for the Scottish Universities.

John Buchan judged that MacDonald would have made 'a heroic Jacobite refugee'. There was something Jacobite-like in his last years. He was a man who had 'done the State some service'. He had made the Labour Party a Parliamentary force and the natural opposition to the Conservatives. In 1931, he had done his duty as he saw it, a duty that had cost him much that he valued. Like Macbeth he could not look to have 'that which should accompany old age – honour, love, obedience, troops of friends'. Yet, like Tennyson's Lancelot, 'his honour rooted in dishonour stood'. He was, if not a great man, a man to be greatly admired. 'Two things', Buchan wrote, 'never failed him: courage and courtesy.' There are worse epitaphs, and MacDonald deserves a good one.

Charles Rennie Mackintosh
(1868–1928)

We are often said to have a liking for paradox and the case of Charles Rennie Mackintosh would seem to bear this out. It is not just that his work should have enjoyed in the 1980s a vogue that it hardly had in his lifetime – that is common enough – but that his new-found popularity should arise at a time when the Modern Movement in architecture, of which he was one of the fathers, was not only worn out but resented and reviled. In spite of that, in the 1980s even those who couldn't say exactly what was meant by Art Nouveau knew enough to associate the term with Mackintosh. At the same time the man himself and his strange, broken career remained shadowy; he was a name rather than a personality. Even the failure of his career awaited adequate assessment.

Mackintosh was born in Glasgow, the son of a police superintendent, and grew up in the golden afternoon of Glasgow's prosperity. His working life in the city is spanned by the great international exhibitions of 1888, 1901 and 1912. He was thirty-three and had already designed his masterpiece, the School of Art, when the 1901 exhibition in Kelvingrove Park drew attendances of 11½ million (or three times the current population of Scotland) and marked what Professor Sydney Checkland called 'Glasgow's Great Apogee'.

In 1900 Mackintosh had married Margot Macdonald, herself an artist and designer of rare talent. Her influence in his career was considerable, as was that of her sister Frances, who married the artist Herbert McNair. Mackintosh was no isolated pioneer.

He had already won a reputation in Europe. His School of Art had achieved what his biographer called 'the synthesis of traditional craftsmanship and twentieth century engineering'. This made it seem appropriately Glaswegian. It has been called 'the first important monument to the new movement in Europe'. He had also built

Queen's Cross Church, Glasgow, in Art Nouveau Gothic and a house, Windyhill, in Kilmacolm. In 1902 he built Hill House in Helensburgh, now owned by the National Trust for Scotland. These two houses were summed up by Pevsner: 'They are in their general outline descendants of the Scottish manor-houses, . . . [not a Scottish term] . . . but their combination of windows, chimney stacks, and oriels is of a subtle irregularity, at first appearing arbitrary, but then revealing itself as most sensitively placed and scaled – very much what Le Corbusier did in his later works – but without the brutality.'

'The Modern Movement without brutality': was that where Mackintosh was heading? He had already achieved a remarkable fusion of a national style with modern theory. He had made his impression on Europe in the Vienna Secessionists exhibition of 1900 and the *Haus Eines Kunstfreundes* competition in 1901 but of major works at home only the Scotland Street School of 1904 and Miss Cranston's Willow Tearoom were still to come. Thereafter there was nothing of moment.

The constraints under which he was working were recognised abroad. A Viennese art magazine stated in 1906 that 'it is indeed a great delight to oppose an all-powerful enemy, and that is precisely why Charles Mackintosh is working in Glasgow'. It was perhaps a delight more easily experienced from a distance. Mackintosh felt his powers and knew they were unused. There was doubtless delight in working for Miss Cranston who gave him and his wife freedom to design everything right down to the cutlery; but it was hardly enough for a man whose foreign friends had fortified his conviction that he was a pioneer of genius.

New commissions did not come. Mackintosh, disillusioned perhaps, began to drink heavily. His work grew disorganised and his behaviour eccentric. His lunch hour would stretch beyond the time when Miss Cranston's customers would be straightening their large hats before the Mackintosh mirrors, preparing to take the late afternoon trams to the terraces of the Great Western Road and the villas of Pollokshields.

His work deteriorated. He had temporarily lost the power of concentration. When his firm decided to enter a competition to design Jordanhill demonstration school, his drawings were found to be impractical. Some of his corridors, like his career, ended in mid-air. In 1913 he left Glasgow and never again worked in the city of his birth.

Something had fizzled out. It is easy to reproach Mackintosh but it may be that the failure of nerve and energy was Glasgow's. When looking at the achievements of Alexander 'Greek' Thomson, it is natural to wonder what Mackintosh might have done if he had worked in the years of Glasgow's blossoming rather than at the time when the fruit was ripe and beginning to rot.

He went to England. He had never had a reputation there, as that complacent country took little note of either Glasgow or Vienna. For the rest of his life he was a studio artist. He retired to France and devoted himself to painting, especially in watercolour. The results were exquisite, delicate and accurate renderings of flowers and a perceptive and imaginative treatment of light on rock formations. They show that he was a master of that medium also but, in some way, they must also be regarded as a retreat. Mackintosh had recovered the balance that he had lost in his last years in Glasgow but he had done so by scaling down his ambitions. His recovery owed much to his wife, who had never lost confidence in his genius. During the dark wartime years, when they worked on textile designs in London, her contribution was equal to his.

To contemplate Mackintosh's career is to know a sense of waste. After 1918, Glasgow began to replace the worst slums in Europe with the worst architecture in Europe. The man who might have brought a civilising imagination to this work was exiled. After the next war came the tower blocks, stark examples of an architectural barbarism which recalls only the first half of Le Courbusier's definition of a house as being 'a machine . . .' and forgets the words that follow 'for living in'. If Mackintosh's career had not been broken, could that have been avoided? Might not that brutalism have been tempered by his awareness that 'all great and living architecture has been the direct expression of the needs and beliefs of man at the time of its creation'? Glasgow and Scotland are now proud of the few examples of Mackintosh's work but the absence of much work that *might* have been is cause for shame. The results of the failure to employ fruitfully the talents of the greatest Scottish architect of the last hundred years can be seen in our cities and towns.

John Wheatley
(1869–1930)

John Wheatley was the most capable of the Clydesiders, that remarkable group of Labour MPs (belonging in fact to the Independent Labour Party, the ILP) who were elected to Parliament in 1922, and whose departure from St Enoch's Station, when they were seen off by a huge and excited crowd, has become one of the fixed points in the myth, legend and history of Labour Scotland.

Wheatley was not, of course, a Scot. He was born of Irish parents in County Waterford but, in the year of his birth, the family removed to Lanarkshire, where his father worked in the mines. They belonged to that great body of Irish immigrants who changed the character of the west of Scotland and helped to form its present one. Nobody would now challenge the right of their descendants to call themselves Scots. Indeed, by a curious irony, many of the grandchildren and great-grandchildren of these immigrants seem to have apportioned to themselves the status of representative Scots. Yet it is worth remarking that as recently as 1923 a sub-committee of the General Assembly of the Church of Scotland charged them with being aliens, who responded to Irish rather than Scottish interests. The whole question of race and nationality is of course a vexed one. More nonsense has been talked about it than about any other subject, and so it is probably most sensible to say simply that people who live in a country and come to identify themselves with it, belong to it more certainly than those whose attachment is only ancestral and who now live elsewhere. This process of assimilation began in Wheatley's lifetime. Although his early political interests were directed to Ireland as a member of the United Irish League, he did more than any other individual to wean the Irish in the west of Scotland from that cause and to encourage them to immerse themselves in the politics of Scotland and mainland Britain.

As a boy, Wheatley's intellectual promise was noted and encouraged by a Dutch mission priest who was attached to his local Catholic School. However, he followed his father down the mines and worked for nine years in the dangerous and old-fashioned pits of Baillieston. He found time to pursue a course of self-education and attended night-classes at a charitable institution, called the Athenaeum, which devoted itself to the education of working-men. He became briefly a publican (though, like most of the ILP and other Scottish Socialists, he was a teetotaller) and then a grocer. Next he collected advertising copy for a Catholic newspaper, the *Glasgow Observer*. In 1906 he went into business on his own account. In partnership with a friend, he launched a printing and publishing company. It originally handled advertising material and published devotional tracts but them moved into newspaper publishing, both in the west of Scotland and Ireland. Wheatley's most successful paper was the *Glasgow Evening Standard*, which ran from 1923 to 1960.

These enterprises proved Wheatley's practical capabilities, something which marked him off from most of his colleagues. They also made him a comparatively wealthy man, able to send his children to fee-paying Catholic schools and to live in a solidly bourgeois house overlooking a golf course. When he died, he left over £16000. Business success might have been expected to influence his politics; after all, it is a truism that the upwardly-mobile move also to the right. That it did not is surely a tribute to his heart and to his commitment to a radical Christianity. He declared that his Socialism emanated 'from that spirit of brotherhood which is ever present in the hearts of men but which is often suppressed by the struggle for existence'. This was a long way from Marx, but it owed much to the Encyclicals of Pope Leo XIII, particularly *De Rerum Novarum*, which sharply attacked Capitalism from a Catholic viewpoint. That was always Wheatley's position.

He was elected to the Glasgow Town Council in 1912. His main interest lay in housing problems and Glasgow's housing, despite attempts at reform, which had gone on intermittently since Chadwick's *Reports on the Sanitary Conditions of the Labouring Population of Scotland* (1842), was a disgrace to humanity. Wheatley advocated using the profits from municipal enterprises, such as the tramways (which did indeed make a profit), to subsidise the building of cottages. His pamphlet, *Eight-Pound Cottages for Glasgow Citizens* (1918), began thus: 'Dr Chalmers, Chief Medical Officer of Health for Glagow, has just issued his report for last year. Commenting on it the *Glagow Herald* remarks that it "reflects a year of normal experience". In this case the normal is horrible.' Professor T. C. Smout observes that 'this understanding that "the normal is horrible" in working-class experience, and the faith that something could be done by the working-class to change it, was the key to the appeal of Wheatley's party'. The conviction that Wheatley was competent enough to initiate such a change was the key to his appeal.

He had his feet firmly on the ground. He opposed the First World War but never attacked the working-class patriotism that was very evident in Glasgow and had led to the city producing a number of volunteers much above the average. He opposed the attempts by the Government to suppress the Labour movement on the Clyde but helped Kirkwood to negotiate an agreement with Beardmore's that resulted in improved working conditions, the abandonment of a policy of 'dilution of Labour' and an increased production of shells. He supported the campaign for Maclean's release from prison but had no time for his apocalyptic and revolutionary rhetoric. He was confident that the vastly increased working-class electorate would return a Labour Government in time and would facilitate the introduction of Socialism by constitutional means.

He became Minister of Health with responsibility for Housing in MacDonald's Minority Government of 1924. His Housing (Financial Provisions) Act was the administration's only legislative achievement. It provided for central government funding of local authorities which undertook the building of houses to approved standards but stipulated that these houses should be built for rent only and not for sale. The houses were unfortunately far from the cottages he had called for. The bleak housing estates, many of which were themselves to be slums in less than thirty years, were distantly derived from the garden suburbs proposed by Ebenezer Howard in England in the 1890s; the distance was more marked than the resemblance. Nevertheless, they provided homes which were very welcome at the time. This extension of municipal socialism, which made Town Councils landlords on a scale, and with a power over their citizens, such as no private landlord could have dreamed of, was to be one of Wheatley's two lasting legacies. The other was, of course, the winning of the Irish to the Labour Party.

Out of office between 1924–29, Wheatley became increasingly impatient with what he saw as the lukewarm commitment to Socialism displayed by MacDonald and Philip Snowden. He supported the General Strike of 1926 and withdrew to the back benches. He opposed the formation of another minority government in 1929 and was not offered a post. He had lost support even within the ILP, though he had at least one contact in the Cabinet, Sir Oswald Mosley, who shared his impatience with Snowden's timid and orthodox economic policy. He was an increasingly isolated figure. Beatrice Webb, by no means a reliable witness where the Clydesiders are concerned, decided that 'as a rebel in the party he has been a failure, his expression is sullen, his words are bitter, his lips are blue and his complexion is patchy and he closes his eyes at you. He says he has lost faith in political democracy, the common people have no will of their own. . . . He would be a Communist if he were not a pious Catholic.'

He died suddenly of a brain haemorrhage in 1930. It is tantalising to wonder where this most able of the Clydesiders would have found himself in the crisis of the following year. He was only sixty-one.

Sir Harry Lauder
(1870–1950)

Hugh MacDiarmid detested Lauder, and his detestation has become the obligatory response of the Scotch intellectual to this particular and most famous Scotch comic (though not, curiously enough, to his modern equivalent Billy Connolly, despite the fact that the case against Lauder could be made equally cogently against Connolly). For MacDiarmid, Lauder represented a debasement of the idea of Scotland. He had constructed for himself a stereotype – the Kilted Clown – and this persona was particularly directed beyond Scotland, to please and flatter the English and other foreigner by displaying Scotland to them in the guise of a caricature. Worse still, this caricature was really, it might be claimed, of English origination, for Lauder's pawky, close-fisted, sentimental Scot was the Scotchman of innumerable *Punch* cartoons. 'Lauderism', Alan Bold has written, 'was a powerful enough threat to Scotland's dignity for MacDiarmid to allude to it in many poems (including his masterpiece).' Lauder's 'special gift', according to Bold, 'was to make the caricature available for export'. In support, he quotes Lauder's own words: 'I decided that if ever I got a footing in England I would not use words or idioms which would only befog my audience. I would sing my songs in English, I determined, but with a Scottish accent.' This, the commonsense decision of a professional performer, which is also, one might add, a form of good manners, is easily construed as subservient, fawning, insincere, and an insult to Scotland. Well, well.

The first thing to be said about Lauder is that he was, within the limits of his craft, a consummate artist. He held his position at the top of the music-hall bills for more than half a century; no one can do that in a business so wholly dependent on popular flavour without being a master. He worked extremely hard: even the wild laugh in the song 'Stop Yer Ticklin' Jock' was rehearsed daily for ten weeks before he first sang the song in public. Every gesture he made was calculated.

His timing was impeccable. He played to audiences all over the world with consistent success. He could command £1,000 a week, at a time when half that sum was a fair professional income for a year. His attention to technique might shame many whose aspirations were much higher, including, it may be said, Hugh MacDiarmid, for Lauder would never have insulted his public with a performance as technically careless or even inept as some of MacDiarmid's work.

He was, of course, sentimental and he did rely on stereotypes. That is the nature of the music hall. In this Lauder was no different from Maurice Chevalier, Edith Piaf or Gracie Fields. A music-hall act or song must make an immediate impression and yet leave one which lasts. Lauder brought this off time and again. His best songs are simple, for there is no room for complicated emotions in popular art. But the emotion they express is a true one. 'Roaming in the gloaming' or 'Keep right on to the end of the road' express sentiments we have all experienced, which there is no need to disparage, and which Lauder does not cheapen. The melodies are simple but memorable. There can be few Scots who have not found themselves humming a Lauder song. His patter was self-consciously humorous, but it was also rich in self-mockery, and only someone who took himself with consistent solemnity could find it offensive. His Scottish types are, of course, caricatures, but they are caricatures of reality, and they are friendly and affectionate. They were recognised as such by most Scots.

For this is perhaps what especially irritates his critics. He may have made the Kilted Clown for export, but it was nowhere more popular and successful than in Scotland. It was not Lauder's falsity with aroused patriotic anger, but his truthfulness. He represented a side of Scotland which those who called themselves Scottish patriots could have done without. His was a warm, comfortable, boozy, sentimental Scotland that didn't take itself consistently seriously, but which was able to laugh at itself, because in the last resort it was very sure of itself: you could call it small-town Scotland and accuse it of smugness and lack of ambition, but however you might deplore it, it was very firmly there. It still is. Lauder's songs remain popular and a re-creation of Lauder's act by Jimmy Logan fills theatres. Lauderism is still alive in Scotland's most successful newspaper, the *Sunday Post*. Perhaps the silliest of many silly remarks by Scotch intellectuals was Tom Nairn's: 'as far as I'm concerned Scotland will be reborn the day the last minister is strangled with the last copy of the *Sunday Post*.' That is merely an expression of dislike of the Scotland in which most of his compatriots live. It is as silly as deploring Harry Lauder, as silly as saying there is no place for sentiment; 'they're a' oot of step but oor Jock'; Lauder could have seen the joke.

John Buchan, Lord Tweedsmuir
(1875–1940)

Born in Perth, where his father was a Free Kirk minister, John Buchan was brought up in Fife, Glasgow and the Borders and educated at Hutchesons' Grammar School, Glasgow University and Brasenose College, Oxford. He was novelist, historian, critic, lawyer, publisher, civil servant engaged in the reconstruction of South Africa after the Boer War, director of Propaganda in the First World War, Member of Parliament for the Scottish Universities, Lord High Commissioner to the General Assembly of the Church of Scotland, Advocate of Empire and Governor-General of Canada, in which post he died. His life might be interpreted as the perfect paradigm of the Scotsman on the Make; he even married a Grosvenor and was raised to the peerage as Lord Tweedsmuir.

Buchan's life was stranger and more complicated than that, however. He was full of contradictions. He was a fervent Scot who lived all his adult life out of Scotland and sank his Scottishness in the larger entities of the United Kingdom and the British Empire. He was a democrat who was accused of being a snob. He was forever recalling the Hebrew prophets but was charged with anti-Semitism. He was a classicist who had little interest in Europe or the Mediterranean world and whose novels breathed the spirit of the high romance of lonely roads, waste places and wild adventures. He had a naturally critical mind but his imagination was captured by the windy rhetoric of Cecil Rhodes and the Imperialist cause. He was a lover of peace who celebrated warfare. He was the author of fifty-five books who, while being immensely successful, was never merely a professional writer. He was the serious scholar who is remembered for stories which he wrote for his own entertainment and called 'shockers'.

The contradictions abound but he contained them. He was indeed all of these things and yet – here is another paradox – few men have seemed to be more all of one piece. In everything he wrote there is the authority of a man certain of his own position. This is both his strength and his weakness. It gives him a marvellous and readable lucidity and a remarkable understanding. At the same time his mind closed early. As he wrote himself, 'some time in my early twenties the arteries of my taste seemed to narrow and harden'. He had been remarkably precocious, having edited Bacon's Essays for a London publisher at the age of seventeen. This early formation of his intellect and the closing of his curiosity was the price he paid. He was indifferent to the perplexities of his age because they did not touch him. He could recognise them but, set against his massive certainties, they appeared trivial and self-indulgent. To some extent they were, but Buchan's disinclination to develop was self-indulgent too. It blinded him to the dangers of some of the political developments of his own time and allowed him to persist in beliefs such as imperialism or the fundamental unity of the British Empire and the United States, when these beliefs had either lost their validity or had never possessed any.

Yet he could not be called complacent. Thanks partly to his Calvinist inheritance, he firmly believed in the reality of evil and Man's sinful and destructive nature. He saw Man, divorced from God and tradition, as wilful and in thrall to his own ego. His Calvinism, however, was tempered by his Classicism, which kept him from the improper pride of the Elect. He never forgot what the Greeks taught of Hubris and the working of Nemesis. He believed too that privilege and position had to be justified by a man's life and works. Time and again he enunciated the doctrine of challenge. He recognised the fragility of civilisation and was aware how easily it could be destroyed by either the barbarians without or the anarchic impulses lurking within each soul. For Buchan, every action was a matter of moral choice and he knew how attractive it was to choose the evil course. In his novels he always granted a certain glamour to his villains, since he could not deny the enticements of the primrose path. He was a Conservative in politics because he recognised the need for a tradition and distrusted experiments that had their root in theory.

He was an accomplished biographer, Sir Walter Scott, Montrose and Augustus being his best subjects, and, as an historical novelist, had a rare ability to bring the past to life. His masterpiece in this genre was *Witch Wood*, a story of seventeenth-century Scotland which rivals Hogg's *The True Confession of a Justified Sinner* as a dramatic analysis of the dark excesses of the Calvinist spirit. But it is his 'shockers' by which he most surely survives. They are rapid, inventive, and have a rare feeling for landscape, place, the moods of weather and the romance of sudden journeys; they are admirably constructed, even though he was inclined to rely on splendid improbabilities in his use of coincidence. The reason for their survival goes deeper, however. He struck a nerve because he reminded his readers of the dark places of the earth and the dark side of their own nature. It is his awareness of evil which sets him apart from most practitioners in the genre, which has won him the admiration of Graham Greene and which recalls Conrad. It is this quality which has enabled these novels to last better than the works of 'serious' contemporaries who never questioned the assumptions of their civilisation and who now seem myopic and complacent in comparison.

Much of Buchan's best writing was set in Scotland. He also compiled a delightful anthology of Scots verse, *The Northern Muse*. He started and edited a magazine, *The Scottish Review*, while working in Edinburgh before the First War as a Director of the publishing firm Nelson's. He never lost touch with Scotland but, having made his home in Oxfordshire in 1919, thereafter only visited Scotland for holidays and occasional political or public purposes. In one sense he moved away from Scotland and may be seen as representative of that drift to the South which has impoverished Scotland by depriving the country of many of its most able and ambitious children. Buchan remained fervently Scottish, however. He saw a role for Scotland within the United Kingdom and the Empire; he saw no incompatibility between Scottish and British and even imperial patriotism. Nevertheless, a career such as his illustrates the disadvantages or deprivation that Scotland may suffer from the Union.

William Douglas Weir, Viscount Weir of Eastwood

(1877–1959)

In 1901 the International Engineering Congress was held in Glasgow. No city could have been a more appropriate host. There were then fifty-one civil, mechanical and electrical engineering firms with more than 250 employees on Clydeside; and this figure did not include firms engaged in shipbuilding or marine or locomotive engineering. Such figures explain the boast that the Clyde was the workshop of the world.

Among these firms, that of G. & J. Weir, was well-established. Its founder, James Weir, was an inventive genius, and the firm concentrated on the production of pumps and auxiliary gear for marine engines. Weir pumps and their design for condensers went into battleships in most of the navies of the world. But success in engineering could be short-lived. The industry experienced rapid technical development, which has never indeed abated, and it was easy for a company to be outstripped by competitors. Continuing success depended on keeping in the van of progress, in both techniques and working methods, on high efficiency in salesmanship, and on constant alertness. The industry survived only in a state of perpetual challenge, and it was a challenge which many once-flourishing firms failed to meet. That Weir's survived it was due largely to the founder's heir, William Weir; yet his story is also one of repeated false starts and unsuccessful projects.

In the Glasgow manner, he served an apprenticeship in the family firm straight from the High School of Glasgow. He was managing director in 1902 and chairman ten years later, a job he was to hold till 1954. He was the greatest figure in Scottish engineering for half a century, and he became also a public man with extensive connections in Government and much experience of Government service himself.

He was constantly aware of the dangers for the firm of over-specialisation, and his life was a long search for profitable diversification. Most of these efforts failed in the long run, but that does not mean that they were not often useful, helping to tide the firm over years when demand for their primary product dropped.

His first enthusiasm was for motor cars and he established a connection with the French firm of Darracq. This was no more than a sideline in the years leading up to the First World War, for then demand for Weir pumps was great. Weirs were not content with this success, but were careful to adapt their technology to oil-fired ships and later turbines. William Weir gave close attention also to working practices: introducing work study, standardisation and payment by results. The last of these was only popular with the unions in good times.

The First World War saw Weirs diversify into aircraft and munitions. They became the principal Clydeside producer in both these fields, though they neither designed nor developed aircraft, and contented themselves with assembling them by mass-production techniques. This was ominous, one of the first examples of branch-line manufacturing by a Scottish company, probably the first by an indigenous one. (The Singer sewing machine factory was already long established.)

Weir himself was Controller of Aeronautical Supplies from 1917, and later Secretary of State for Air. He was made a Viscount in 1918, but returned to the firm after the war.

Post-war years were difficult, though the invention of a new design for a regenerative condenser with a closed feed was successful, and was to be their staple product for many years. Nevertheless employment fell back by two-thirds, and the capital in the business was also reduced. Naturally Lord Weir again looked for means to diversify. He tried to promote prefabricated steel houses for local authorities, but ran into opposition from building trades. This was a good illustration of the difficulties encountered in a contracting economy: products could only be promoted at the expense of established ones. This must always be the case to some extent, but when the economy is expanding, the effect is felt less. Other attempts at diversification were more successful: a nickel-copper alloy, called monol metal, suitable for use in propellors; auto-giros and helicopters. Though none of these was to be outstandingly successful, they helped Weir's to sustain the Depression. The company was still there, and healthy, when demand for its traditional products revived in the late 1930s. Many of its old rivals had disappeared.

All this time Weir involved himself also in public affairs, particularly in aviation. He was a special adviser at the Air Ministry from 1935–8, with the responsibility of ensuring that the RAF, whose survival as a separate service he had done much to secure, should have the necessary resources for the coming war. G. & J. Weir put up the money which made Sir Frank Whittle's jet engine possible. When war broke out he became Director-General of Explosives, and was later on Chairman of the Tank Board. He returned to his company in 1945 to see it through the difficult post-war years.

It is hard to disentangle Weir's life from that of his company, but that it survived to remain a great engineering company (despite severe troubles in the 1970s) is in large measure due to his restless foresight. He worked in a business which required constant adaptability, where today's success was obsolete tomorrow.

John Maclean
(1879–1923)

John Maclean was the Bonnie Prince Charlie of Scottish Socialism, the hero of the Revolution that never was. Partly because he achieved so little, his name has all the sad resonance of heroic failure and, like Prince Charlie, he has been celebrated in song and poetry. Hugh MacDiarmid called him 'one of the few true men in our sordid breed,/A flash of sun in a country all prison-grey'. Hamish Henderson made him the hero of his ballad, 'Freedom Come All Ye'. Sorley Maclean and Sydney Goodsir Smith also wrote admiringly of him.

He was born, and lived all his life, in Glasgow but he belonged to the dispossessed peasantry of the Highlands. He was an inheritor of a broken culture thrust by economic circumstances into an industrial city. His father was a potter, who died when the boy was nine. His mother, a McPhee, worked as a weaver, then kept a shop, then took in lodgers. John Maclean wrote that 'it was the sacrifices she made . . . to enable me to be educated . . . which made me resolve to use my education in the service of the workers.'

He trained as a teacher in a Free Church College and also took a degree in Political Economy at Glasgow University. He was a founder member of the Glasgow Teachers' Socialist Society. Working as he did for most of his life as an educationalist, giving lectures in economics on Sunday afternoons and helping to found the Scottish Labour College, his socialism was always dogmatic and didactic.

An inherited antipathy to landlords and landlordism helped to make him a Socialist, as did his loss of religious faith. Having been brought up in the Calvinist Original Secession Church, he became an atheist under the influence of T. H. Huxley and Herbert Spencer and because he regarded the churches' attitude to social reform as hypocrticial. But the name of Christ always came easily to his lips. He seems to have regarded Him as a proto-Socialist agitator. In 1918 he told the Durham miners that 'the mantle of Jesus Christ has fallen upon the Bolsheviks'.

By his own account he was converted to Socialism by reading Robert Blatchford's *Merrie England* but from there proceeded to

Marx. This led him to join the Socialist Democratic Federation (SDF), the most Marxian of the many Labour Groups, which had been started by the eccentric Old Etonian, H. M. Hyndman. Before the First World War, Maclean was best known as a lecturer and organiser of the unemployed and unskilled workers. It was the war which made him a figure of more than local importance. He opposed it from the outset. In his view, it was merely the outcome of the struggle for markets between imperialist powers. As a logical theoretician he might have welcomed the war as a step towards the disintegration of the capitalist world but he found repellent the idea that workers should be killed to make capitalists rich. At first he merely called for a negotiated peace; within a couple of years he was demanding 'a socialist revolution'. Not surprisingly he soon found himself in trouble with the authorities. He was dismissed from his teaching post by the Govan School Board after he had been charged 'with using language likely to cause a breach of the peace' and a few months later was arrested and charged under the Defence of the Realm Act. He was alleged to have tried to discourage recruitment to the armed forces and to have impeded the production of war materials. He had clearly done both of these things, however high-minded his motives, but pled not guilty. He was sentenced to three years' penal servitude. *The Scotsman* newspaper expressed its approval: 'He is a representative of a poisonous set of parasites . . . who talk treason instead of working.' He was released fifteen months later, partly in response to massive demonstrations in Glasgow and the Government's consequent desire to appease unrest.

He was overjoyed by the Bolshevik Revolution of November 1917: 'too overcome with emotion even to speak', according to one biographer. The Bolsheviks responded by honouring him, naming him an honorary president of the First Congress of Soviets and also Bolshevik Consul to Scotland. The Government, which had not recognised the Bolshevik Government, not surprisingly refused to accept its consul.

In March 1918 Maclean was again arrested and charged with sedition. This time he refused to plead. Instead he told the court that he was not there as the accused: 'I am here as the accuser of Capitalism dripping with blood from head to foot.' This did not impress the court and he was sentenced to five years' imprisonment. It has been said that 'this was an indication of how seriously the Government took Maclean and his politics' but it may rather have been only an indication of how seriously the judges took the crime of sedition.

The sentence aroused fury and outrage among the Labour movement in the west of Scotland. The Clyde District Defence

Committee demanded Maclean's release. The Gorbals Labour Party chose him as their parliamentary candidate, even though there was already a Labour Member. He alleged that his food was poisoned and went on hunger strike. He was forcibly fed, a vile practice. His wife warned that 'he cannot much longer endure the torture of body and mind to which he is daily being subject'.

He was released on 3 December 1918. It should be noted that, although Maclean was arrested and sentenced on six occasions, only on the fifth did he serve anything like the full term in gaol; dissidents in the Bolshevik State were less fortunate.

After the war, as the Labour movement advanced to the centre of politics, Maclean found himself in a more and more peripheral position. This was partly because his views had grown wilder and his grip on reality was weakening. In a pamphlet, *The War after the War*, he foretold intense competition between the capitalist countries for a shrinking world market, and a war between Britain and the USA over the ownership and control of the Pacific Ocean. Few people can have thought this likely. He called for a 'revolution in Britain no later than this year' as the best way to protect the Bolshevik Revolution and to avoid a new war. He supported the campaign for Irish Home Rule although he also argued 'that Irish labour would not be free under a Sinn Fein Republic'. Nevertheless he was encouraged by events in Ireland to call for the establishment of a Workers' Republic of Scotland: 'Glasgow [could be made] a Petrograd, a Revolutionary centre second to none', he wrote in his magazine *Vanguard*, 'Scotland must have independence. The Communism of the clans must be re-established on a modern basis. Scotland must therefore work itself into a Communism embracing the whole country as a unit. Back to Communism and Forward to Communism.' Moreover, it was only by establishing a Scottish Workers' Republic that Scotland could avoid involvement in the coming war in the Pacific between England and the USA.

This was wild talk and it was no wonder, though doubtless sad, that couthier figures on the Left, such as Willie Gallacher, should have concluded that he had become mentally unbalanced. Hugh MacDiarmid later had no difficulty in 'dismissing this atrocious story. It was obviously manufactured to discredit his advocacy at this time of Scottish Workers' Republicanism.' Perhaps so; but Maclean in his last years sounds like a man whose sense of reality was limited to what went on in his own head and who took less and less notice of the world around him.

He stood in a local election and the General Election of 1923. In both contests he was well beaten. He then resigned his post as a tutor with the Scottish Labour College, when the National Committee refused to accept his draft constitution. He called this an act of 'ingratitude and treachery'. In April 1923 he was arrested again and charged with a breach of the peace but this time the charge was dropped. His health was broken, and perhaps his will also; he died of pneumonia while campaigning in the Gorbals in December 1923.

That Maclean in his way was a great man cannot be doubted; his abiding influence is proof of that, when the memory of those on the Left who defeated him in his lifetime is fading. He was a good man, too, and an honest one, with no humour but with a deep attachment to what he saw as the cause of human betterment. He never came close to success; his failure was even more complete than Prince Charles Edward's and surely no more to be regretted.

He has become the hero-martyr of the Scottish Left, although he abandoned the constitutionalism that the Scottish Labour Party has always followed. His terms of imprisonment, however, have provoked a strange response from his admirers; strange because, on Maclean's own terms, they were surely justified. If Maclean was, as his admirers insist, a serious revolutionary, then the State had a right to defend itself against him. If it was wrong for the State to exercise that right, then Maclean was not to be taken seriously. To applaud Maclean and yet refuse to recognise that the State was justified in imprisoning him, is ridiculous. It is also to diminish him. Can anyone claim that had he been successful, he would himself have been more tender than Lenin? It is absurd to pretend that in a revolutionary situation, only the revolutionists are justified in advocating force.

John Orr, later Lord Boyd-Orr
(1880–1971)

Swift's King of Brobdingnag gave it as his opinion that 'whoever could make two ears of corn, or two blades of grass, to grow upon a spot of ground where only one grew before, would deserve better of mankind, and do more essential service to mankind, than the whole race of politicians put together'. Few sensible men would dissent from this opinion, adding only that it is the business of the politicians to arrange matters so as to allow such work to be done. If one accepts the king's judgement, few Scotsmen have done more for their fellow-countrymen or for mankind in general than John Boyd-Orr.

He was born in Ayrshire, the son of a quarry-owner, and first attending the village school at Kilmaurs where he judged that 'the children of the poor were probably as well educated as those of the wealthy in rudimentary subjects like reading, writing and arithmetic'. But if their mental food was as good, their real food was decidedly inferior, especially in the cities; it was to be his lifework to try to correct this. He was one of the first fully to appreciate the importance of nutrition.

At Glasgow University he became a friend of the future politician Walter Elliot, whose co-operation and assistance between the wars was to be invaluable. He served in the First World War winning a DSO and MC, and like many who suffered that experience emerged from the war not only determined that such lunatic waste should never again be inflicted on mankind, but also that the survivors should return to, and their children grow up in, a better world.

He saw that there were two important aspects of nutrition. There was the question of production, and the question of how to establish what was in fact a satisfactory diet, who failed to obtain one, and how to correct this. The problems were distinct and yet closely connected. It was certainly impossible to correct deficiencies unless you set yourself to improve agricultural productivity. Health in the cities depended on prosperity in the countryside, and this depended on being able to help farmers to effect a second, scientific, revolution in agriculture. Modern problems of over-production and surpluses are in part at least, evidence of his success.

In 1920 he went to the recently founded Rowett Research

Institute outside Aberdeen to work on the mineral requirements in animal diet. This led on to an investigation of pastures. The institute procured samples of pasture from every sheep-farming district in Britain and many abroad, even from as far off as the Falkland Islands. Analysis revealed a correlation between the chemical and physical composition of soils and the protein and mineral content of the pasture; this enabled a connection to be made between the composition and quality of the pasture and the rate of growth of the stock; diseases were often found to be attributable to mineral deficiences. From such work stemmed the scientific farming of today which has seen such an enormous increase in productivity. It was the basis of the near self-sufficiency in food which Britain has attained. Much of the research was funded by the Empire Marketing Board which Stanley Baldwin had set up.

The Board also financed a controlled experiment in feeding milk to schoolchildren in the Scottish cities which Orr organised in 1927. This showed that the children who had been supplied with milk began to grow as quickly as the children of the rich, who had been on average four inches taller at the age of fourteen. It was this experiment which led, at Elliot's insistence, to the supply of free milk in schools.

Orr was then able to broaden his investigation. In the early 1930s he began what was to be a classic survey of the relationship between income and food consumption, concluding that 'in Britain a diet completely adequate for health, according to modern standards, is reached at an income level above that of 50 per cent of the population'. This was not a popular judgement, but his evidence was cogent.

His career might have been checked when his friend and ally Elliot, to whom he was rather elaborately related by marriage, was omitted from Churchill's coalition in 1940, but he found a new ally in Lord Woolton who became Minister for Food. It was largely as a result of Orr's work, and the application of his ideas, that the quite remarkable feat was achieved of improving the nutritional standards, and therefore the health, of the people during a time of total war and food rationing. But the evidence was incontrovertible.

At the end of the war, Orr, now MP for the Scottish Universities, acquired some notoriety (and the nickname 'dismal Johnny') on account of his forecasts of imminent world famine. This was, of course, alarmist talk but deliberately so. The outcome was the establishment of the Food and Agriculture Organisation of the United Nations, and Orr, now created a peer, became its first Director. He was now able to promulgate his ideas on a global scale. FAO, which had its headquarters in Rome, became an exception among UN organisations; a success. The rise in food production in countries such as India was the consequence of the application of the work initiated by Boyd-Orr in Scotland, and if politicians in many Third World countries adopted policies which might have been intended to encourage the fulfilment of his prophecies of famine, enough was achieved to avert the global disaster he had warned against.

Even a brief survey of his career bears out the truth of Swift's words. Few men have done more for mankind, or deserved our gratitude more.

Thomas Johnston
(1881–1965)

Thomas Johnston was perhaps the most effective Secretary of State Scotland has had. Certainly the way that Scotland has been governed since the Second War owes much to him. However, the wisdom and effectiveness of his work has become more open to question as the years have passed.

He began on the fringe and all his life was a steady progress to a centrist position. In 1909 he published *Our Scots Noble Families*, an intemperate attack on the landed gentry whom he denounced as 'tax-gatherers [who] sucked the life-blood of the nation . . . that they might live in idleness and luxury. . . . Time and again they have sold our land to the invader'. In the 1940s, by now sitting on numerous quasi-governmental boards with representatives of our Scots noble families, Johnston busied himself trying to buy up all unsold copies of his book.

Of course, Johnston, for all the violence of his early opinions, was always respectable. He inherited a printing business and two weekly papers from his mother's cousin. He attended Glasgow University and in 1906 founded the magazine *Forward*, which was financed partly by Roland Muirhead, a wealthy tanner and enthusiast for Scottish Home Rule. *Forward* advocated nationalisation of the railways and of land. It was outspoken and puritanical – Johnston, a teetotaller, refused to accept advertisements for alcoholic drinks. He was also active as a town-councillor in his native Kirkintilloch. In this role he already showed the dirigiste tendencies which were to mark his whole public life: he founded a municipal cinema, a municipal pig-feeding scheme, municipal kitchens and shower-baths, and even municipal jam-making. In the 1940s Johnston was to show that he thought that the Gentlemen in St Andrews House knew best how Scotland should be run; forty years earlier the Gentleman in Kirkintilloch Town Hall had been equally certain.

He opposed the First World War at first, and so *Forward* was briefly suspended. However, by 1916, he supported the war effort and was again free to publish. He entered Parliament in 1922 as Member for Clackmannan and West Stirlingshire, though he was reluctant to go to London and always remained suspicious of the English.

Much of his activity in the 1920s, however, was directed to imperial and colonial affairs. He became converted to the idea that the Empire could be 'the greatest lever for human emancipation the world has ever known' and he was rightly suspicious of Indian nationalists. After a visit to India to investigate the conditions of jute workers, he observed that they were exploited more by Indian capitalists than by British. He mocked the pretence of the nationalists that 'the starvation and robbery of the poor peasant would cease if they and their friends were in control'. However, he never fully confronted what Orwell was to see as the dilemma of socialists: the knowledge that the prosperity of British workers might depend on the exploitation or restriction of colonial workers. In 1926, for instance, he opposed a Bill to grant a loan for the building of the Zambesi bridge and the extension of the railway to the Tetso coal-fields for fear that this would lead to the import of cheap African coal.

He supported Ramsay MacDonald and was made Under-Secretary for Scotland in the 1929 Labour Government. He was associated with Mosley in efforts to combat the Depression and consequent unemployment, though he later played down his part in the Mosley Memorandum. Out of Parliament from 1931–35, he was then returned again for his old seat and showed a characteristic and contradictory indecision over questions of re-armament and foreign policy. He wanted to resist Hitler without re-arming.

In 1941 Churchill made him Secretary of State for Scotland and the great part of his life began. He was certainly a powerful and persuasive minister. He established a Council of State consisting of all the past Secretaries and he arranged that Scottish MPs should meet in Edinburgh to discuss policy and to liaise with officials in St Andrews House. In 1942 he set up the Scottish Council on Industry, drawing on business, the trade unions and local government for its membership. The Council was able to improve the allocation of wartime industry to Scotland. At a time when the State, engaged in a great war, was arrogating to itself new powers and control over large areas of economic life, Johnston at least ensured that many of these new powers would be retained in Edinburgh and not exercised from London. His administration finally established the Scottish Office as a quasi-autonomous organ of Government.

In doing this Johnston headed off political nationalism. He had himself supported the Home Rules Bills of 1924 and 1927 but this now seemed to him an unnecessary measure. He had warned the Cabinet that 'there was a strong nationalist movement in Scotland and that it could be a potential danger if it grew through lack of attention to Scottish interests'. The answer was to strengthen the home-based administration. Thus in an atmosphere where the idea of beneficient activity of the State in economic and social affairs attracted more and more support in all political parties, Johnston was able to print his stamp on the country.

In effect, by concentrating State activity in Edinburgh, Johnston may be seen to have given a new vitality to the Union. Whether this had a generally beneficial effect on the economy of Scotland is open to doubt. Johnston certainly encouraged the belief, which has remained paramount in Scotland, that little may be achieved without State aid and State regulation. Moreover, in some respects Johnston's own policy was myopic. His colleague on the Council of State, the Tory Walter Elliot, pointed out that 'the expansion of industry in Scotland was ephemeral, being almost entirely confined to munitions and war industries which would, from their very nature, decline rapidly after the war, while more permanent industries were attracted to England'. There is no evidence that Johnston fully grasped the gravity of this criticism. Instead, he was too often carried off on irrelevant hobby-horses, such as the iniquity of printing Scottish telephone directories in England and the possibility of using Scottish nettles in paper-making. From 1942 he was much concerned with the establishment of what was to be the North of Scotland Hydro-Electric Board, the effect of which, as its critics had foretold, was to reduce the demand for Scottish coal without achieving the promised diversification of the economy of the Highlands.

Johnston retired from party politics in 1945 to become head of the Hydro Board, head of the Scottish Tourist Board and Head of the Scottish Division of the Forestry Commission. He became one of the 'great and guid'; almost no public board seemed right without him. For better or worse, he shaped the development of Scotland. The guided economy of post-war Scotland, which has brought some benefits and much painful waste, owes more to Johnston than to any other individual. His work weakened the argument for a national parliament for a generation; he made Scotland safe for bureaucracy. He represented the modern State's trust in the rule of the expert and the consensus of 'informed' opinion. Nevertheless, it is fair to record the verdict of a distinguished historian: 'the fruits of the collectivist State, of the rule of the expert, and of a policy of welfare determined from above and afar, are to be seen in the steadily improving quality of life for the Scottish people between the 1940s and the mid-1970s'. (T. C. Smout: *A Century of the Scottish People*.) One might only add the rider that in parts of Britain, which have not enjoyed these benefits, the quality of life has often improved more.

Sir James Lithgow
(1883–1952)

Sir James Lithgow was for half a century the greatest figure in Scottish industry. His biography is not only of intrinsic interest but also reveals the central and enduring problems that the Scottish economy has experienced and continues to experience.

His father, William Todd Lithgow, had in 1874 established himself as a partner in the shipbuilding firm of Russell & Co in Port Glasgow. The firm concentrated on building bulk-carriers for grain, coal, sugar, oil and wood and employed a system of building to semi-standard designs. This firm was hugely profitable – William Lithgow was to die a millionaire. He was able to offer his son James the choice of living as a country gentleman, divorced from the business which created his wealth, or of entering the yard as an apprentice. James Lithgow chose the latter course, as did his younger brother Henry, with whom he worked closely for the next forty years and on whom he depended greatly, as he himself became more and more involved in the politics of wider industrial affairs and eventually became the spokesman for manufacturing industry in Scotland.

William Lithgow died in 1908, so that James inherited the company at the age of twenty-five. Fortunately this coincided with a boom in shipbuilding and the years up to the outbreak of war in 1914 saw a steady expansion. By then, Lithgows were Port Glasgow and Port Glasgow was Lithgows. Already James Lithgow had begun his career of wider public service, being President of the Clyde Shipbuilders Association.

A keen Territorial soldier, he served fifteen months in France, leaving Henry to manage the yard and to pursue at the same time a policy of acquisition of other firms. During the war, Lithgows bought Robert Duncan & Co and the Glasgow firm of marine engineers, David Rowan & Co. In 1917 James Lithgow was made Director of Merchant Shipping. His job was to see that the merchant yards met the demands made on them by the war.

The first post-war years were good ones, as there was much shipping to be replaced. Lithgows bought other companies and also involved themselves for the first time in steel-making, to ensure supplies that were endangered by a world shortage.

The post-war boom lasted only a short time and very soon shipbuilding entered a difficult period. Lithgow believed that British industry was in danger of pricing itself out of the market. The pound was overvalued, all the more so after the ill-advised decision to return to the Gold Standard. At the same time, labour was making new demands which did not reflect the prosperity of the industry. Lithgow considered that 'when labour leaders instruct their members to welcome changes designed to reduce total costs and to work up to the reasonable capacity of their skill, realising that the laws of supply and demand in a democratically governed country are an ample safeguard against exploitation, there will be some real hope of maintaining wages at a higher level'. This is a tune that could have been played, indeed has been played, at any time in the sixty years since.

There was gross over-capacity in shipbuilding and a process of 'readjustment' was necessary. Lithgow disliked the prospect. He regarded it as evidence of failure to come to terms with the problem. Nevertheless, it was true that, throughout the post-war decade, shipyards had been working at only half capacity. The National Shipbuilders Security Ltd was founded with the intention of restructuring the industry by bringing capacity closer to likely demand. Lithgow was involved also in a similar exercise in the steel-making industry, particularly at Beardmore's.

Naturally, none of this made Lithgow popular, as it was impossible to reduce shipbuilding and steel-making capacities without at the same time creating even more unemployment as yards closed. Yet he could see no other possible course of action. It was better to have a smaller industry, which was able to compete in world markets, than a large one which was heavily and, so it seemed, irredeemably in debt. Some clamoured for Protection but he saw no solution there. He was by upbringing and conviction a Free Trader and believed that Protection would result in the further shrinkage of world markets. In the Thirties, however, he arrived at a compromise by supporting Imperial Preference, seeing in the Empire a large Free Trade area that might benefit from protection against external interests.

His position on restructuring was strengthened, however, by his own character and philosophy. In the first place, he took nothing himself from Lithgows; his general policy had been not to take dividends but to keep money within the company. He could hardly be accused of stripping industry for his own personal profit. Indeed it is interesting that, when he died, his estate was less than half that of his father.

More importantly, perhaps, he believed that it was his duty to work for the establishment of industries that might replace those that were contracting. He was one of the founders of the Scottish National Development Council in 1931 and was its chairman from that date till 1939. He believed that Scottish industrialists had a duty towards their country: 'It may be taken for granted', he said, 'that those who have made their money in Scotland have an obligation to keep it there and to use their best endeavours to develop and keep the health of the industry to which they owe their prosperity.' This high sense of duty gave him authority.

This sense of duty was bolstered by his religion. He was a devout and generous member of the Church of Scotland. He had a keen sense too of civic duty and of duty to his own workforce. No doubt this would be condemned by many as paternalist but it informed Lithgow's life. He recognised that he held a privileged position and he believed that this could only be justified by the return he made. He was a great industrialist but, being that, he had to be also a public servant. No-one was ever further from the picture of the robber capitalist than Lithgow. He believed that 'industry and commerce, even life itself, can only be carried on by giving value for money received, and that can only be achieved by hard work and application by each one in his particular sphere'. There was much in Lithgow that Carlyle would have recognised and honoured.

Other honours came his way, of course: he was knighted in 1935, received honorary degrees and was made the first honorary citizen of Port Glasgow. But work was the heart of his creed and his labours were extraordinary. During the Second World War he was Controller of Merchant Shipping and Repairs, Deputy Chairman of the Industrial Capacity Committee of the Production Council, and President of the Iron and Steel Federation. Despite these responsibilities he still occupied himself with Lithgows and with Beardmore and Fairfields of which he was also Chairman. His brother Henry saw to the day-to-day management of the family firm but, even so, Lithgow's workload was staggering.

He died in 1952, before Britain's position as the greatest shipbuilding nation had been eroded. It is possible to see his life as a long struggle against inevitability – there is heroism in that – but it is perhaps truer to see him as one of the last exemplars of a peculiarly Scottish virtue. P. H. Scott has drawn attention to the Scottish cult of the old Roman virtue of *severitas*: 'The *severitas* in question', he wrote, 'is *severitas* towards oneself.' This was certainly manifest in Lithgow.

Sir Compton Mackenzie
(1883–1972)

Compton Mackenzie was for a long time the best-known Scottish writer. He was one of the founders of the Scottish National Party; he appeared in whisky advertisements; his pronouncements on public affairs were frequently sought by newspaper editors who knew they could rely on him to produce good copy; he was the doyen of the literary corps.

Yet there was more than one paradox in this. In the first place, Mackenzie was a Scot by adoption rather than by birth or upbringing; he never lived in Scotland till he was nearly fifty. He belonged to a famous theatrical family. His father, Edward Compton, was a well-known actor-manager and his sister became the actress Fay Compton. He was educated in England, at St Paul's and Magdalen College, Oxford, and his first reputation – one might almost say his first career – was as an English novelist. The second paradox was that his eventual popular reputation depended on his least substantial works: the Highland comedies, romps and farcical extravaganzas of which *Whisky Galore* was the best known. They already seem rather dated.

His early novels, *The Passionate Elopement, Guy and Pauline* and *Carnival*, are full of that peculiarly Edwardian and English country lyricism that was soon to pretend to modernity by calling itself Georgian. They are lush and sensuous prose equivalents of Rupert Brooke's poetry. Today they are, perhaps, chiefly of historical interest as being so perfect an expression of that flower of English certainty in the rightness of the world's arrangement that was to disintegrate forever in Flanders. They were successful, however, in their time. They attracted the admiring attention of Henry James who, in a celebrated article in the *Times Literary Supplement* in 1914, picked out Mackenzie as 'very much the greatest talent of a new generation'.

The previous year Mackenzie had published his first masterpiece, *Sinister Street*, which seemed to justify James's judgement. Ford Madox Ford (still at that time called Hueffer) also thought it 'possibly a work of real genius'. Henry James said Mackenzie 'had emancipated the English novel'. The booksellers W. H. Smith showed the literary taste ever associated with the firm by banning the book from their circulating library. The novel had a success in America too; it made Mackenzie the idol of the young Scott Fitzgerald whose early novels reek of his influence.

During the First World War, Mackenzie served with British Intelligence in the Aegean. It was a period which marked his life, both by giving him a lasting contempt for officialdom that is apparent in much of his fiction and also by reinforcing the love of Greece that had been nurtured by his classical studies. He wrote several volumes of war memories.

With the return of peace, Mackenzie slid out of fashion. He was out of sympathy with the modern movement, as he detested the psychological investigation of character and had no interest in experimentation. Scott Fitzgerald, visiting him on Capri (Mackenzie always loved islands), spent 'half the night talking to my old idol Compton Mackenzie. You get no sense from him that his work has gone to pieces. I think he is just tired. The war wrecked him as it did Wells and many of his generation'.

Nevertheless, the wreck recovered, with two sparkling comedies set on Capri: *Vestal Fire* and *Extraordinary Women*. Both books show the influence of his friend, Norman Douglas, who indeed appears, very thinly disguised, as a character in the first of them. Both books have abundant energy and good humour; they sparkle with life and remain, for some of his admirers, his finest fiction.

In 1928 he came to live in Scotland, on the island of Barra, and from then on identified himself with his ancestral country. Although it might seem a sudden decision and an abrupt volte-face, it had been brewing for a long time and there is no reason to question his sincerity. He had become a Roman Catholic in 1914. This contributed to his Jacobite enthusiasm for Scotland but there were older impulses at work. In his Rectorial Address to Glasgow University, he explained how, at the age of eight, he was given a copy of Scott's *Tales of a Grandfather* and how 'it happened that soon after I came possessed of this talisman to live in the past of that race from which I sprung that I travelled northward alone. It was near dusk on an evening of earliest Spring. Somebody in the railway-carriage announced that we were crossing the border, and I craned my head out of the window to enjoy the magical sensation. Down the long train came a faint sound of cheering and from windows far ahead I could see hats being waved. An austere landscape in the fast-fading dusk, a stream of flamy smoke from an engine, a few cheers ringing above the roar of the train, a few hats waving; not much perhaps, but enough for a child of eight to sit back again in a dim railway-carriage and dream over, his heart blazoned like a herald's tabard with the bright symbols of his country's life, his heart draped like a hatchment with the sombre memories of defeat upon defeat. Thence onwards I lived secretly in the past of my country . . .' To both the Church of Rome and Scotland, Mackenzie brought all the often uncritical enthusiasm of a convert. There was another element too. He had become an enthusiast for the renaissance of small or historic nations. The influence of Greece was paramount and he rejoiced at the recreation of Poland and Ireland. Why should Scotland not recover its independence in like manner? His dreams went further. He pondered the possibilities of a Pan-Celtic Federation.

If he was never more than an amateur politician, he remained a very professional writer. The late thirties were occupied by the writing of his most ambitious work, *The Four Winds of Love*. It was published from 1937 to 1945 in four parts, with six volumes, some 3000 pages and perhaps a million words. The American critic Edmund Wilson admired it greatly; it 'escaped the provinciality that was the bane of most English fiction'. The action extends from 1900 to 1940. Its theme is how the social, economic, political and ideological development of the modern world has impinged on traditional and inherited culture. The hero, John Ogilvie, is exposed to English public school and university education, to Irish, Scottish and Greek nationalism, to the First World War and Fascism in Italy, to conversion to Catholicism, to Zionism and Communism; in short, to almost everything in the modern world. Ogilvie confronts them all, argues about them, comes to a conclusion and teaches others, since he is endlessly loquacious and didactic. At the same time each wind brings him a different love; the erotic themes shadow the public ones. His private and public lives are intertwined and interest is maintained on both levels. A complicated structural symbolism operates throughout. However, the weaknesses are also obvious. Mackenzie's disinclination to explore at any depth the tensions in the main characters means that they are less than the significant emblematic figures that they are meant to be; none is capable of interesting development. Nevertheless, these weaknesses are subsumed in the richness, vitality, wit and intelligence of the novel. Mackenzie's willingness to tackle themes of real and central importance to the modern world is admirable. It is a novel on a great scale, which still offers, amid certain longueurs, intense delights.

While working on this book Mackenzie began also to write the Highland farces which were to make him so popular and the best-known Scottish writer. There was, however, one last novel of real quality. *Thin Ice*, published in 1956, is the story of a homosexual Tory politician. It is in some ways an uncharacteristic book, being told with dry spare economy. It is a true work of art.

Some still doubt whether Mackenzie ever fulfilled his early promise. They point to the facility with which he wrote and to the self-satisfaction that he displayed as evidence of shallowness. Nevertheless, *Sinister Street, Vestal Fire, Extraordinary Women, The Four Winds of Love*, and *Thin Ice* represent a body of remarkable quality. If he had written only these books, his reputation would be higher than it is.

Edwin Muir
(1887–1959)

In a much-resented passage of a much-resented book, 'Scott and Scotland', Edwin Muir wrote 'Scotland can only create a national literature by writing in English.' He made this pronouncement when Hugh MacDiarmid's Scottish Renaissance was in the full, if deceptive, flower of its youth. It was natural that those who had committed themselves to restoring the old Scots tongue to full and flexible usage should find this judgement hard either to accept or forgive. Muir became a target for the darts of literary nationalists. His own Orcadian origins were stressed, and no doubt they had in fact something to do with his views, for in Orkney he had grown up speaking a dialect which he could hardly recognise in written Scots. This was unfortunate for it meant that his argument was never really confronted, and it was unfortunate also for it meant that Muir's own poetry received less than its due, and so his achievement, which was to be simultaneously a great Scottish poet, and a great modern European one, was largely ignored.

Muir's experience and development were alike remarkable. He was brought up on the little island of Wyre, where his father farmed, neither skilfully nor successfully. He would look back on his childhood as idyllic, which is common enough; its significance, however, went beyond his personal happiness. He grew up, as he understood it, in a pre-industrial world, which was based on the principle of co-operation. In his autobiography he wrote: 'I was born before the Industrial Revolution, and am now about two hundred years old. But I have skipped a hundred and fifty of them. I was really born in 1737, and till I was fourteen no time-accidents happened to me. Then in 1751 I set out for Glasgow. When I arrived there I found that it was not 1751, but 1901, and that a hundred and fifty years had been burned up in my two days' journey. But I myself was still in 1751, and remained there for a long time. All my life since I have been trying to overhaul that invisible leeway.' This was not fanciful; it was the central fact of Muir's life. He had been reared in Eden, and driven out.

The family's experience of Glasgow was vile. They could hardly adapt. His parents and two brothers died in a very short time. He worked as a clerk, most miserably in a factory where bones were made into glue. However, he read voraciously to educate himself, and, remarkably, succeeded in doing so. He began to contribute to magazines, and in 1918 published a collection of aphorisms, 'We Moderns', using the pseudonym Edward Moore.

He married in 1919. His wife, Willa Anderson, came from Shetland, though she had been brought up in Montrose, and he described his marriage as 'the most fortunate event in my life'. It rescued him from despair, possibly suicide. She was a very strong-minded woman, whom some found difficult; she was a rock to Muir.

They moved first to London and then to Prague. Muir was now writing for American magazines, and they taught themselves German, and began to make a living as translators. Together they translated Feuchtwanger and, more importantly, Kafka. Muir found an affinity with Kafka, the great explorer of alienation in a world stifled by the bureaucratic machine and divorced from God. He also began to write poetry.

His early poetry sprang from his childhood memories. It is, of course, unusual for a poet to begin in middle-life, and Muir found his first verse awkward and stiff. A fairer comment might be that he had not yet found his own voice; echoes of Eliot and Yeats are powerful. Yet there is no clean break in his work; it is all of a piece, and the later poetry, though deeper and more accomplished than his early work, is recognisably from the same stamp.

For much of the 1930s and throughout the war, he lived in Scotland, seldom happily. Though he had some sympathy with the aspirations of Scottish Nationalism, he could not believe in it as a practical possibility. He had always called himself a socialist and never ceased to do so, but his socialism was idiosyncratic, for he believed in the immortality of the soul and called himself 'a man who believes that people . . . should bring about on this earth a society fit for immortal souls'. This was not to be found on the agenda of any political party. Moreover, he was extremely hostile to the materialistic determinism of Communism, which he found as repellent as the theological determinism of Calvin; and this, he held, had inflicted a sore wound on Scotland. His pessimism did not appeal to more ardent spirits, and his analysis of the condition of Scotland as displayed in 'Scottish Journey' and poems such as 'Scotland 1941' alienated many.

Yet he was working towards a tenable position, and as he did so his poetry gained in richness, depth and authority. It was his brief spell in Italy after the war, when he was Director of the British Council in Rome, which brought him to a full expression of Christian Humanism which makes his last poetry so moving and cogent. In his autobiography he told how he had come on a plaque representing the Annunciation: 'An angel and a young girl, their bodies inclined towards each other, their knees bent, as if overcome by love, *tutto tremante*, gazed upon each other like Dante's pair; and that representation of human love so intense that it could not reach further seemed the perfect earthly symbol of the love that passes understanding.' He was no longer hankering after a lost Eden. It is easy to imagine the young Muir, in the wet gas-lit horror of Glasgow, looking back to summer evenings on Wyre where 'time seemed finished ere the ship passed by', and from that point drifting into a debilitating nostalgia. But he had come, like Dante, to see life as a journey, and so to go beyond Eden; in doing so he found a fuller realisation of the value of human experience:

> 'But famished field and blackened tree
> Bear flowers in Eden never known.
> Blossoms of grief and charity
> Bloom in these darkened fields alone.
> What had Eden ever to say
> Of hope and faith and pity and love
> Until was buried all its day
> And memory found its treasure trove?
> Strange blessings never in Paradise
> Fall from these beclouded skies . . .'

This is great poetry, lucid and complex at the same time. Muir had called the first version of his autobiography, 'The Fable and the Story', the story being what happens in a man's life, the fable its deeper significance. Now, under the influence of Orkney and Italy, the story and the fable came together; in reading his last poems we can experience what he called 'the free environing warmth of human kindness' and a powerful sense, as if we were brushed with an angel's wing, of the love and mercy of God.

John Logie Baird
(1888–1946)

The exact status of an inventor is rarely certain. He is hardly ever alone in his field, and it may be claimed that inventions exist in the general air; if one man does not pluck them down, another will. Nevertheless this does not invalidate the claims of the pioneers. One such was John Logie Baird, whose claim to be the inventor of television is as good as anyone's, even though it was not to be his system that was employed when the BBC started the world's first television service in 1936. Of course, there are many who would say that the invention of television is a matter for regret rather than pride, but, on balance, whatever the harm done by Baird's invention, it has probably added to the general store of human happiness.

Baird was, like so many Scots of energy and ambition, a son of the manse. His father was parish minister of Helensburgh, and Baird grew up in the halcyon days of the West of Scotland, when Glasgow's energy and imaginative capability seemed to promise an endlessly sunny future. It was a society where interest in technology was normal, and Baird himself went to the Royal Technical College, having early shown an inventive bent. Thence he proceeded to Glasgow University to study for a BSc. He volunteered for the army in 1914 but was rejected owing to his chronic ill-health. He took a job as an electrical supply engineer, but his health failed, and he set up as a professional inventor.

His early efforts were diverse, but generally unsuccessful. A cure for haemorrhoids was a flop; so was an attempt to manufacture synthetic diamonds. The Baird Undersock 'keeping the Feet Warm in Winter and Cool in Summer' made him a little money, but involved him in production difficulties. His health poor, he emigrated to Trinidad, and then, briefly to the United States, but was back in Britain soon after the war, by which time he was already experimenting with television. By 1926 he was ready to offer a demonstration, and pictures were transmitted from one room to another. Baird had demonstrated that television was a practical possibility, and he was certainly the first man to do so. Then, with the help of the Chief Engineer of the BBC he sent pictures along telephone wires to a BBC studio which then put them on the air,

Baird himself receiving them on his set in Frith Street 'practically unaltered'.

Despite this, the BBC, still itself an infant and fully engaged in the much more practical and immediate problem of radio, showed no interest in developing Baird's idea. If he was going to pursue his project, he would have to raise money, form a company and build his own transmitter. He proceeded to do so, and licensed his television station – again this was the first to come into existence. He moved into a larger studio near Leicester Square, found backers, and set up Baird Television Ltd. He continued to make technical progress, even transmitting a picture across the Atlantic and to the liner *Berengaria* en route for New York. However, his partners lost hope, seeing no sign of an early financial return. He became disillusioned: 'If any inventor reads these pages,' he wrote, 'let him by this be warned, and do what Graham Bell, inventor of the telephone did, and sell for cash. Inventors are no match for financiers where stocks and shares are concerned, and will, if they hold on, find that the financiers have the cash and they have the paper.' In fact, of course, Baird's invention was, despite apparent similarities, of a different type from Bell's, which could early be seen to have a clear commercial value. Baird really required to have persuaded Reith at the BBC or the heads of one of the big American radio stations that television was a medium of communication comparable to radio and the cinema. He failed to do so. He failed to make money either, even though at one time he was offered more than £100000 for his shares in Baird Television. Such an offer could surely have been used to impress others with the commercial possibilities of the medium. It seems that Baird was an example of the pure inventor, a man with very little sense of organisation. He continued to develop varieties of television, experimenting with colour, large-screen television, telephone television, and what he called stereoscopic TV, but the mainstream of television exploitation passed him by.

He was unfortune to be a loner and to live at a time when the link between industry and invention which had helped sustain Kelvin had been weakened. Moreover, unlike Kelvin, he had no real academic background. He never worked in a university beyond undergraduate level, and one can only surmise what he might have achieved with the advantage of the backing of a university department. There is something tragic in his life – a sense of wasted powers – but the tragedy extends beyond the personal. Here after all was a Scot who must be considered the most remarkable innovator of his generation, a man who had created what was to be the most powerful and influential means of communication of the second half of the twentieth century, and his own country was blind to his genius, and unable to produce any man, institution or company capable of exploiting it. In Baird's success, we can see the enduring vitality of Scotsmen; in his failure, the economic lassitude of our country.

Walter Elliot
(1888–1958)

There have been a number of Scottish Prime Ministers. In this century Balfour, Campbell-Bannerman, MacDonald and Sir Alec Douglas-Home were incontrovertibly Scots; Bonar Law was an Ulster Scot who made his money in Glasgow; while Harold Macmillan rarely allowed his Highland grandfather and Hebridean ancestors to be forgotten. Despite this, Scots MPs have rarely been highly considered, and this is even truer on the Conservative side. Very few have been men of any distinction other than social, and even that has become rarer. One exception was Walter Elliot. Many between the wars picked him as a future Prime Minister. He never came near it. He held Cabinet Office only as Secretary of State for Scotland, Minister of Agriculture and Minister of Health. He was out of office for the last twenty years of his life. His career might be described as a failure, and probably disappointed him. Yet he made a deep impression on all who came in contact with him; one fellow-Tory, Sir Beverley Baxter, wrote: 'When Churchill formed his Government in 1951, and left Elliot out, the House watched him take his seat among the rank and file and suddenly realised that this Ministerial cast-off was a great man, whose presence in the Chamber lent dignity to us all.' Few deserve such a tribute; Elliot did.

He was born in Lanark, where his father was a farmer and auctioneer, and he was properly proud of his Border ancestry. He once said, 'When I hear people – Americans, Indians – speaking of old feuds with England, it makes me smile. I suppose the English have hanged more Elliots alone – certainly more Borderers . . . than the total of all people who were killed in the War of Independence.' This memory aroused in him no animosity towards the English. He was in the fullest and most exact sense of the word a Unionist, capable of dismissing complaints of Scottish nationalists about English domination as 'whining formulae'; but no one could doubt that he was a Scottish patriot, rooted in our heritage and proud of our achievements. He took pleasure in pointing out that Scotland was 'a microcosm of Europe', as England had never been, and of reminding his English friends that a Scotsman had painted the banner of Joan of Arc. He read Scott and Stevenson insatiably, but he was also never without a copy of Gibbon's *Decline and Fall*.

He was educated at Glasgow Academy and Glasgow University in its great days. Like his friend O. H. Mavor ('James Bridie') he qualified as a doctor in the intervals of editing the Glasgow University Magazine. (Later he claimed to have been the only editor of it to have become Rector of the University.) It was as a doctor that he served in the war, with the Scots Greys. He won the MC at Wancourt near Arras in April 1917, and a bar to it six months later. The war left him with a dislike of Germans, which he struggled to overcome after 1945, and a contempt for those who thought they had been badly treated by the Treaty of Versailles.

He was elected for Lanark in the Khaki Election of 1919. The legend has it that, on being invited to stand, he replied by telegram 'Yes, which party?' In fact he could never have been anything but a Tory. He had no time for the doctrinaire theories of Socialism, and, though a Free Trader, saw too clearly the need for State intervention in matters of public health and certain industries to be a classical Liberal. More important still, he held an organic view of social development which inclined him to Toryism.

Throughout the period between the wars, Elliot's star remained in the ascendant. There was only one hitch, when he lost Lanark by 250 votes in 1923, but the following year he was returned for Kelvingrove, which, though a marginal, he held till 1945. He soon made his mark by his speeches on Health matters, but it was recognised that he was not restricted to this professional interest. He advocated agricultural research, in which he maintained a lifelong interest, and helped his friend John Boyd-Orr to establish the Rowett Institute in Aberdeen.

He was a success in each of the Ministries he occupied. As Minister of Agriculture he established the system which gradually rescued farming from a long depression, and which was to give it conditions of stability which ensured a steady growth. It was essentially by Elliot's system that British agriculture was run till we entered the Common Market.

At the Scottish Office he developed policies of administrative devolution, set up the Scottish Special Housing Association, and encouraged the Scottish National Development Council. The Scottish Economic Committee was created in 1936 and promoted the Empire Exhibition in Glasgow in 1938. The post-war form of Scottish Government owes more to the initiatives undertaken by Elliot from 1936–8 than to any other politician, and during the war he was equally effective in Tom Johnston's Council of State. In this he took the leading role in the important areas of industrial and housing policy, and an examination of the Council's Minutes has led the historian Dr Christopher Harvie to conclude that 'while Johnston's energy and persistence emerge, what is most striking is the role of Elliot'.

As Minister of Health Elliot was not only able to emphasise the importance of nutrition ('man is what he eats' was a favourite saying), but also had the responsibility of preparing the Health Services for war and organising plans for the evacuation of children from the cities. Characteristically, he was determined that there should be no class distinction in this.

Munich wrecked Elliot's career. He was no appeaser by nature, and he had always distrusted the Germans. He has recognised that Hitler's occupation of the Rhineland in 1936 should have been opposed, and in retrospect that this was the moment when he should have resigned. But he had the ability, unfortunate for a politician, of being able to see both sides of a question. He had no personal responsibility for Munich, he was doing work which he enjoyed and considered important, and he was bound to Chamberlain by loyalty, affection and respect. He was one of those Conservatives omitted by Churchill when he formed his Coalition, and never achieved Government office again. It was a waste. Churchill and he were antipathetic. Churchill observed of him, 'He talks too much', the criticism of a monologuist. He did include Elliot in his Shadow Cabinet, when Elliot returned to the House as member for the Scottish Universities in 1946, but seems to have felt no compunction on leaving him out of the Cabinet in 1951. He offered Elliot a choice of ministries below Cabinet rank, but cannot have been surprised when this was refused.

Elliot did not repine. He remained an active and influential politician, whose mind seemed endlessly fertile. He defended Scottish interests, worked for Western Europe and Zionism, concerned himself with colonialism in Africa, was a prolific journalist and broadcaster. The sense of talents unused remains.

He has been credited by Dr George Davie with coining the phrase 'the Demoractic Intellect' to define a Scottish ideal. (He would have made a remarkable Minister of Education – for Scotland anyway.)

In 1932 he described the Scottish political heritage in words still worth pondering:

'It is a heritage wherein discipline is rigidly and ruthlessly enforced, but where criticism and attack are unflinching, continuous, and salt with a bitter and jealous humour. It is a heritage wherein intellect, speech and, above all, arguments are the passports to the highest eminence in the land. These traditions we should study, and their histories are the annals of the parishes, their ministers, and their elders.'

One of his first speeches in the Commons advocated the admission of women to the House of Lords. It is a pleasing irony that one of the first Life Peeresses to be created was his widow, Katherine Tennant, the daughter of Sir Charles Tennant and the present Baroness Elliot of Harwood.

Lord Reith
(1889–1971)

Churchill is said to have remarked of Sir Stafford Cripps, 'There, but for the grace of God, goes God.' He might have said it of John Reith, a man whom he also disliked, but had to respect. Reith has one achievement to his name of enduring importance: he made the BBC. In the fifty years since he left it, no other Director-General has ever attained his authority or marked the stamp of his personality so completely on the Corporation. It is not too much to say that almost everything which is good in the BBC, and which has contributed to its worldwide reputation for high standards and trustworthiness, derives from Reith. One has also to confess that its worst faults, self-satisfaction and an almost intolerable self-righteousness, were also characteristic of him.

Reith was born in Stonehaven, and educated at Glasgow Academy and Gresham's School in Norfolk. He trained as an engineer, and may be taken as representative of a continuing strain of pragmatic Calvinism. Everything he did throughout his life was informed with a sense of high moral purpose – you could see it in his craggy face – and an equal sense of his own virtue. The fact that he really was virtuous and really possessed noble ideals only added to the irritation with which many came to view him.

He served and was decorated in the First War, of which he was to write in old age a vivid memoir, *Wearing Spurs*. In 1923, at the age of thirty-four, he was appointed Director-General of the new BBC. He had no experience of radio, but then no one else had. It is reasonable to suppose that it was partly his ability as an engineer which commended him, but it soon became clear that he had very definite ideas of what a national broadcasting service should be. 'In other countries,' as Malcolm Muggeridge has put it, 'the voice might be monopolised by a party, and made to utter only its slogans, or put up for sale, precious moments purchased to praise a pill, explain a soap's excellence, but in England' (he should have said 'Britain') 'in Sir John Reith's words, what was aimed at was an expression of British mentality at its best.' This was no mean ambition.

The BBC was to be an oddity, an anomaly among broadcasting services. It was to be free of commercialism, at the mercy of no special interest, financed through the licence system by public funds, the level of that finance determined by Parliament, yet at the same time independent of Government, the voice of Britain, not of His Majesty's Ministers.

The 1926 General Strike gave him an opportunity to put his principles into action. Very much against the wishes of Churchill, then Chancellor of the Exchequer, Reith refused to allow the BBC to be used against the strikers. This was a remarkable expression of strong-mindedness and independence. It made the BBC's reputation for fair dealing. Reith had a great respect for authority (and expected his staff to show a similar respect for his), but he conceived himself as being responsible to a higher authority than the Government of the day. At a time when the country's leading newspaper, *The Times*, was often seen by foreigners as a Government organ, and indeed saw itself in the same light, Reith proclaimed that the BBC could not be used for any party political purpose, unless the other side was given a fair hearing too. The reputation for trustworthy news which the BBC gained, and was to keep for half a century, was the direct result of Reith's principles.

It could be argued that his position was logically unsound. The BBC did after all depend on the Government for its supplies, and it could be argued that he who pays the piper should call the tune. It is a measure of Reith's achievement that he elevated the young corporation above that argument. He made the BBC into a national asset. He made it seem as impartial as the Crown. At a time when people already said 'you can't believe what you read in the papers', 'I heard it on the wireless' became an asseveration of ultimate truth. That was Reith's achievement.

It was possible to mock some aspects of his governance. The requirement that radio announcers should wear dinner-jackets seems absurd today. But Reith defended it as a mark of respect, not only for distinguished guests who might appear in the studio, but for the medium the announcers served. Likewise, in its desire to be fair and to give weight to all points of view, Reith's BBC could seem bland, too eager to stifle controversy. (One sign of his caution was his insistence that everything, even debates, should be scripted in advance, and the script approved.) Furthermore the BBC under

Reith seemed to many pervasively middle-class, though this was hardly his intention.

Reith only served fifteen years at the BBC, but the impression he made was so great that for a quarter of a century after his resignation, it was still recognisably his institution. That was extraordinary, and inasmuch as the BBC has played so great a part in contemporary culture, Reith's influence has been enormous. He stood for public decency and morality; he could be stuffy – for a time divorce debarred a man from the role of announcer. He was even in his time a little old-fashioned, but that he was a force for good cannot be doubted. No one in a position of authority has since Reith quite so clearly and cogently articulated the ethos of Scots Presbyterianiam.

He was not yet fifty when he left the BBC, but he found no subsequent post worthy of his talents. He ran an airline (Imperial Airways), served briefly in Churchill's wartime Government as Minister of Information, and was Chairman of the Overseas Development Corporation. He performed much useful public service, but the last part of his life leaves the impression of a great man wasted.

Hugh MacDiarmid
(1892–1978)

Hugh MacDiarmid was, of course, Christopher Murray Grieve and many of his friends always referred to him as 'Grieve' or 'Chris'. However, it was as MacDiarmid that he chose to present himself to the world and as MacDiarmid that he offered himself as the Voice of Scotland, so it seems best to call him by that name.

Everything about him was contradictory and he liked it that way. He was a Nationalist who was expelled from the Scottish National Party for Communism, and a Communist who was expelled from the Communist Party of Great Britain for Nationalism. He was a poet who set himself to restore the Scots language, to rescue it by 'adapting an essentially rural tongue to the very much more complex requirements of our urban civilisation' but who abandoned Scots for a peculiarly arid English as soon as he seemed to have won both success and followers. He was a man of the people who was yet a flinty and contemptuous elitist. He was a poet who asked, 'Are my poems spoken in the factories and fields/in the streets o' the toon?/ Gin they're no, then I'm failing to dae/What I ocht to ha' dune.' At the same time he could say in a letter to Iain Crichton Smith: 'you are perfectly correct when you say that I have no more use for the masses than they have for me. There is scarcely anything that appeals to any considerable body of people that I have anything other than comtempt for'. He was a poet of striking originality, who was also capable of plagiary and the regurgitation of half-digested ideas garnered in his wide and often uncritical reading. He could be as good as Wordsworth, having something of Wordsworth's neo-Platonism, and as bad as Wordsworth. He was fiercely independent and an inveterate borrower. He was a man of great kindness, intelligence and charm, who was capable of uttering the most stupid and repellent ideas. He was vain, even for a writer: 'I myself am Scotland today,' he absurdly stated, although the great majority of Scotsmen had probably at most a faint notion of who he was. Yet he was humble before his art. His capacity for scorn was equalled by his capacity for admiration. 'I'll hae nae hauf-way hoose, but aye be whaur/Extremes meet,' he wrote. He was.

MacDiarmid was a poet and an intellectual. These are the first truths about him. He responded with a quivering intensity both to the physical world about him and to abstract ideas. His greatest poetry was written when his imagination contrived a synthesis of idea and object. His poetry was always a quest, which was perhaps why he changed his style so restlessly. He sought a language that could contain all language. He was, in the philosophical sense of the word, an Idealist: 'thought is reality – and thought alone', he wrote in the Third Hymn to Lenin. However, like all poets who strive to reform language, his best poetry is vivid and concrete.

MacDiarmid was born in Langholm, near the border with England. Perhaps the nearness of England sharpened his sense of difference. He was largely self-educated and claimed to have read all the books in the town's library. He had all the confidence in his own judgement that is often revealed by autodidacts, but it was coupled with a tendency to swallow theories whole. His sharp edges were never smoothed off in debate with intellectual equals when young. He trained as a teacher but turned journalist. For some twenty years, except for the period of the First World War when he served as a sergeant in the RAMC, partly in Salonika, he worked as a provincial journalist. It was an experience that his prose style reflected.

His early poetry was written in English and was conventionally Georgian. In the 1920s he turned to Scots. He saw it as 'a vast unutilised mass of lapsed observation made by minds whose attitudes to experience and whose speculative and imaginative tendencies were quite different from any possible to Englishmen and Anglicised Scots today. It is an inchoate Marcel Proust – a Dostoevskian debris of ideas – an inexhaustible quarry of subtle and significant sound'. From this quarry, using learned articles on local dialects and Jamieson's Scots dictionary, he mined a language for himself to use. His long poem, *A Drunk Man Looks at the Thistle*, was an extraordinary feat and, despite some clumsy infelicities, proves MacDiarmid's theory. He called this Synthetic Scots, a term that appealed doubtless to his Hegelianism.

Throughout the 1920s, MacDiarmid identified himself with the movement which became self-consciously known as the Scottish Renaissance. The term was invented by a Frenchman but perhaps those writers to whom it applied should have refrained from employing it themselves. Then, as soon as it was gathering momentum and MacDiarmid seemed to have proved its point, the pace slackened and he was off on a new tack. Although he broke savagely with Edwin Muir, when Muir suggested that MacDiarmid's Scots might be no more than an interesting and unique success which did not alter the fact that the future for Scots writers lay in writing in English, MacDiarmid was soon diluting the congested and literary Scots he had employed. The *First Hymn to Lenin* was written in much thinner language, as if the urgency of his ideas forbade him to seek their deepest expression. From there he moved to what he would call Synthetic English, a language capable of incorporating a wealth of scientific material and one which lent itself to discursive, argumentative and didactic verse. Many admirers of MacDiarmid find his development disappointing or distressing but he had no sense of having lost his way, even though many of his more ambitious projects remained unfinished.

The 1930s were a bad decade for him. His first marriage ended, painfully. He was unable to find employment. He suffered a nervous breakdown. Only the care of his second wife, Valda Trevlyn, and his consciousness of his own genius and mission pulled him through. For much of the time he lived in dire poverty on Whalsay, one of the Shetland Islands. In these years he felt himself to be a prophet in the wilderness. He wrote incessantly but found it hard to produce anything complete, as his projects spiralled more and more ambitiously. His letters of this time combine vast claims for himself and his work in progress with requests for small loans to pay the local shops and details of his daily life – cutting peat or gathering gulls' eggs to pickle for winter. Nevertheless, he came through, when a lesser man would have cracked or gone off his head.

He spent part of the Second World War in an engineering works in Glasgow. Afterwards he pursued his lonely battle against what he saw as the cultural establishment, until, suddenly as it were, the tables were turned. MacDiarmid himself became the revered and representative figurehead of Scottish culture. In his last two decades he was the Grand Old Man of Scottish Letters, the object of study in universities world wide, the proof that Scotland too had a Great Poet and one who had never troubled himself to seek popularity.

The year before MacDiarmid died, the Russian poet Yevtushenko remarked, 'MacDiarmid, he's a great poet, but politically he's crazy'. The greatness was recognised and the craziness forgiven. His advocacy of a Scottish Fascism in the Twenties was dismissed as an aberration; his decision to rejoin the Communist Party in 1956, after the suppression of the Hungarian Rising, was seen only as characteristically contrary. In fact both were absolutely of a part; he was a man who lived largely in the mind, besotted with the purity of ideas. How could the facts of murder and oppression be allowed to sully the pure theory of Communism? His Communism might owe more to Nietzsche than to Marx, since he had indeed cast himself as the Nietzschean *übermensch*, but it was an essential part of his poetic mind. Norman McCaig perhaps summed it up when he said it 'was not so much an ideology as a convenient mythology, something as mythical as Yeats's gyres or Graves's White Goddess'.

MacDiarmid was a poet or he was nothing. In a letter in 1973 he wrote: 'my concern with politics and poetry is not the shallow thing most people mean when they aver that they have their own opinions and likes and dislikes, but a veritable matter of life and death'. He deceived himself up to a point because taken out of the context of his poetry, his politics *were* actually shallow and a mere matter of likes and dislikes. But fundamentally what he wrote was true, since everything that came into his mind was valuable to him because of what he was. It had, therefore, to go towards the making of his poetry. Besides that, nothing mattered.

MacDiarmid became the part he acted. It was absurd that the little journalist in Montrose should advance himself as the Voice and Saviour of Scotland but, if we examine the part he played in the history of Scottish literature, it is hard not to deny that that is just what he became. The country's literature had slid into a cosy and sentimental provinciality. MacDiarmid insisted that a Scottish writer was capable, within the context of Scotland, of engaging with any and every theme. Others joined him in this ambition but he was the most prominent. After MacDiarmid there was no call for any Scottish writer to be timid or apologetic. Like Walter Scott a hundred years before, he was a reviving and reinvigorating force. He insisted, like Scott, that Scotland was a serious matter.

Eric Linklater
(1899–1974)

Eric Linklater has strong claims to be considered Scotland's best novelist since Stevenson and, like Stevenson and indeed Scott and Byron, he combined a lifetime's devotion to the craft of writing with the suspicion that this was something hardly worthy of a proper man. This had, however, certain advantages: for one thing it gave him a varied experience – he served in both Wars, travelled widely, and took part, somewhat ineffectively, in politics – and in this way he acquired a store of experience that enabled him to write fuller novels.

He came from an Orkney family, though he was in fact born in South Wales. The Orkney heritage, its Norse influence and farming and fishing folk, acted as an anchor. His prose is always hard and lucid when he writes of Orkney. Orkney controlled the exuberance of his fancy and checked his tendency to exaggeration. He was to describe himself as 'a peasant with a pen'; if so, it was an Orkney peasant. Orkney plays a large part in two of his early novels, *White-Man's Saga* and *Magnus Merriman*. In the latter, the Orkney scenes have an authority that is not to be found in the more obviously amusing first part of the novel set in London and Edinburgh.

Linklater was under age when he served with the Black Watch in Flanders. He always retained a love for the Regiment. His last book, finished by his younger son, Andro, was to be its history. He always had a romantic admiration for soldiers; he wrote splendidly, for instance, about Lord Wavell. After the war, he went to Aberdeen University to read medicine but abandoned the attempt to be a doctor. In the 1920s he spent two years as a journalist on the *Times of India* and another two years as a Commonwealth Fellow in the United States. This second experience bore fruit in the novel, *Juan in America*, a comic extravaganza recording the adventures there of his hero, a putative descendant of Byron's Don Juan. It was published in 1931 and established his reputation. It combines sharp observation with wild farce. The language is rich and the novel breathes enjoyment of life.

Returning to Scotland, he engaged in Nationalist politics, standing as a candidate at a by-election in Fife. This was an experience which he used to good effect in *Magnus Merriman*.

Many of his pre-war novels were in picaresque vein. They established Linklater as a comic writer of great gusto and inventiveness. After the war he achieved a success with *Private Angelo*, written in similar style but with more sympathy and depth of understanding. It showed Linklater to be one of the best writers about war, fully alive to its horrors and destructiveness but at the same time conscious of the humanity which can emerge from it. One of Linklater's strengths was his ability to admire what many intellectuals might shun and despise. He was aware of the splendours as well as the miseries of war and, for him, courage was the supreme virtue.

In the post-war years he was one of the best known men in Scotland. He was in demand as a radio performer and he even appeared in whisky advertisements with his friend Sir Compton Mackenzie. In the Fifties, however, his work began to slide out of fashion. The Linklater qualities of gallantry and wit hardly belonged to that earnest time. Moreover, his attitude to his work was not such as to attract the attention of academics. He was essentially a craftsman. He believed, like his friend Evelyn Waugh, that books were objects made to delight their authors and their readers. He despised the idea of self-expression. He came to be seen as a maker of elegant entertainments.

It was absurd. He had had the misfortune to go out of fashion when he was at the height of his powers. He did not repine, but continued to work. There were still occasional novels, such as *Laxdale Hall* and *A Merry Muse*, in the old vein but much of his work, though still witty, was darker. *Mr Byculla, The House of Gair, The Dark of Summer, Roll of Honour, A Terrible Freedom*, and *A Man Over Forty* represented a remarkable body of fiction. In each of these novels he set himself a formidable technical problem. In each he departed from a strictly linear narrative. In each he concerned himself with the questions of what we inherit and of how, in the light of that heredity, we live our lives. The finest is *The Dark of Summer*, an unregarded masterpiece which moves, with an ease that perhaps only a fellow-novelist can fully appreciate, between Shetland in the eighteenth and twentieth centuries and between London, the Faroes, the Italian campaign and the Korean War. It is a study of courage and cowardice, treachery and loyalty, egoism and selflessness, damnation and redemption. It is written with a hard elegance and a compassion that never verges on sentimentality. Its climax has reduced me on every reading to tears of joy and wonder. If I were allowed to preserve only one Scottish novel of this century, it would be *The Dark of Summer*. It combines the craftsmanship of Stevenson with the humanity of Scott.

That said, it is fair to add that Linklater's own favourite among his novels was *Position at Noon* (1958). It is graceful and witty in its tracing of the heredity of an English family over three centuries. Each chapter is a perfect short story and yet they add up to a coherent and satisfying whole.

Perhaps his variety and lucidity told against him. Literary reputations have, to some extent at least fallen into the hands of academics who relish books which lack these qualities. Yet Linklater deserves study. He was fully alive, for instance, to the problems facing the Scottish writer, observing that our 'novelists may avoid Scottish themes; or deal with them in a parochial spirit which diminishes what is already small enough; or confine themselves to some remote parcel of geography, to some distant fragment of life, and find in that solitary corner a significance that is clearly lacking in the whole'. Aware of this as he was, Linklater, nevertheless, challenged his bleak diagnosis. In many ways apparently out of the mainstream – being a Tory and Imperialist as well as a Nationalist, and a craftsman always conscious of his obligation to the public – he achieved a body of work which was essentially Scottish, yet never narrowly nor exclusively so. He was an accomplished amateur historian and a stimulating essayist and travel-writer, but it is his novels which will live. Indeed they sing with life and with zest.

Lewis Grassic Gibbon

(1901–1935)

Gibbon was born James Leslie Mitchell but his most important work, *A Scots Quair*, was published under the pseudonym of Lewis Grassic Gibbon, so it seems most sensible to refer to him as such.

He was born in Aberdeenshire and brought up in the Mearns where his father farmed. He was encouraged to write by his first schoolmaster, Alexander Gray, at Arbuthnott village school and, as a young man, worked as a reporter in Aberdeen and Glasgow. In the 1920s he served in both the RSAC and the RAF before settling himself to the life of a professional writer in, of all places, Welwyn Garden City. His writing career lasted less than ten years but he was splendidly prolific, publishing fourteen books under his own name, as well as the three novels that make up the *Quair* and a book called *Scottish Scene* written in collaboration with Hugh MacDiarmid; all this between 1928 and 1935.

The books published under his own name show an interest in prehistory, travel and the romance of distant civilisations. He subscribed to the myth of Diffusionism, evolved by an Australian professor called Smith; which held that primitive man, the hunter and fruit-gatherer, lived in a golden age that civilisation, marked by the use of metals, destroyed. Gibbon translated this into Scottish terms and found there (in his imagination) happy hunters whose descendants were the Picts. Inasmuch as our ignorance of the Picts and their predecessors is both vast and deep, this agreeable theory may be maintained. It was useful to him. He also affirmed that the last vestiges of this primitive tribe could be discerned in North-East Scotland until the First World War. The Mitchell books include science fiction, a study of the explorer Mungo Park, the historical novel *Spartacus* and an autobiographical novel, *The Thirteenth Disciple*, which traces his own spiritual and intellectual development towards a romantic Communism.

He would, however, be little more than a literary curiosity but for *A Scots Quair*. To say this is not to disparage his other work; it is merely that it would be unlikely ever to have been republished in different circumstances, and so he would be remembered only as an eccentric footnote and as a promise cut short. *A Scots Quair* made Gibbon a writer of importance.

It was published in three volumes: *Sunset Song* (1932); *Cloud Howe* (1933) and *Grey Granite* (1934). The central figure in all three books is the girl Chris Guthrie, the crofter's daughter of Kinraddie. In *Sunset Song* Gibbon powerfully evokes the working of the land and the compulsion it exerts. Chris marries a farmer, only to see him killed and his way of life destroyed by the Great War. The novel is heavy with symbolism. The frequent and insistent intrusuion of symbols may mar the novel and irritate readers but it does not outweigh the book's feeling for the physical world in which its strength lies.

In *Cloud Howe* Chris, who has a son by her first marriage, now marries a Church of Scotland minister, whose charge is in a small town hit by the post-war Depression. Gibbon offers a picture of malice, narrow-mindedness, bigotry and class-consciousness, which is intended to be an antidote to the couthy Kailyard depiction of small-town Scotland. It is harsh and bitter and yet some sentimentality intrudes in the characterisation of Chris's husband, broken by the self-righteousness and meanness of his leading parishioners.

Grey Granite is set in Aberdeen, the city scarcely disguised. Chris, who has been widowed again and whose only child of her second marriage was still-born (a piece of clumsily obvious symbolism), now marries a displaced agricultural labourer. The picture of city life is bleak; these are people deprived of their birthright. The focus shifts to Chris's son Ewan who, like the young Mitchell, becomes a Communist. At the end of the novel, when Chris returns to the country, he sets off for London.

Gibbon's style is an obstacle to many readers. Eschewing Scots and the clumsy and ugly orthography it enjoins, he wrote in standard English with a strong Scots accent. It is, of course, an artificial language but it is a solution of a sort to the problem of how to register a Scottish consciousness in a manner accessible to a wide range of readers. At its best, Gibbon's style rises to a real nobility. It is capable of accommodating a variety of expression, including a sardonic humour wholly characteristic of North-East Scotland. At other times, however, it seems feebly and wilfully mannered, sinking close to self-parody. It is a style that demands from the reader a willing suspension of his critical faculties, a complete surrender to the tone of voice. Because it is artificial, however, it is frequently fatiguing to read. And yet it may fairly be claimed that no-one has come as close as Gibbon to resolving what is indeed a real problem confronting all Scottish novelists and especially those who wish to write of the working-class, whether in the city or in the countryside.

His feeling for the land is real and his use of Chris, as a symbol for its enduring strength and resilience and its cruelty too, works because

Chris is also thoroughly realised as a woman and is not just a representative figure. Yet here too, in his treatment of the land, his writing is uneven; it often comes close to the 'Dark Earth', portentous sentimentality of English rural novelists.

A Scots Quair has had no real successor, partly because the society he depicted in its strongest passages was dying, partly because of the very success of the book. It remains a lonely landmark in Scottish Literature. For all its faults, there is nothing else quite like it and it remains perhaps the most ambitious fiction written about Scotland this century.

Eric Liddell
(1902–1945)

I first heard the name of Eric Liddell in church, and I suppose that was a common experience for many of my generation; for my children he is the hero of that surprising success of the British Film Industry, *Chariots of Fire*. This says something of the change that has come over Scotland in the last four decades, the most marked feature of which has been the displacement of the Kirk from its central position in the life of the nation; a displacement with which neither the Kirk nor Scotland has fully come to terms.

I cannot remember now which aspect of Liddell's life was held up for admiration in that distant sermon. It might have been his refusal to compromise his principle of observing the Sabbath; it might have been his decision to put earthly rewards behind him, and devote his life to mission work; it might have been his death in a Japanese prison camp. Most probably his whole life was displayed as a model.

He was a man of unusual distinction, probity and courage. He was born in Tientsin in Northern China, the son of a missionary couple; that is to say, he was born into the consciousness of the missionary role of the Church of Scotland, and this was to be his lodestar. He was educated at Eltham College in Surrey, a public school established for the children of those engaged in mission work. The number engaged in missionary work may be gauged from the existence of such a school. Curiously, an older contemporary of Liddell's there was one A. L. Gracie, whose parents were missionaries in Ceylon, and who would captain Scotland at rugby, playing as Liddell's partner in 1923. Neither Liddell nor Gracie had a close connection with Scotland, though Liddell did spend some time at the village school in Drymen.

He attended both Edinburgh University and Heriot-Watt College, and while at Edinburgh began to make a name for himself as an athlete and rugby player. Though his style was described as awkward and ungainly, he was a remarkable competitor; in half a dozen athletics seasons in Scotland he was only once beaten in a race, at distances between 100 and 440 yards. His speed made him a very valuable wing-threequarter at rugby, and he played seven times for Scotland in 1922–3. These games included a win at Cardiff, Scotland's first victory there for thirty-three years, in which game Liddell scored a try, when 'zooming', as Gracie put it, 'along the horizon, he picked up the ball without the slightest check and ran over in the left corner'.

1924 was an Olympic year and the greatest Britain was to experience till Moscow in 1980. Liddell's best event was thought to be the 200 metres, but the final of this was scheduled to be run on a Sunday, and Liddell therefore declined to participate. One wonders what grounds would be necessary to persuade a modern athlete to forego the chance of an Olympic medal. It is worth repeating that Liddell was an extremely competitive athlete, whose distinguishing feature was his refusal to admit defeat; by this decision, however, he showed where sport ranked in his scale of values. He did, however, run in the 400 metres, winning the Gold Medal and breaking the world record at the same time, something no other Scottish athlete has ever managed to do.

He retired from athletics the following year, and returned to China to take up mission work. It was often thankless and, as the Sino–Japanese War intensified, increasingly dangerous. He took as a text St Luke 16:10, 'he that is faithful in that which is least is faithful also in much: and he that is unjust in least is unjust also in much', and added that 'it was as if God had said to me, "Be honest and straight"'. He endured four years' privation in a Japanese camp before dying just before the end of the war. He was only forty-three.

Liddell's life is a thing complete in itself, like a work of art. One can see why he was elected as the paradigm of the missionary Christian. Yet, wondering what might have become of him had he survived the war, one also finds it hard to avoid the question of the relationship between this work and Scotland. The missionaries set themselves a great task; but even as they set their face to it, they had turned their backs on another. They set out to win China, Africa and India for Christ; and while they were so engaged, the Church was losing Scotland. It seems possible that for several generations the noblest spirits in the Church turned away from their home country to evangelise the world. What might someone of Liddell's integrity and energy have achieved in the Scotland of the Depression? The question is tempting, but even to pose it requires one to imagine a different sort of Liddell. Yet it is fair to ask it, for the missionary movement was the spiritual equivalent of imperialism. Scotland was enriched, both materially and spiritually, by its commitment to the empire; but this commitment was not all enrichment. There was a price to be paid, and this was often the impoverishment of Scotland by the withdrawal to the periphery of empire of so many of its most capable sons and daughters.

John M. Bannerman,
Lord Bannerman of Kildonan
(1902–1969)

If you were to choose a figure to represent the best of twentieth-century Scotland, you might well settle on John M. Bannerman; you might do so even though – and perhaps because – in certain important areas of his life, he might be judged a failure.

He belonged to the great family of dispossessed Gaeldom, and his consciousness of this was perhaps the impelling influence in his life. The family roots were in the Strath of Kildonan, but Bannerman's great-grandfather married a MacDonald from South Uist, and the girl returned to live there with her children after her husband's death. John M. Bannerman's own father migrated to Glasgow, where he worked in the Post Office, eventually becoming a senior superintendent, but he was extremely active in Gaelic organisations, one of the founders of the *Ceilidh Nan Gaidheal*, and later President of the National Mod. The family language was Gaelic, and the young John worked for the language throughout his life.

He was educated at Glasgow High School, Glasgow University, and Balliol College, Oxford, where he did a post-graduate scholarship course in Agricultural Economics. He played rugby for Scotland from 1921–9, winning thirty-seven international caps, a record that stood till the 1960s. By modern standards, he was too small, too light and too slow to be an international forward, but he was recognised as the greatest forward of his day, a masterly controller of the ball in the foot-rushes which marked the Scottish game, a player as tireless and aggressive as he was skilful. He played at a great period – perhaps the greatest – of Scottish rugby, and he was the cornerstone of the pack throughout it. He took part in a rare and famous victory at Cardiff in 1923, and the Grand Slam triumph of 1925. Later, in 1954–5, he served as President of the SRU, and cogently advocated the revival of a traditionally robust Scottish forward game. The adjective 'raw-boned' has often been applied to Scottish forwards; no one deserved it more than Bannerman.

He became farm manager and factor to the Duke of Montrose, with whose son, the Marquis of Graham, he had been friendly at Oxford. This job was to supply both his livelihood and his base, but he was never restricted to it, nor by it. His energies seemed boundless, and he was active in the Gaelic movement, in broadcasting (and later television), in forestry and in politics. His loyalty to the Graham family was complete; when he eventually reached the House of Lords as a Life Peer, he defied Party instructions to vote for the renewal of sanctions against Rhodesia, because his old friend was a Minister in the Rhodesia Front Government.

Bannerman became a Liberal because he believed in Home Rule; a second motive was that the Tory Party represented the Highland landlords and he had an inherited antipathy to landlordism. He was a fervent Scottish patriot, though one who saw nothing to be gained by separation from the United Kingdom; but everything to be desired in the establishment of a Scottish Government. He believed that Scotland had suffered from the abdication of responsibility for its own affairs, and that no part of the country had suffered more from the remoteness of Government than the Highlands. Much of what he advocated in the twenty years after the war has become more widely accepted today: the Highlands and Islands Board was constituted as he would have wished, even though he disagreed with many of its priorities, such as the proposed establishment of an industrial conurbation around Invergordon: 'the basic economic fabric of the whole Highlands,' he wrote, 'is tattered and torn and needs repair'. The countryside already exported people: 'why add another magnet?' He believed that 'light industries should be established in country areas, so that farmers of land which does not yield a living wage should have the chance of augmenting their income at the local factory'. The 'industrial crofter' was 'worth planning for'. He was in favour of land reclamation schemes, and the encouragement of farm forestry and forest holdings. In the light of the EEC agricultural surpluses, his support for part-time farming makes good sense.

He fought seven elections and lost them all, though he came near to winning Inverness-shire in 1955 when he reduced the Conservative majority to 966, and almost brought off a sensational by-election victory at Paisley when he reduced a Labour majority from 7,000 to 1,600. He was Chairman of the Scottish Liberal Party from 1955–65, a period which saw a resurgence in the Party's fortunes. When he became Chairman Jo Grimond was the only Liberal MP in Scotland; when he left office he had been joined by four others. Bannerman's enthusiasm and obvious benevolence contributed greatly to this revival. He advocated electoral pacts with the SNP, but could convince neither his own party nor the Nationalists, and he was no more successful in persuading Liberals that they should stand as Scottish Liberals, even though the Scottish Liberal Party had its own identity. In 1967 he was made a Life Peer.

Bannerman's influence depended partly on the great affection in which he was held; he was so obviously a good man and a kind one. This didn't prevent him from acquiring enemies, for he never shrank from outspoken attacks on vested interests. It was his business to draw attention to the long neglect, and frequent oppression of the Highlands, and he didn't care on whose toes he trod in doing so.

'It has been the attitude,' he wrote, 'of succeeding London governments to shrug off the blame for the present situation and to sneer, albeit circumspectly, at the remnant of people left. The Highlander has been condemned as lazy and always waiting for someone to help him. But the blame rests squarely on apathy and neglect of the Highlands by governments over the generations. If there are sneers, they should be reserved for Westminster.'

He wanted to keep the best of the Past alive to nurture the Present and the Future: to destroy a culture was to deprive those who should be its inheritors.

Lord Fraser of Allander

(1903–1966)

Hugh Fraser, who became Lord Fraser of Allander, was a businessman of remarkable skill, who in his later years was extremely active in wider schemes for the development of the Scottish economy; the creation of Aviemore as a tourist centre owed much to him, and he gave his name (and a lot of money) to the principal economics institute in Scotland. He was hard-working, decent and honourable, and though scandal involved some of his associates like the architect John Poulson and the civil servant George Pottinger, it never touched Fraser. Yet for all his personal qualities Fraser was principally important as a symbol. His career saw the coming together of two trends, both of which may be held to have involved as much loss as gain for the country.

Napoleon or Voltaire or Louis XIV (or perhaps all of them; why not?) called the English (or the British) 'a nation of shopkeepers', but the description was premature. Shopkeeping on anything more than a trivial scale had to wait till the Industrial Revolution had created a large middle-class possessed of a quantity of disposable income, and had made possible improvements in transport which would allow of the extensive distribution of goods. These conditions were not realised until the middle of the nineteenth century. Even then, however, shops were modest family businesses, serving their localities and content to do so. They were also either specialists or small general merchants; the department store was an American invention, coming only at the end of the century.

Very soon, however, department stores had been established in all the larger towns and cities. They were distinct, each with its own character and loyal customers; women were as attached to their favoured store as their husbands to a football, rugby or cricket club. These businesses were usually managed by the family which owned them, and they reflected, to some extent anyway, not only their own individual character, but something of the character of the town or city in which they were established. Necessarily vague and difficult to articulate, these distinctions were nevertheless remarked by visitors. The four great cities of Scotland, and many of the larger towns, were proud of their department stores.

Curiously, this development attracted relatively little attention from political economists. There is, for instance, no mention of the retail trade in Dr James Bowie's *The Future of Scotland,* published in 1939, even though it was already one of the largest employers in the country, particularly of women. This absence was characteristic of a peculiarly blinkered Scottish view of economic relations; it still continues today: the retail trade is conspicuously absent also from T. C. Smout's *A Century of the Scottish People 1830–1950.*

Hugh Fraser inherited a family draper's business in his native West of Scotland. He realised that by standardising his buying policies and encouraging a quick turnover of goods, he could undercut his immediate competitors. His success was rapid and great. In the early 1950s he embarked on a programme of expansion by takeover which soon made him the most successful businessman in Scotland. In such a trade it was, of course, impossible to achieve a monopoly, though Fraser was essentially a monopolist in concept. He realised that the market was expanding rapidly as a result of the post-war prosperity which had increased the numbers in the middle class, and once he had bought one store in a city high street, he attracted to it such a volume of business that other competitors, often complacently managed, soon became his victims too. Only a few independents survived, and he was not yet challenged by English chain stores. For almost twenty years he dominated the Scottish market in what the Americans call 'dry goods'. He bought the Newcastle-based North of England firm Binns, which had itself expanded into Scotland in the 1930s, and then reached the summit of his ambition when he bought the great Knightsbridge store, Harrods.

Harrods was an untypical purchase, and was not treated like other Fraser stores, though it was soon contributing almost half the profits of House of Fraser. The rest of the empire was, however, more ramshackle than it appeared. Many of the stores which Fraser had bought were old-fashioned in their design and ill-suited to modern trading. He had acquired surplus capacity in many towns, though of course by doing so, he had eliminated competition. But a new competition was emerging, for by the end of the 1960s the department store had, except for those at the top end of the market, begun to seem old-fashioned; it was being challenged by specialist boutiques, soon themselves organised in nationwide chains. Finally Fraser's purchases had created many dissatisfied customers, for his success was based on selling mass-produced goods, often of inferior quality and design.

Nevertheless, though his company was to experience difficulties after his death, Fraser was a very considerable figure, whose success was remarkable. He contributed, however, to a depressing standardisation and lowering of quality; at the same time he was alive to a truth which eluded many earnest economists and planners: that the prosperity of a modern economy, and the maintenance of a high level of employment, might depend as much on a buoyant service industry as on manufacturing. In the light of this, the interest he showed in his last years in the development of the Scottish tourist industry, and his encouragement of the arts, seem natural corollaries of his original insight. Between the wars the representative figure of Scottish life was the shipbuilder Sir Jame Lithgow; in the 1950s and 1960s it became the shopkeeper Hugh Fraser.

Benny Lynch
(1910–1943)

The Depression struck the West of Scotland hard in the 1930s, all the more because the previous decade had seen the contraction of the Clyde's staple industries. In these twenty years between the wars the vision of Glasgow as the Second City of the Empire began to wither; not even the Empire Exhibition of 1938 could revive it. From being a city which, whatever its problems, had been one of restless and exuberant promise, Glasgow turned in on itself. It became more conscious of its vices than its virtues. Much, of course, remained and Glaswegians never stopped being proud of their city, but at the same time they felt some shame and less and less assurance. It was the era of the Gorbals razor-gangs, of Alexander McArthur's *No Mean City*: in this time, according to Alan Bold, in his survey *Modern Scottish Literature*, 'the really lasting fictive image of Glasgow is of a vast slum, a frightening vicious place populated by gangsters, morally angelic hardmen, loyal but downtrodden wives, sluttish but well-meaning mistresses and domestic tyrants of all ages'. This Glasgow of the poor quarters experienced unemployment levels of more than 30 per cent; infant mortality in 1937 was 104 in every thousand births; overcrowding in Scotland as a whole was six times worse than in England, malnutrition was common, and many children still suffered from rickets.

There were a few ways out. Intelligence, as always, offered one escape route: professional sport another. A man might rise above his condition because of the skill he possessed in his feet or in his fists. But such an escape was precarious, not only because the career of a professional footballer or boxer was likely to be short, but because it placed great stress on the character, a degree of stress indeed which broke many of the most gifted. One such was Benny Lynch.

He was a representative figure, only to be differentiated from thousands of his fellows by reason of his speed of foot and fist, and his extraordinary and innate ability to fight. He was very small, a natural flyweight (under 8 stone) and, as the current cant term has it, disadvantaged in almost every other way. He grew up in poverty, flashed across the scene like a brilliant light, and disappeared into miserable darkness.

He early learned that he could fight his way out of trouble and professional boxing offered him all he could hope for. He was not a great craftsman like his Welsh predecessor as World Flyweight Champion, Jimmy Wilde, but he was very fast and, unusually for a flyweight, had a genuine knock-out punch. That was the sensational thing about Lynch: he could punch as hard as a man a couple of stone heavier, and this ability took him to the world title. In doing so he seemed to strike a blow for all the deprived and oppressed of his class and country, and was adopted not just as a national hero, but as their representative.

He had this astonishing talent, but he had nothing else. He had neither solid family background, nor character. Having attained his ambition, he was lost. There was nowhere to go and he had no means of living satisfactorily at the point where he had arrived. Lacking cultural background, for he belonged to a peasantry which had been thrust by circumstance into a proletariat, and had lost its stability and much of its sense of values in the process, he found only one means of expressing himself in his celebrity; he had no ballast, but he had the bottle. The worst days of urban drunkenness were past; nothing in Glasgow of the 1930s approached the horror of eighty or ninety years previously; but whisky was nevertheless both the refuge and the stimulus many men sought; poor Benny Lynch more than most. He began then to drink heavily. Training was neglected. He was unprepared for fights, and below his best when he entered the ring. His timing of a punch – that mysterious ability which had carried him to glory – deserted him. Help was offered, but he did not know how to accept it. Soon his admirers turned away from him in shame, dismay and disgust; it was as if they, who had seen in his glory the expression of their own vitality, swagger and indomitable refusal to submit to the indignities of life, now recognised their own weakness in his decline, and they shrank from it in horror. When they spurned him, they were throwing stones at the mirror where they saw themselves reflected. His fall was rapid, though slow and agonising compared to his rise. He was dead at the age of thirty-three, a miserable derelict.

Jock Stein
(1920–1985)

'Freedom an' whisky gang thegither' said Burns, and most twentieth-century Scots would add football. It has been the main passion of the Scottish working-class, and their principal means of self-expression and self-assertion. The Scots' attitude to football has been a mixture of arrogance and infirmity. The old tag 'in victory more than men, in defeat less than women' might be held to apply. Scots believe that we play with a passion and artistry denied to less fortunate nations; at the same time our confidence is easily shattered. The weight of events oppresses the fantastic dreams.

Jock Stein gained a special place in the affection of his compatriots precisely because he proved, however briefly, that we were capable of making magic dreams come true.

He not only did that. He underlined the belief that football was the true heritage of the working-class Scot, the career really open to talent. It was even more satisfying that there was nothing flash about him, though often 'flash' has been just what was demanded of our heroes. The ideal of Scottish football has been the 'tanner-ba'' player, the man of intricate and ingenious skills, who performs as if for his own enjoyment. On a slightly grander scale this figure was represented by Rangers' Jim Baxter, toying with the English, beating a man for the sake of doing just that, rather than for any tactical advantage it might bring.

Stein wasn't like that. He came up the hard way. He went down the Lanarkshire pits as a boy, and he never forgot what football meant to his fellow-miners. He was always to insist on the importance of the football follower to the game. The best match in the world, he said, was no sort of match at all if there wasn't a crowd.

His football career was undistinguished for years. He played for the Coatbridge side Albion Rovers, then went to non-league football in Wales. He was on the slow side and awkward, but it happened that Celtic were going through a difficult period, and someone there remembered this cool and steady centre-half who had played for Albion. He was brought back to fill a gap in their defence, and did so excellently. Even so, he was never a great player, merely a useful one. It was as a manager that he was to fulfil himself.

He began with Dunfermline Athletic, an unfashionable club, and took them to win the Scottish Cup. Then he went to Hibs, a club which had fallen from its high estate, and promised to do the same job there. But his old club Celtic stepped in and Stein returned to Parkhead.

It was a time when football seemed to be strangled by the twin doctrines of efficiency and caution. The first was displayed by the England team which won the World Cup in 1966, the second by the Italian clubs which dominated European competitions. Stein's Celtic changed all that; his philosophy encouraged audacity and self-expression. He created a team whose whole was more than the sum of its parts. Few members of his side were regular international players, though most did in fact play for their country on several occasions, but together they played with a pace and imagination which delighted the crowds and brought success. Their greatest hour was in Lisbon in 1967 when they won the European Cup by beating Internazionale Milano.

Football matches are won by the players on the field and it is easy to exaggerate the contribution made by the manager. But no one had any doubt that Stein had been important. As *The Scotsman*'s football correspondent John Rafferty put it: 'The winning of that final had been impregnated with Stein's personality . . . There was a point about Jock Stein which was overlooked and probably because of its simplicity. He just knew more about football than the others. It is strange but your ordinary fellow will admit that somebody can know more about horse-racing or even medicine or music, but he finds it hard to understand that such as Stein could know so much more about football and to a decisive degree. But that was the way it was.'

That was Stein's first contribution – to satisfy dreams of how football should be played. His second was as important; it was to restore Scotland's self-respect.

In 1978 Scottish football suffered from its ineffable conceit. The national team's manager, one Ally McLeod, persuaded the nation that we could win the World Cup in Argentina. This was folly such as the Greeks termed 'hubris', and it was punished. Scotland were laughed out of the tournament and wafted home on a gale of mockery and disillusion. At this point Stein, in poor health since a serious car crash, was invited to take over the national side. He did so. His teams showed little of the flair his Celtic side had displayed, but they played worthily, within the limits of their ability. He brought dignity and seriousness to the job. He restored the pride bruised in Argentina.

His commitment was complete, and he died in office, suffering a heart attack in the last minutes of an international match in Cardiff. He had achieved much, but even more important had been the example of his character. He had proved that we could win without vainglory, and lose without whining: that one did not have to behave like a spoiled adolescent to commit oneself to a game.

Index